# Alphabet
# Soup

RET.

## Also published by Bloomsbury Reference:

| | |
|---|---|
| ⁻nglish Dictionary | 0 7475 6243 1 |
| A no-nonsense guide to easily confused words | 0 7475 7231 3 |
| tionary of Euphemisms | 0 7475 5045 X |
| Good Word Guide  0 7475 6524 4 (hb) | 0 7475 7232 1 (pb) |
| Bloomsbury Grammar Guide | 0 7475 5035 2 |
| Dictionary of Word Origins | 0 7475 5448 X |
| Eating out en français | 0 7475 6975 4 |
| Eating out in five languages | 0 7475 6977 0 |
| Oddbins Dictionary of Wine | 0 7475 6641 0 |
| A Cook's Dictionary | 0 7475 7226 7 |

### Specialist dictionaries:

| | |
|---|---|
| Dictionary of Accounting | 0 7475 6991 6 |
| Dictionary of Banking and Finance | 0 7475 6685 2 |
| Dictionary of Business | 0 7475 6980 0 |
| Dictionary of Computing | 0 7475 6622 4 |
| Dictionary of Economics | 0 7475 6632 1 |
| Dictionary of Environment and Ecology | 0 7475 7201 1 |
| Dictionary of Hotels, Tourism and Catering Management | 1 9016 5999 2 |
| Dictionary of Human Resources and Personnel Management | 0 7475 6623 2 |
| Dictionary of Law | 0 7475 6636 4 |
| Dictionary of Marketing | 0 7475 6621 6 |
| Dictionary of Medical Terms | 0 7475 6987 8 |
| Dictionary of Military Terms | 0 7475 7477 4 |
| Dictionary of Nursing | 0 7475 6634 8 |
| Dictionary of Politics and Government | 0 7475 7220 8 |
| Dictionary of Science and Technology | 0 7475 6620 8 |

### Easier English™ titles:

| | |
|---|---|
| Easier English Basic Dictionary | 0 7475 6644 5 |
| Easier English Basic Synonyms | 0 7475 6979 7 |
| Easier English Intermediate Dictionary | 0 7475 6989 4 |
| Easier English Student Dictionary | 0 7475 6624 0 |

Visit our website for full details of all our books
**www.bloomsbury.com/reference**

# Alphabet Soup

## An A to Z of Abbreviations

Rosalind Fergusson

BLOOMSBURY

A BLOOMSBURY REFERENCE BOOK
**www.bloomsbury.com/reference**

First published 2004

Bloomsbury Publishing Plc
38 Soho Square, London W1D 3HB

Copyright © Bloomsbury Publishing Plc 2004

British Library Cataloguing-in-Publication Data
A catalogue record for this book is available from the British Library

ISBN 0 7475 7230 5

*Text Production and Proofreading*
Katy McAdam, Joel Adams, Heather Bateman

All papers used by Bloomsbury Publishing are natural, recyclable
products made from wood grown in well-managed forests.
The manufacturing processes conform to the
environmental regulations of the country of origin.

Text processed and computer typeset by Bloomsbury
Printed in Great Britain by Clays Ltd, St Ives Plc

# Introduction

We live in an age of haste. Everything has to be done the day before yesterday and at breakneck speed. This need for speed, fuelled by technology, has led to a corresponding demand for conciseness in language. The formal, rather verbose and formulaic business letter is being increasingly replaced by the less formal, more concise – and frequently misspelt – e-mail.

This desire for conciseness has provided the perfect breeding ground for that traditional space-saving device, the abbreviation. The invention of the mobile phone, or rather the popular use of its keypad to send messages, known as text messaging, has done even more to promote it.

Several expressions found in basic text messaging are formed in the same way that traditional abbreviations are – by using the initial letters of the relevant words. Thus, we find **YNK** ('you never know'); the not very polite **MYOB** ('mind your own business'); and **HAND** (the abbreviation of the most annoying phrase ever borrowed from American English, 'have a nice day').

Text messaging, however, takes a few liberties with the traditional system of abbreviation. Many of the shortened forms are abbreviations, but not as we know them. Letter sounds, for example, are much used, as in **THNQ** ('thank you'), **CUL** ('see you later') and **RU?** ('are you?'). Even more confusing to the uninitiated is the use of numbers in text messaging, as in such expressions as **GR8** ('great') and **F2T** ('free to talk').

The recent growth in abbreviations is not restricted to these trendy texting forms however. Indeed, there has been a proliferation of them wherever you look and no area of life is immune from them. They have infiltrated not only the newer disciplines such as ecology and computing, but also the older, more staid disciplines of the law and medicine. I will not quote any of them here because the text of the book is crammed with them. Take your pick!

It is, of course, this sheer volume of abbreviations in modern times that is really novel. Abbreviations, in fewer numbers, have been with us for a considerable time. Indeed, medieval scribes used them when penning their parchments as a means of saving space and reducing effort.

These early abbreviations were in Latin and some of these have survived until the present day. Thus, most of us would be familiar with abbreviations such as **a.m.**, **p.m.**, **e.g.** and **i.e.**, and we would also be likely to know that they mean, respectively, 'before noon', 'after noon', 'for example' and 'that is'. Of course, we might not know what Latin words the abbreviations actually stand for, but this does not come between us and our comprehension of the abbreviated expressions.

As Latin waned and people began to write in the vernacular language, the practice of abbreviating expressions continued at a gradual pace, increasing rapidly in the nineteenth century. But, before that, as *Fowler's Modern English* reminds us, the practice was condemned by some well-known writers and critics.

We find Joseph Addison writing in the *Spectator* in 1711 that 'It is perhaps this Humour of speaking no more than we needs must which has so miserably curtailed some of our Words … as in mob., rep., pos., incog., and the like.' Just slightly later, in 1712, in his *Proposal for Correcting, Improving and Ascertaining the English Tongue*, Swift proposed an annual expurgatory publication which would 'condemn those barbarous mutilations of vowels and syllables' including the curtailment of words referred to by Addison, known to us as abbreviations.

However, even criticism from great minds did not stem the habit of abbreviating words, and the nineteenth century brought us shortened forms (not strictly abbreviations) such as **specs** (1826), **cab** (1827), **flu** (1839), **ad** (1841), **zoo** (1847), **pub** (1859), **photo** (1860), **vet** (1862), **pro** (1866), **gym** (1871), **bike** (1882), and **phone** (1884). It also saw the rise of a vogue for informal and humorous abbreviations such as **OK** (all correct) and **PDQ** (pretty damned quick). The first of these has survived and even transcended its abbreviation status to become a word with various parts of speech. The latter has also survived on the lips and pens of the peremptory, but it is now dated.

The twentieth century got off to a good start, as far as shortenings were concerned, with **taxi** (1907), **fridge** (1935) and **telly** (1942). But quite far into that century shortened forms still did not enjoy anything like the status they enjoy today. Until the last quarter of the twentieth century, many dictionaries still tended to relegate abbreviations to the back pages together with such add-ons as the table of chemical elements: they did not belong in the main text among the 'real' words.

In the closing decades of the twentieth century, abbreviations began to proliferate. They were aided in this spawning by the fact that more and more public and private bodies came into being and were given names which defied memorizing. Soon abbreviations stopped just being names of organizations or part of the jargon of some professions and trades which most of us could happily ignore. They became part of our everyday lives. The early 1980s brought us **Aids** and, slightly later in the decade, **HIV** and **BSE,** all of which relate to life-and-death issues.

In the second part of the 1980s began the trend towards forming humorous, or facetious, acronyms. Many of these came and went, as they deserved to do, but **Yuppie** (a 'young upwardly mobile professional') and **Nimby** ('not in my backyard', the cry of the not-so-concerned environmentalists) have hung on in there.

Abbreviations have much in common with jargon in that they have become part of the language that is exclusive to a particular profession or group. Language used in this way, as a convenient shorthand, can easily become a kind of barrier – a way of reinforcing people's sense of belonging to an in-group. The scale of abbreviations now is such that there is absolutely no possibility of remembering the huge number that are circulating in the wider world, and dictionaries cannot possibly spare the space to accommodate even a fraction of these.

Abbreviations are one of the most daunting features of the English language. They can be both obscure and contrived and, because they have become so omnipresent in our lives, we need a guide to help us penetrate them. So it is that they have been accorded a whole volume to themselves, a volume which takes the pain out of abbreviations and makes them approachable, interesting and, at times, entertaining. Abbreviations have certainly come a long way since they were simply a space-filling list in the back pages of dictionaries.

Betty Kirkpatrick

# Editor's note

This book covers the four main types of abbreviation – shortenings, contractions, initialisms, and acronyms – but does not label them explicitly. These four types are as follows:

*Shortenings* of words usually consist of the first few letters of the full form and are usually spelt with a final full stop when they are still regarded as abbreviations, for example **cont**. = continued, **etc**. = et cetera. They may also consist of the stressed syllable of the shortened word, e.g. **bus** or **gym**. In cases where they form words in their own right, the full stop is omitted, for example **hippo** = hippopotamus. Such shortenings are often but not always informal. Some become the standard forms, and the full forms are then regarded as formal or technical, for example **bus** = omnibus, **pub** = public house, **zoo** = zoological garden.

*Contractions* are abbreviated forms in which letters from the middle of the full form have been omitted, for example **Dr** = doctor, **St** = saint or street. Practice varies with regard to adding a full stop, but in modern British usage it is increasingly usual to omit it. Another kind of contraction is the type with an apostrophe marking the omission of letters: **can't** = cannot, **didn't** = did not, **you've** = you have.

*Initialisms* are made up of the initial letters of words and are pronounced as separate letters: **CIA** (or **C.I.A.**), **pm** (or **p.m.**), **US** (or **U.S.**). Practice again varies with regard to full stops, with current usage increasingly in favour of omitting them, especially when the initialism consists entirely of capital letters.

*Acronyms* are initialisms that have become words in their own right, or similar words formed from parts of several words. They are pronounced as words rather than as a series of letters, for example **Aids**, **NATO**, **FIFA**, and do not have full stops. Some become so established they are no longer recognized as acronyms, for example **radar**, **laser** and **scuba**. In many cases the acronym becomes the standard term and the full form is only used in explanatory contexts.

# Pronunciation Guide

The following symbols have been used to show the pronunciation of abbreviations in the dictionary.

Stress is indicated by a main stress mark ( ' ) and a secondary stress mark ( , ). Note that these are only guides, as the stress of the word changes according to its position in the sentence.

| Vowels | | Consonants | |
|---|---|---|---|
| æ | back | b | buck |
| ɑː | harm | d | dead |
| ɒ | stop | ð | other |
| aɪ | type | dʒ | jump |
| aʊ | how | f | fare |
| aɪə | hire | g | gold |
| aʊə | hour | h | head |
| ɔː | course | j | yellow |
| ɔɪ | annoy | k | cab |
| e | head | l | leave |
| eə | fair | m | mix |
| eɪ | make | n | nil |
| eʊ | go | ŋ | sing |
| ɜː | word | p | print |
| iː | keep | r | rest |
| i | happy | s | save |
| ə | about | ʃ | shop |
| ɪ | fit | t | take |
| ɪə | near | tʃ | change |
| u | annual | θ | theft |
| uː | pool | v | value |
| ʊ | book | w | work |
| ʊə | tour | x | loch |
| ʌ | shut | ʒ | measure |
| | | z | zone |

# Dialect Labels

This book uses the following labels to indicate the geographical area where an abbreviation is used:

ANZ = Australia and New Zealand
Aus = Australia
Can = Canada
N Am = North America

NZ = New Zealand
S Africa = South Africa
S Asia = South Asia
US = United States of America

# A

**a 1.** PHYSICS acceleration **2.** MEASUREMENTS are **3.** TRANSPORT arrives

**A 1.** COMPUTING 10 (*used in hexadecimal notation*) **2.** ROADS a main road other than a motorway (NOTE: The abbreviation **A** is used before the road number, as in *A28*.) **3.** CHEMISTRY activity **4.** BIOCHEMISTRY adenine **5.** MEASUREMENTS, PHYSICS ampere **6.** MEASUREMENTS, PHYSICS angstrom **7.** PHYSICS mass number

**Å** MEASUREMENTS, PHYSICS angstrom

**A2** EDUCATION in England, Wales, and Northern Ireland, the second year of a full A-level course, or the examination taken at the end of that year

**AA 1.** HEALTH Alcoholics Anonymous **2.** SOCIAL WELFARE a state benefit paid to disabled people to cover the cost of constant care or supervision. Full form **attendance allowance 3.** AUTOMOTIVE Automobile Association

**AAA 1.** /ˌtrɪp(ə)l ˈeɪ/ ATHLETICS Amateur Athletic Association **2.** ACCOUNTING American Accounting Association **3.** AUTOMOTIVE American Automobile Association **4.** ARMS antiaircraft artillery **5.** AUTOMOTIVE Australian Automobile Association

**AAD** MONEY Arab accounting dinar

**a.a.e.** HUMAN RESOURCES according to age and experience (*used in job advertisements*)

**AAIA** ACCOUNTING Associate of the Association of International Accountants

**AAM** ARMS air-to-air missile

**AAMOF** ONLINE as a matter of fact (*used in e-mails*)

**A & E** HEALTH SERVICES the official name of the hospital department traditionally known as casualty. The US equivalent is ER (emergency room). Full form **accident and emergency**

**A & M** CHRISTIANITY (Hymns) Ancient and Modern

**A & R** RECORDING artists and repertoire

**AARF** ACCOUNTING Australian Accounting Research Foundation

**AAS** ACCOUNTING Australian Accounting Standard

**AASB** ACCOUNTING Australian Accounting Standards Board

**A'asia** Australasia

**AAT** ACCOUNTING Association of Accounting Technicians

**AAVE** LANGUAGE African American Vernacular English

**AB 1.** NAVY able-bodied seaman **2.** Alberta **3.** *US* EDUCATION Bachelor of Arts **4.** BUSINESS a type of company in Swedish-speaking countries. The abbreviation is equivalent to plc or Ltd. Full form **Aktiebolaget**

**ABA 1.** BOXING Amateur Boxing Association **2.** BANKING American Bankers Association **3.** LAW American Bar Association

**ABB** MANAGEMENT activity-based budgeting

**abbr.** abbreviation

**ABC 1.** MANAGEMENT activity-based costing **2.** BROADCASTING American Broadcasting Company **3.** BROADCASTING Australian Broadcasting Corporation **4.** the alphabet, especially in referring to basic reading and writing

**ABCs** BUSINESS Audit Bureau of Circulations

**ABEND** /ˈæbend/ **1.** COMPUTING a sudden failure of a computer program or system. Full form **abnormal end 2.** ONLINE absent by enforced Net deprivation (NOTE: The abbreviation **ABEND** is used in the subject line of e-mails to warn correspondents of the sender's imminent loss of Internet access.)

**ABI** INSURANCE Association of British Insurers

**ABM 1.** MANAGEMENT activity-based management **2.** ARMS antiballistic missile

**abn** airborne

**ABN** BUSINESS a numeric code assigned to a business so that it can be identified by the Australian Taxation Office and other government departments. Full form **Australian Business Number**

**ABR** COMPUTING available bit rate

**ABS 1.** INDUSTRY a type of strong plastic used to make moulded casings, pipes, and car parts. Full form **acrylonitrile-butadiene-styrene 2.** AUTOMOTIVE a system of electronically controlled brakes that prevents a vehicle's wheels locking if the driver brakes suddenly. Full form **antilock braking system** (NOTE: The abbreviation **ABS** was originally an abbreviation of the German term *Antiblockier-System*.) **3.** COMMERCE Australian Bureau of Statistics

**ABTA** /'æbtə/ TRAVEL Association of British Travel Agents

**abv** WINE alcohol by volume

**ac** ONLINE academic organization (NOTE: The abbreviation **ac** is seen at the end of Internet addresses, preceded by a dot.)

**Ac** CHEMICAL ELEMENTS actinium

**AC 1.** WINE a Portuguese wine-making cooperative. Full form **adega cooperativa 2.** air conditioning **3.** AIR FORCE Aircraftman **4.** ELECTRICITY alternating current **5.** METEOROLOGY altocumulus **6.** CALENDAR ante Christum (*used before dates*) **7.** WINE a certification for French wine that guarantees its origin and verifies that it meets production regulations. Full form **appellation contrôlée 8.** ATHLETICS Athletic Club (*used in club names*) **9.** Companion in the Order of Australia

**a/c 1.** COMMERCE account **2.** BANKING account current

**A/C 1.** COMMERCE account **2.** BANKING account current **3.** air conditioning

**ACA 1.** ACCOUNTING Associate of the Institute of Chartered Accountants in England and Wales **2.** COMMUNICATION Australian Communications Authority

**ACAS** /'eɪkæs/ HUMAN RESOURCES an organization that mediates between employers and employees or trade unions in industrial disputes. Full form **Advisory, Conciliation, and Arbitration Service** (NOTE: Sometimes written **Acas**, the acronym has entered the language as a noun; the full form is rarely encountered in general usage.)

**ACAUS** ACCOUNTING Association of Chartered Accountants in the United States

**acc. 1.** COMMERCE account **2.** GRAMMAR accusative

**ACCA** ACCOUNTING **1.** Associate of the Association of Chartered Certified Accountants **2.** Association of Chartered Certified Accountants

**ACCC** /ˌeɪ ˌtrɪp(ə)l 'siː/ COMMERCE Australian Competition and Consumer Commission

**ACCI** COMMERCE Australian Chamber of Commerce and Industry

**acct** COMMERCE account

**ACD** BUSINESS authorized corporate director

**AC/DC** an offensive term meaning bisexual

**ACDI** COMPUTING asynchronous communications device interface

**ACE 1.** EDUCATION Advisory Centre for Education **2.** MILITARY Allied Command Europe **3.** /eɪs/ BIOCHEMISTRY an enzyme that increases blood pressure. Full form **angiotensin-converting enzyme** (NOTE: The acronym **ACE** has entered the language as a noun, also used in *ACE inhibitor*, denoting a drug that blocks this enzyme.)

**ACE inhibitor** a drug that blocks an enzyme that raises blood pressure

**ACF** COMPUTING advanced communications function

**ACH** E-COMMERCE a wholesale payment network for interbank clearing and payment settlement, accessible through points of sale or cashpoints. Full form **automated clearing house**

**ACL** COMPUTING access control list

**ACLU** LAW American Civil Liberties Union

**ACM 1.** AIR FORCE Air Chief Marshal **2.** COMPUTING Association for Computing Machinery **3.** MANUFACTURING Australian Chamber of Manufactures

**ACR** HOUSEHOLD audio cassette recorder

**ACRS** ACCOUNTING accelerated cost recovery system

**ACT 1.** FINANCE a tax paid by any company that pays a dividend, calculated by deducting the basic rate of income tax from the grossed-up value of the dividend. Full form **advance corporation tax 2.** Australian Capital Territory

**ACTH** BIOCHEMISTRY a pituitary hormone that stimulates the adrenal cortex to produce steroid hormones. Full form **adrenocorticotrophic hormone**

**ACTU** HUMAN RESOURCES Australian Council of Trade Unions

**ACT-UP** /ˈækt ʌp/ HEALTH an activist organization concerned with the rights and treatment of people with Aids. Full form **Aids Coalition To Unleash Power**

**ACU** MONEY Asian currency unit

**ACVE** EDUCATION Advanced Certificate of Vocational Education

**ACW** AIR FORCE Aircraftwoman

**ad 1.** TENNIS advantage **2.** ONLINE Andorra (NOTE: The abbreviation **ad** is seen at the end of Internet addresses, preceded by a dot.)

**AD 1.** MEDICINE Alzheimer's disease **2.** CALENDAR anno Domini

The abbreviation **AD** in this sense is used to indicate a date that is a specified number of years after the birth of Jesus Christ. AD is traditionally put before the year number (*AD 435*), but it is normally acceptable to put it after the identification of a century (*the fifth century AD*). **PE** (Present Era) and **CE** (Common Era) have been suggested as non-Christian alternatives.

**A/D** ELECTRONICS analogue to digital

**Ada** /ˈeɪdə/ COMPUTING a high-level computer-programming language that is used mainly for military, industrial, and scientific applications (NOTE: Sometimes spelt **ADA**, this is not an abbreviation: it is named after the English mathematician Augusta *Ada* Byron, Countess of Lovelace (1815–52).)

**ADB** BANKING **1.** African Development Bank **2.** Asian Development Bank

**ADC** ELECTRONICS analogue-to-digital converter

**ADD** MEDICINE attention deficit disorder

**add. 1.** addendum **2.** MATHEMATICS addition **3.** address

**ADDACS** BANKING Automated Direct Debit Amendments and Cancellation Service

**ADF** BANKING Approved Deposit Fund

**ADH** BIOCHEMISTRY antidiuretic hormone

**ADHD** MEDICINE attention deficit hyperactivity disorder

**ADI** HEALTH acceptable daily intake

**adj. 1.** GRAMMAR adjective **2.** MATHEMATICS adjoint **3.** LOGIC adjunct **4.** INSURANCE adjustment **5.** MILITARY adjutant

**Adjt** MILITARY Adjutant

**ADLs** MEDICINE activities of daily living

**Adm.** NAVY **1.** Admiral **2.** Admiralty

**ADP 1.** BIOCHEMISTRY a chemical compound derived from ATP that is involved in energy transfer reactions in living cells. Full form **adenosine diphosphate 2.** COMPUTING automatic data processing

**ADPCM** COMPUTING adaptive differential pulse code modulation

**ADR** BUSINESS American Depositary Receipt

**ADSL** COMPUTING a high-speed telephone line that can transmit voice and video data over copper wires. Full form **asymmetrical digital subscriber line**

**ADT** *N Am* TIME Atlantic Daylight Time

**adv. 1.** GRAMMAR adverb **2.** GRAMMAR adverbial **3.** MARKETING advertisement **4.** advisory

**ad val.** FINANCE in proportion to the value. Full form **ad valorem** (NOTE: From Latin.)

**advt** MARKETING advertisement

**AE 1.** BUSINESS aggregate expenditure **2.** ECOLOGY assimilation efficiency

**AEA** INDUST Atomic Energy Authority

**AEC** INDUST Atomic Energy Commission

**AEEU** HUMAN RESOURCES Amalgamated Engineering and Electrical Union

**AER** FINANCE annual equivalent rate

**aero** ONLINE aviation industry (NOTE: The abbreviation **aero** is seen at the end of Internet addresses, preceded by a dot.)

**AEST** TIME Australian Eastern Standard Time

**AEU** *Aus* EDUCATION Australian Education Union

**AEX** STOCK EXCHANGE Amsterdam Stock Exchange

**af** ONLINE Afghanistan (NOTE: The abbreviation **af** is seen at the end of Internet addresses, preceded by a dot.)

**AF 1.** AIR FORCE air force **2.** Anglo-French **3.** ELECTRONICS audio frequency **4.** PHOTOGRAPHY autofocus

**Af. 1.** Africa **2.** African

**AFAANZ** FINANCE Accounting and Finance Association of Australia and New Zealand

**AFAIK** ONLINE as far as I know (*used in e-mails and text messages*)

**AFBD** STOCK EXCHANGE Association of Futures Brokers and Dealers

**AFC 1.** AEROSPACE automatic flight control **2.** ELECTRONICS automatic frequency control

**AFIPS** COMPUTING American Federation of Information Processing Societies

**AFL** Australian Football League

**AFL-CIO** HUMAN RESOURCES a federation formed in 1955 by the merging of the American Federation of Labour and the Congress of Industrial Organizations. ◊ **CIO**

**AFLP** BIOTECHNOLOGY a rapid method for detecting variations in DNA sequences between individuals. Full form **amplified fragment length polymorphism**

**AFM** PHYSICS atomic force microscope

**AFNOR** /ˈæfnɔː/ the French industrial standards authority. Full form **Association française de normalisation**

**AFP 1.** BIOCHEMISTRY alpha-foetoprotein **2.** POLICE Australian Federal Police

**Afr. 1.** Africa **2.** African

**AFTA** /ˈæftə/ COMMERCE ASEAN Free Trade Area

**AFV** MILITARY armoured fighting vehicle

**ag** ONLINE Antigua and Barbuda (NOTE: The abbreviation **ag** is seen at the end of Internet addresses, preceded by a dot.)

**Ag** CHEMICAL ELEMENTS silver

**AG 1.** ARMY adjutant general **2.** BUSINESS a type of company in German-speaking countries. The abbreviation is equivalent to plc or Ltd. Full form **Aktiengesellschaft 3.** LAW attorney general

**AGC** ELECTRONICS a radio receiver control system by which the amplifier is adjusted to compensate for variations in the volume of the signal, so that the volume of the output is constant. Full form **automatic gain control**

**AGI** BUSINESS **1.** adjusted gross income **2.** annual gross income

**AGM** BUSINESS annual general meeting

**AGN** ASTRONOMY active galactic nucleus

**AGP** COMPUTING a computer interface that allows the display of three-dimensional graphics. Full form **accelerated graphics port**

**AGR** INDUST advanced gas-cooled reactor

**AH 1.** MEASUREMENTS, PHYSICS ampere-hour **2.** CALENDAR anno Hegirae (NOTE: The abbreviation **AH** is used to indicate the number of years from the Hegira (AD 622), a key date in the Islamic calendar.)

**A.h.** MEASUREMENTS, PHYSICS ampere-hour

**AHA** CHEMISTRY alpha-hydroxy acid

**AHF** BIOCHEMISTRY antihaemophilic factor

**AHI** COMMERCE the Afrikaans chamber of commerce. Full form **Afrikaanse Handelsinstituut**

**AHST** TIME Alaska-Hawaii Standard Time

**ai** ONLINE Anguilla (NOTE: The abbreviation **ai** is seen at the end of Internet addresses, preceded by a dot.)

**AI 1.** CHEMISTRY active ingredient **2.** MEDICINE artificial insemination **3.** COMPUTING artificial intelligence **4.** AEROSPACE attitude indicator

**AIA** ACCOUNTING Association of International Accountants

**AICPA** ACCOUNTING American Institute of Certified Public Accountants

**AID 1.** MEDICINE acute infectious disease **2.** INTERNATIONAL RELATIONS Agency for International Development **3.** MEDICINE artificial insemination by donor

**Aids** /eɪdz/ MEDICINE a disease of the immune system caused by infection with the retrovirus HIV, which destroys some types of white blood cells and is transmitted through blood or bodily secretions such as semen. Full form **acquired immune deficiency syndrome**

> The acronym **Aids** has entered the language as a noun, and the full form is rarely encountered in general usage. A number of other English words originated in a similar way and are now so well-established in the language that they are no longer regarded as acronyms. These include *laser* 'light amplification by stimulated emission of radiation', *quango* 'quasiautonomous nongovernmental organization', *radar* 'radio detection and ranging', *scuba* 'self-contained underwater breathing apparatus', and *sonar* 'sound navigation ranging'. The noun *flak*, denoting anti-aircraft fire or strong criticism, comes from the German phrase *Fleiger Abwehr Kanone*, meaning 'aeroplane defence canon'.

**AIFA** FINANCE Association of Financial Advisers

**AIH** MEDICINE artificial insemination by husband

**AIL** ECOLOGY aesthetic injury level

**AIM** /eɪm, ˌeɪ aɪ 'em/ BUSINESS alternative investment market

**AIMA** BUSINESS Alternative Investment Management Association

**ain't** /eɪnt/ a contraction of 'am not', 'is not', 'are not', 'have not', or 'has not'

**AIR** RADIO All India Radio

**AIRC** HUMAN RESOURCES Australian Industrial Relations Commission

**AITC** FINANCE Association of Investment Trust Companies

**AJA** PRESS Australian Journalists' Association

**AJK** HORSERACING Australian Jockey Club

**AK** MAIL Alaska (NOTE: The abbreviation **AK** is part of the US sorting code on the last line of an Alaska address.)

**a.k.a.** also known as (NOTE: The abbreviation **a.k.a.** is used to introduce a pseudonym or nickname: *Sean Combs a.k.a. Puff Daddy.*)

**al** ONLINE Albania (NOTE: The abbreviation **al** is seen at the end of Internet addresses, preceded by a dot.)

**Al** CHEMICAL ELEMENTS aluminium

**AL** MAIL Alabama (NOTE: The abbreviation **AL** is part of the US sorting code on the last line of an Alabama address.)

**al. 1.** alcohol **2.** alcoholic

**ALA** all letters answered (NOTE: The abbreviation **ALA** is used in personal advertisements.)

**Alb. 1.** Albania **2.** Albanian

**ALBM** ARMS air-launched ballistic missile

**alc. 1.** alcohol **2.** alcoholic

**ALCM** ARMS air-launched cruise missile

**A level** EDUCATION in England, Wales, and Northern Ireland, the advanced level of any subject studied to gain a General Certificate of Education qualification. Full form **Advanced level** (NOTE: The abbreviation is used as a noun to denote both the level (*studying biology at A level*) and the qualification (*candidates with two or more A levels*).)

**ALF** Animal Liberation Front

**Alg. 1.** Algeria **2.** Algerian

**ALGOL** /ˈælgɒl/ COMPUTING a high-level computer programming language that uses algebraic symbols in solving mathematical and scientific problems. Full form **algorithm-oriented language**

**ALMO** /ˈælməʊ/ PUBLIC ADMINISTRATION arm's length management organization

**ALP** POLITICS Australian Labor Party

**ALS** MEDICINE amyotrophic lateral sclerosis

**Alt** COMPUTING a computer key that is held down while another other key or sequence of keys is pressed, to perform a particular function or produce a particular character. Full form **alternate (or alternative) key** (NOTE: Some computer keyboards also have an **Alt Gr** (alternative graphics) key, which is used in a similar way.)

**ALT** BIOCHEMISTRY alanine aminotransferase

**alt. 1.** alteration **2.** BOTANY alternate **3.** altitude **4.** MUSIC alto

**Alta** Alberta

**ALU** COMPUTING a circuit in a computer's central processing unit that makes decisions based on the results of calculations. Full form **arithmetic logic unit**

**am 1.** RADIO amplitude modulation **2.** ONLINE Armenia (NOTE: The abbreviation **am** is seen at the end of Internet addresses, preceded by a dot.)

**Am** CHEMICAL ELEMENTS americium

**AM 1.** MILITARY Albert Medal **2.** RADIO amplitude modulation **3.** anno mundi **4.** TIME ante meridiem. ◊ **a.m. 5.** ACCOUNTING asset management **6.** associate member **7.** *US* EDUCATION Master of Arts **8.** Member in the Order of Australia

**Am. 1.** American **2.** BIBLE Amos

**a.m.** TIME in the period between midnight and noon. Full form **ante meridiem** (NOTE: The abbreviation **a.m.**, from the Latin, 'before noon', is used after a specific time in the 12-hour clock. It is sometimes written AM or am.)

**AMBA** MANAGEMENT Association of MBAs

**Amer.** American

**Amex** /ˈæmeks/ STOCK EXCHANGE American Stock Exchange

**AmEx** /ˈæmeks/ FINANCE American Express

**Amicus** /ˈæmɪkəs/ HUMAN RESOURCES a trade union formed by the merger of the AEEU and MSF in January 2002 (NOTE: **Amicus** is not an abbreviation: the name was chosen principally because it is Latin for 'friend'.)

**AMP** BIOCHEMISTRY a compound involved in energy transfer reactions in living cells. Full form **adenosine monophosphate**

**AMPS** FINANCE auction market preferred stock

**AMT** MANUFACTURING advanced manufacturing technology

**amu** MEASUREMENTS, PHYSICS atomic mass unit

**AMU** MEASUREMENTS, PHYSICS atomic mass unit

**AMVETS** /ˈæmvets/ MILITARY in the United States, a private organization of veterans of World War II and subsequent conflicts. Full form **American Veterans**

**an** ONLINE Netherlands Antilles (NOTE: The abbreviation **an** is seen at the end of Internet addresses, preceded by a dot.)

**anal.** 1. analogous 2. analogy 3. analysis 4. analytic

**anat.** MEDICINE 1. anatomical 2. anatomy

**ANC** 1. POLITICS a South African political party that fought against apartheid and formed the country's first multiracial government in 1994. Full form **African National Congress** 2. CHEMISTRY acid-neutralizing capacity

**ANLL** MEDICINE acute nonlymphocytic leukaemia

**ANN** COMPUTING artificial neural network

**ann.** 1. PUBLISHING annals 2. annual 3. FINANCE annuity

**anon.** anonymous (NOTE: The abbreviation **anon.** often follows a quotation of unknown authorship.)

**ANSI** /ˈænsi/ American National Standards Institute

**ANSI C** /ˌænsiˈsiː/ COMPUTING a standard version of the C programming language

**ant.** 1. antiquarian 2. antiquity 3. LANGUAGE antonym

**Ant.** Antarctica

**anthrop.** 1. anthropological 2. anthropology

**antiq.** 1. antiquarian 2. antiquity

**ANU** EDUCATION Australian National University

**Anzac** /ˈænzæk/ ARMY (member of the) Australia and New Zealand Army Corps
The abbreviation **Anzac** originally applied to soldiers who served with the Australia and New Zealand Army Corps in World War I. It was subsequently used to denote any Australian or New Zealand soldier.

**ANZCERTA** COMMERCE Australia and New Zealand Closer Economic Relations Trade Agreement

**ANZUS** /ˈænzəs/ INTERNATIONAL RELATIONS a defence treaty negotiated between Australia, New Zealand, and the United States in 1951. Full form **Australia, New Zealand, and the United States**

**ao** ONLINE Angola (NOTE: The abbreviation **ao** is seen at the end of Internet addresses, preceded by a dot.)

**AO** 1. *Aus* STOCK EXCHANGE All-Ordinaries Index 2. Officer in the Order of Australia

**a/o** ACCOUNTING account of

**AOAI** ENVIRONMENT Area of Archaeological Importance

**AOB** usually the last item on the agenda of a meeting. Full form **any other business**

**AOC** WINE a certification for French wine that guarantees its origin and high quality. Full form **appellation d'origine contrôlée**

**AOL** COMPUTING America Online

**AOM** ENVIRONMENT active organic matter

**AON** STOCK EXCHANGE describing an order that must be executed in its entirety or not at all. Full form **all or none**

**AONB** ENVIRONMENT an area of countryside officially designated as being special and deserving of protection. Full form **Area of Outstanding Natural Beauty**

There are 41 AONBs in England and Wales. The first AONB to be designated was the Gower peninsula in Wales, in 1956. Other abbreviations connected with nature conservation include **ESA** (environmentally sensitive area), **SAC** (special area of conservation), **SPA** (special protection area), and **SSSI** (site of special scientific interest)

**AOR** MUSIC adult-oriented rock

**AP 1.** MILITARY Air Police **2.** *US* TRAVEL accommodation and all meals at a hotel: the US equivalent of full board. Full form **American plan 3.** MILITARY antipersonnel **4.** PUBLISHING Associated Press

**a.p. 1.** FINANCE additional premium **2.** PUBLISHING author's proof **3.** PHARMACOLOGY before a meal. Full form **ante prandium** (NOTE: The abbreviation **a.p.** is used in prescriptions.)

**APA** COMPUTING all points addressable

**APACS** BUSINESS Association for Payment Clearing Services

**APB 1.** ACCOUNTING Accounting Principles Board **2.** *US* CRIME a message broadcast to all police in a particular area, usually containing urgent information or a warning. Full form **all-points bulletin 3.** ACCOUNTING Auditing Practices Board

**APC** COMMERCE average propensity to consume

**APD** MEDICINE adult polycyclic disease

**APEC** /'eɪpek/ FINANCE Asia-Pacific Economic Cooperation

**Apex** /'eɪpeks/ TRAVEL a system whereby air or rail tickets are available at a reduced price when bought a specific period of time in advance. Full form **advance-purchase excursion**

**APH** MEDICINE antepartum haemorrhage

**API 1.** INDUST American Petroleum Institute **2.** COMPUTING application programming interface

**APM 1.** COMPUTING a specification that allows an operating system such as earlier versions of Windows to control the power management features of a computer. Full form **advanced power management 2.** COMMERCE average propensity to import

**A.P.Nr** WINE an indication that a German wine has met the minimum standards required by law. Full form **Amtliche Prüfungsnummer** (NOTE: From the German, 'official test number'.)

**Apoc.** BIBLE **1.** another name for the book of Revelation. Full form **Apocalypse 2.** Apocrypha

**APP 1.** MEDICINE amyloid precursor protein **2.** COMMERCE average physical product

**app. 1.** apparatus **2.** PUBLISHING appendix **3.** applied **4.** appointed **5.** apprentice **6.** approved **7.** approximate

**APPC** COMPUTING advanced program to program communications

**approx. 1.** approximate **2.** approximately

**appt** appointment

**APR** FINANCE **1.** the annual equivalent of an interest rate quoted for a different interval, usually monthly. Full form **annual percentage rate 2.** annual purchase rate (NOTE: The abbreviation **APR** is used to show repayment rates in hire-purchase schemes.)

**Apr.** CALENDAR April

**APRA** /'æprə/ FINANCE Australian Prudential Regulation Authority

**APS** COMMERCE average propensity to save

**apt** apartment

**APT** RAIL advanced passenger train

**APV** FINANCE adjusted present value

**APY** FINANCE annual percentage yield

**aq** ONLINE Antarctica (NOTE: The abbreviation **aq** is seen at the end of Internet addresses, preceded by a dot.)

**AQ** EDUCATION achievement quotient

**aq. 1.** PHARMACEUTICAL INDUSTRY water. Full form **aqua 2.** PHARMACEUTICAL INDUSTRY a solution made in water. Full form **aqua 3.** CHEMISTRY aqueous

**AQS** ECOLOGY air quality standards

**Ar** CHEMICAL ELEMENTS argon

**AR 1.** ACCOUNTING a record that shows how much is owed to a company by customers who have purchased supplies or services on credit. Full form **accounts receivable 2.** MAIL Arkansas (NOTE: The abbreviation **AR** is part of the US sorting code on the last line of an Arkansas address.) **3.** MEDICINE attributable risk

**ar.** TRAVEL **1.** arrival **2.** arrive

**Ar. 1.** Arabia **2.** Arabian **3.** LANGUAGE Arabic

**ARA** ARTS Associate of the Royal Academy

**Arab. 1.** Arabia **2.** Arabian **3.** LANGUAGE Arabic

**arb.** STOCK EXCHANGE arbitrageur

**ARC** MEDICINE **1.** the set of symptoms associated with infection by HIV, including weight loss and fever. Full form **Aids-related complex 2.** Aids-related condition

**arch. 1.** archaic **2.** archaism **3.** archery **4.** GEOGRAPHY archipelago **5.** architect **6.** architecture

**archd. 1.** CHRISTIANITY archdeacon **2.** archduke

**archit.** architecture

**ARD** MEDICINE acute respiratory disease

**ARDS** /ɑːdz/ MEDICINE adult respiratory distress syndrome

**ARELS** /ˈærəlz/ EDUCATION Association of Recognized English Language Schools

**aren't** /ɑːnt/ **1.** am not **2.** are not

**arg** COMPUTING a value that modifies how a command or junction operates in a computer program. Full form **argument**

**ARL** RUGBY Australian Rugby League

**ARLL** COMPUTING advanced run-length limited

**ARM** *US* FINANCE adjustable-rate mortgage

**ARP 1.** ECOLOGY acreage reduction programme **2.** COMPUTING address resolution protocol **3.** /ɑːp/ MILITARY air-raid precautions

**ARPANET** /ˈɑːpənet/ COMPUTING a wide area network (WAN) of the late 1960s linking government, academic, business, and military sites. Full form **Advanced Research Projects Agency Network** (NOTE: **ARPANET** was a precursor of the Internet.)

**ARPS** STOCK EXCHANGE adjustable-rate preferred stock

**ARQ** COMPUTING automatic repeat request

**arr. 1.** MUSIC arranged **2.** TRAVEL arrival **3.** TRAVEL arrived **4.** TRAVEL arrives

**ART** MEDICINE assisted reproductive technology

**art. 1.** article **2.** artificial **3.** ARMS artillery **4.** artist

**arty** MILITARY artillery

**as** ONLINE American Samoa (NOTE: The abbreviation **as** is seen at the end of Internet addresses, preceded by a dot.)

**As** CHEMICAL ELEMENTS arsenic

**AS 1.** BANKING a term used for defining how long a person has to settle a bill after having been presented with it, e.g. *30 days AS*. Full form **after sight 2.** LANGUAGE Anglo-Saxon **3.** MILITARY antisubmarine

**As. 1.** Asia **2.** Asian

**ASA** MARKETING Advertising Standards Authority

**ASAP** /ˈeɪsæp/ as soon as possible

**a.s.a.p.** /ˈeɪsæp/ as soon as possible

**ASAT** MILITARY antisatellite

**ASB** ACCOUNTING Accounting Standards Board

**ASBO** LAW antisocial behaviour order

**ASC** ACCOUNTING Accounting Standards Committee

**ASCAP** PUBLISHING American Society of Composers, Authors, and Publishers

**ASCII** /ˈæskiː/ COMPUTING full form **American Standard Code for Information Interchange**

**ASD** MEDICINE autistic spectrum disorders

**ASEAN** /ˈæziən/ POLITICS Association of Southeast Asian Nations

**ASF** COMPUTING Active Streaming Format

**ASH** HEALTH Action on Smoking and Health

**ASI** AEROSPACE airspeed indicator

**ASIC 1.** COMPUTING application-specific integrated circuits **2.** FINANCE Australian Securities and Investments Commission

**ASIO** /ˈeɪziəʊ/ MILITARY Australian Security Intelligence Organization

**ASIS** /ˈæsɪs/ MILITARY Australian Secret Intelligence Service

**ASL** LANGUAGE American Sign Language

**ASLEF** /ˈæzlef/ HUMAN RESOURCES Associated Society of Locomotive Engineers and Firemen

**AS level** EDUCATION in England, Wales, and Northern Ireland, a school examination taken at an advanced level in a subject. It is equivalent to half an A-level. Full form **Advanced Subsidiary level** (NOTE: Before 2000, the full name of the examination was *Advanced Supplementary level*.)

**ASM** ARMS air-to-surface missile

**ASP** COMPUTING **1.** a page in HTML with scripts that are processed on a server before being sent to a user. Full form **active server page 2.** a company that provides one or more program functions (e.g. accounting) on behalf of an enterprise, freeing it to concentrate on its primary business. Full form **application service provider**

**ASR** COMPUTING automatic send/receive

**ASSR** POLITICS Autonomous Soviet Socialist Republic

**asst** assistant

**asstd 1.** assisted **2.** assorted

**AST 1.** /æst/ TIME Atlantic Standard Time **2.** STOCK EXCHANGE automated screen trading

**astrol. 1.** astrologer **2.** astrological **3.** astrology

**astron. 1.** astronomer **2.** astronomical **3.** astronomy

**ASU** HUMAN RESOURCES Australian Services Union

**ASX** STOCK EXCHANGE Australian Stock Exchange

**at** ONLINE Austria (NOTE: The abbreviation **at** is seen at the end of Internet addresses, preceded by a dot.)

**At** CHEMICAL ELEMENTS astatine

**AT 1.** COMPUTING a standard of PC originally developed by IBM that uses a 16-bit 80286 processor. Full form **Advanced Technologies 2.** MILITARY antitank **3.** TIME Atlantic Time **4.** EDUCATION attainment target

**at. 1.** MEASUREMENTS, PHYSICS atmosphere **2.** PHYSICS atomic

**ATAPI** COMPUTING AT attachment packet interface

**ATB 1.** VEHICLES all-terrain bike **2.** EXTREME SPORTS all-terrain boarding

**ATC 1.** AIR FORCE Air Training Corps **2.** AVIAT air-traffic control

**ATM 1.** COMPUTING Adobe Type Manager **2.** COMPUTING asynchronous transfer mode **3.** BANKING another name for a cashpoint. Full form **automated teller machine**

**atm. 1.** MEASUREMENTS atmosphere **2.** atmospheric

**at. no.** CHEMISTRY atomic number

**ATO** /ˈeɪtəʊ/ FINANCE Australian Taxation Office

**A to D** ELECTRONICS analogue to digital

**ATOL** /ˈætɒl/ AVIAT Air Travel Organizers' Licence

**ATP 1.** BIOCHEMISTRY a chemical compound in living organisms that releases energy for cellular reactions when it converts to ADP. Full form **adenosine triphosphate 2.** TENNIS Association of Tennis Professionals

**ATPase** /ˌeɪ tiː piː ˈeɪz/ BIOCHEMISTRY an enzyme that aids the breakdown of ATP into ADP with a release of energy. Full form **adenosine triphosphatase**

**ATS 1.** MEDICINE antitetanus serum **2.** TECHNOLOGY Applications Technology Satellite **3.** BANKING automatic transfer service

**ATSIC** *Aus* POLITICS a federal authority representing the interests of Australia's indigenous peoples. Full form **Aboriginal and Torres Strait Islander Commission**

**att. 1.** attached **2.** attention **3.** LAW attorney

**Att. Gen.** LAW Attorney General

**attn** attention

**attrib.** GRAMMAR attributive

**Atty. Gen.** LAW Attorney General

**ATV** VEHICLES all-terrain vehicle

**at. wt** CHEMISTRY atomic weight

**au** ONLINE Australia (NOTE: The abbreviation **au** is seen at the end of Internet addresses, preceded by a dot.)

**Au** CHEMICAL ELEMENTS gold (NOTE: From the Latin *aurum*.)

**AU 1.** MEASUREMENTS, PHYSICS angstrom unit **2.** MEASUREMENTS, ASTRONOMY astronomical unit

**a.u. 1.** MEASUREMENTS, PHYSICS angstrom unit **2.** MEASUREMENTS, ASTRONOMY astronomical unit

**AUC 1.** ab urbe condita (NOTE: The abbreviation **AUC**, from the Latin, 'in the year from the founding of the city', was used by Roman classical writers to specify dates in terms of the number of years since Rome's foundation in 753 BC.) **2.** EDUCATION Australian Universities Commission

**AUD** MONEY Australian dollar

**aud.** ACCOUNTING **1.** audit **2.** auditor

**Aug.** CALENDAR August

**AUP** COMPUTING acceptable use policy

**AUS** EDUCATION Australian Union of Students

**Aus. 1.** Australia **2.** Australian **3.** Austria **4.** Austrian

**Aust. 1.** Australia **2.** Australian **3.** Austria **4.** Austrian

**AUSTEL** /ˈɒztel/ TELECOMMUNICATIONS Australian Telecommunications Authority

**Austral. 1.** Australasia **2.** Australia **3.** Australian

**AUT 1.** HUMAN RESOURCES Association of University Teachers **2.** FINANCE authorized unit trust

**auth. 1.** authentic **2.** author **3.** authority **4.** authorized

**AUTIF** FINANCE Association of Unit Trusts and Investment Funds

**auto. 1.** automatic **2.** MECHANICAL ENGINEERING automotive

**aux.** auxiliary

**A/UX** COMPUTING a version of the UNIX operating system for the Apple Mac range of computers. Full form **Apple's UNIX**

**AV 1.** MEDIA audiovisual **2.** BIBLE Authorized Version

**av. 1.** average **2.** MEASUREMENTS avoirdupois

**Av.** ROADS avenue

**a/v 1.** FINANCE in proportion to the value. Full form **ad valorem 2.** MEDICINE audiovisual

**AVA** WINE a designated grape-growing area for US wines. Full form **American Viticultural Area** (NOTE: The abbreviation **AVA** is used on US wine labels in a similar way to AC or AOC on French wines.)

**AVC 1.** PENSIONS additional voluntary contribution **2.** BUSINESS average variable cost

**avdp.** MEASUREMENTS avoirdupois

**Ave.** ROADS avenue (NOTE: The abbreviation **Ave.** is used in addresses.)

**avg.** average

**AVM 1.** AIR FORCE Air Vice-Marshal **2.** MEDICINE arteriovenous malformation

**AVPU** MEDICINE a checklist for rating a person's level of consciousness that includes assessing his or her responsiveness to verbal and painful stimuli. Full form **alert, verbal, pain, unresponsive**

**A/W** MEASUREMENTS actual weight

**AWACS** /'eɪwæks/ MILITARY a radar and computer system carried in an aircraft to track large numbers of low-flying aircraft. Full form **airborne warning and control system**

**AWBC** WINE Australian Wine and Brandy Corporation

**AWE** STATISTICS average weekly earnings

**az** ONLINE Azerbaijan (NOTE: The abbreviation **az** is seen at the end of Internet addresses, preceded by a dot.)

**AZ** MAIL Arizona (NOTE: The abbreviation **AZ** is part of the US sorting code on the last line of an Arizona address.)

**az. 1.** ASTRONOMY azimuth **2.** HERALDRY azure

**AZT** PHARMACOLOGY an antiviral drug used in the treatment of Aids. Full form **azidothymidine**

# B

**b 1.** MEASUREMENTS, PHYSICS a unit of nuclear cross section. Full form **barn 2.** MUSIC bass
**3.** MUSIC basso **4.** MEASUREMENTS, ACOUSTICS bel **5.** billion **6.** COMPUTING bit **7.** book **8.** born
**9.** CRICKET bowled **10.** breadth **11.** CRICKET a run scored off a ball that has not been hit
by a batsman, awarded to the team as a whole. Full form **bye**

**B 1.** EDUCATION Bachelor (NOTE: The abbreviation **B** is used in degree titles, as in *BSc*.) **2.**
MUSIC bass **3.** MUSIC basso **4.** PHYSICS a scale for calibrating hydrometers that are used to
ascertain the relative density of liquids. Full form **Baumé scale 5.** GEOGRAPHY Bay (*used
on maps*) **6.** MEASUREMENTS, ACOUSTICS bel **7.** billion **8.** CHESS bishop **9.** black (NOTE: The
abbreviation **B**, when used on pencils, indicates that the lead is soft.) **10.** book **11.**
CHEMICAL ELEMENTS boron **12.** breadth **13.** COMPUTING byte **14.** COMPUTING eleven (*used in
hexadecimal notation*) **15.** PHYSICS the strength of a magnetic field multiplied by the
porosity of a medium. Symbol for **magnetic flux density 16.** ROADS a secondary road
(NOTE: The abbreviation **B** in this sense is used before the road number, as in *B2143*.)

**B2B** E-COMMERCE business-to-business

**B2C** E-COMMERCE business-to-consumer

**B4** ONLINE before (*used in e-mails and text messages*)

**B4N** ONLINE bye for now (*used in e-mails and text messages*)

**Ba** CHEMICAL ELEMENTS barium

**BA 1.** EDUCATION Bachelor of Arts **2.** WINE German term meaning 'selected berries', used
to refer to grapes selected by hand before pressing. Full form **Beerenauslese 3.** British
Academy **4.** British Airways **5.** SCIENCE British Association (for the Advancement of
Science)

**BAA** ACCOUNTING British Accounting Association

**BAC** BIOTECHNOLOGY a sequence of DNA taken from another organism and inserted in a
bacterium to reveal its function. Full form **bacterial artificial chromosome**

**BACS** /bæks/ BUSINESS a system for transferring funds directly from one bank account to
another. It is used, e.g., by companies making payments to regular suppliers. Full form
**Bankers' Automated Clearing System**

**bact.** MICROBIOLOGY **1.** bacteria **2.** bacteriology

**bacteriol.** MICROBIOLOGY bacteriology

**BADC** ACCOUNTING Business Accounting Deliberation Council of Japan

**BAFTA** /ˈbæftə/ CINEMA British Academy of Film and Television Arts

**BAHA** MEDICINE bone anchored hearing aid

**BAL** MEDICINE dimercaprol: an antidote to heavy metal poisoning. Full form **British anti-
lewisite**

**BAN** BANKING a short-term bond issued in anticipation of a larger bond issue. Full form
**bond anticipation note**

**B & B** TRAVEL bed and breakfast

> The abbreviation is sometimes used as a noun to denote a relatively small, informal, and
> inexpensive establishment offering such accommodation, especially a guesthouse or private
> home as opposed to a hotel.

**B and S Ball** DANCE a social event held in the Australian outback for young people,
typically a weekend of music, dancing, and drinking. Full form **Bachelor and Spinsters
Ball**

**B & W** PHOTOGRAPHY, TV, CINEMA black-and-white

**bar. 1.** METEOROLOGY barometer **2.** METEOROLOGY barometric **3.** MEASUREMENTS barrel (NOTE: The abbreviation **BAR** is used in the oil and brewing industries.)

**Bar. 1.** LAW barrister **2.** BIBLE Baruch

**BARB** /bɑːb/ BROADCASTING Broadcasters' Audience Research Board

**BArch** EDUCATION Bachelor of Architecture

**BARS** BUSINESS a method of assessing employee's performance according to their behaviour. Full form **behaviourally anchored rating scales**

**Bart** baronet

**BAS 1.** EDUCATION Bachelor of Agricultural Science **2.** EDUCATION Bachelor of Applied Science **3.** *Aus* BUSINESS a tax statement made yearly by businesses. Full form **Business Activity Statement**

**BASc** EDUCATION **1.** Bachelor of Agricultural Science **2.** Bachelor of Applied Science

**BASIC** /ˈbeɪsɪk/ COMPUTING a high-level computer programming language that uses common English terms and algebra. Full form **Beginners All-purpose Symbolic Instruction Code**

**BASW** SOCIAL WELFARE British Association of Social Workers

**BAT** /bæt/ COMPUTING a filename extension used in MS-DOS systems to signify a batch file (i.e. a computer file containing a series of commands to be processed as if they were entered from the keyboard consecutively). Full form **batch**

**bat. 1.** COMPUTING batch **2.** MILITARY battalion

**BATNEEC** /ˈbætniːk/ ENVIRONMENT a principle applied to the control of emissions into the air, land, and water from polluting processes, minimizing pollution without requiring technology or methods that are not yet available or unreasonably expensive. Full form **best available technology not entailing excessive cost**

**bb** ONLINE Barbados (NOTE: The abbreviation **bb** is seen at the end of Internet addresses, preceded by a dot.)

**BB 1.** Boys' Brigade **2.** ONLINE bye-bye (*used in e-mails and text messages*) **3.** double black (NOTE: The abbreviation **BB**, when used on pencils, indicates that the lead is very soft.)

**BBA 1.** EDUCATION Bachelor of Business Administration **2.** BANKING British Bankers' Association

**BBC** BROADCASTING British Broadcasting Corporation (NOTE: The abbreviation **BBC** itself is sometimes informally shortened to Beeb.)

**BBFC** CINEMA British Board of Film Classification

**bbl** MEASUREMENTS barrel (NOTE: The abbreviation **BBL** is used in the oil and brewing industries.)

**BBQ** FOOD barbecue

**BBS** ONLINE an online forum used to exchange e-mails, chat, and access software. Full form **bulletin board system**

**BC 1.** ONLINE because (*used in e-mails and text messages*) **2.** CALENDAR before Christ **3.** MEDICINE bone conduction **4.** British Columbia **5.** FINANCE budgetary control

The abbreviation **BC** is used to indicate a date that is a specified number of years before the birth of Jesus Christ. The alternative **BCE** (before the Common Era) may be used to avoid the association with Christianity.

**BCA** COMMERCE Business Council of Australia

**bcc** COMPUTING a copy of an e-mail sent to somebody at the same time as the original message without the primary addressee being aware of this. Full form **blind carbon copy**

**BCC 1.** COMPUTING an error detection method for blocks of transmitted data. Full form **block character check 2.** HEALTH Breast Cancer Campaign **3.** COMMERCE British Chambers of Commerce

**BCCS** FINANCE Board of Currency Commissioners

**BCD** COMPUTING a numbering system in which each digit of a decimal is converted into a binary number. Full form **binary coded decimal**

**BCE** 1. *US* EDUCATION Bachelor of Chemical Engineering 2. EDUCATION Bachelor of Civil Engineering 3. CALENDAR before the Common Era (NOTE: The abbreviation **BCE** is used after a date as the non-Christian equivalent of BC.)

**BCG** PHARMACOLOGY an anti-tuberculosis vaccine made from a weakened strain of the tubercle bacillus. Full form **bacillus Calmette-Guérin (vaccine)** (NOTE: The abbreviation **BCG** is used as a noun denoting an injection of this vaccine.)

**BCh** EDUCATION Bachelor of Surgery (NOTE: From the Latin *Baccalaureus Chirurgiae*.)

**BCH code** COMPUTING an error-correcting code. Full form **Bose-Chandhuri-Hocquenghem code**

**BChE** EDUCATION Bachelor of Chemical Engineering

**BCL** Bachelor of Civil Law

**BCNF** COMPUTING a method of structuring information in a database to improve storage efficiency. Full form **Boyce-Codd normal form**

**BCNU** ONLINE be seeing you (*used in e-mails and text messages*)

**BCNZ** BROADCASTING Broadcasting Corporation of New Zealand

**BCPL** COMPUTING a high-level programming language. Full form **Basic Combined Programming Language**

**BCS** COMPUTING 1. a system that runs dedicated programs or tasks for a central computer. Full form **basic control system (satellite)** 2. British Computer Society

**bd** 1. ONLINE Bangladesh (NOTE: The abbreviation **bd** is seen at the end of Internet addresses, preceded by a dot.) 2. NAUTICAL board 3. FINANCE bond 4. PUBLISHING bound

**BD** 1. EDUCATION Bachelor of Divinity 2. MEDICINE Borna disease

**B/D** 1. BANKING bank draft 2. BANKING banker's draft 3. BANKING bills discounted 4. ACCOUNTING brought down

**BDA** DENTISTRY British Dental Association

**bd ft** MEASUREMENTS, CONSTRUCTION a unit of volume for timber, equal to the volume of a board that is one foot square and one inch thick. Full form **board foot**

**BDI** BUSINESS a measure of a brand's sales in an area in relation to the number of people living there. Full form **brand development index**

**Bdr** MILITARY Bombardier

**bds** 1. PUBLISHING bound in boards 2. bundles

**BDS** EDUCATION Bachelor of Dental Surgery

**be** ONLINE Belgium (NOTE: The abbreviation **be** is seen at the end of Internet addresses, preceded by a dot.)

**Be** CHEMICAL ELEMENTS beryllium

**BE** 1. EDUCATION Bachelor of Education 2. EDUCATION Bachelor of Engineering 3. COMMERCE a document setting out an instruction to pay a named person a fixed sum of money on a specified date or when the person requests payment. Full form **bill of exchange**

**BEC** COMPUTING a device that extends an 8-bit bus to accommodate 16-bit add-in cards. Full form **bus extension card**

**BECTU** /'bektuː/ Broadcasting, Entertainment, and Cinematograph Technicians Union

**BEd** EDUCATION Bachelor of Education

**beds** bedrooms (*used in property advertisements*)

**Beds.** Bedfordshire

**BEF** the British Army that served overseas during World War I and World War II. Full form **British Expeditionary Force**

**BER** COMPUTING 1. basic encoding rule 2. bit error rate

**Berks.** Berkshire

**betcha** /ˈbetʃə/ a form of 'bet you' used mainly in conversation

**bf 1.** bloody fool **2.** PRINTING boldface

**BF** Belgian franc

**b/f** ACCOUNTING brought forward

**BFE** STOCK EXCHANGE Baltic Futures Exchange

**BFI** CINEMA British Film Institute

**BFN** ONLINE bye for now (NOTE: The abbreviation **BFN**, now used in e-mails or text messages, predates modern technology, having been in general informal use since the mid-20th century or earlier.)

**BFPO** MILITARY British Forces Post Office

**bg** ONLINE Bulgaria (NOTE: The abbreviation **bg** is seen at the end of Internet addresses, preceded by a dot.)

**BG** *N Am* MILITARY Brigadier General

**BGC** BANKING bank giro credit

**BGP** COMPUTING a protocol that allows routers to share routing information to allow each router to calculate the most efficient path for information. Full form **border gateway protocol**

**bh** ONLINE Bahrain (NOTE: The abbreviation **bh** is seen at the end of Internet addresses, preceded by a dot.)

**Bh** CHEMICAL ELEMENTS bohrium

**BHC** CHEMISTRY benzene hexachloride

**Bhd** BUSINESS a Malay word meaning limited, when referring to businesses in Malaysia. Full form **Berhad**

**bhp** MECHANICAL ENGINEERING brake horsepower

**BHT** CHEMISTRY a crystalline solid used as an antioxidant for fats and oils. Full form **butylated hydroxytoluene**

**bi** ONLINE Burundi (NOTE: The abbreviation **ac** is seen at the end of Internet addresses, preceded by a dot.)

**Bi** CHEMICAL ELEMENTS bismuth

**Bib.** RELIGION **1.** Bible **2.** biblical

**bibl.** PUBLISHING bibliography

**b.i.d.** PHARMACEUTICAL INDUSTRY twice a day (NOTE: The abbreviation **b.i.d.**, from the Latin *ut dictum*, is used in prescriptions.)

**BIM** COMMERCE British Institute of Management

**BIN** BUSINESS a six-digit number used to identify banks for charge-card purposes. Full form **bank identification number**

**BIND** COMPUTING software that provides the functions of a Domain Name Server for server computers running BSD UNIX. Full form **Berkeley Internet Name Domain**

**biog.** LITERATURE **1.** biographer **2.** biographical **3.** biography

**biol. 1.** biological **2.** biology

**BIOS** /ˈbaɪɒs/ COMPUTING a small unerasable computer program that contains the instructions needed to begin operation and controls the data flow between the operating system and application programs and the hardware devices. Full form **basic input-output system**

**BIPS** /bɪps/ E-COMMERCE bank Internet payment system

**BIS** BANKING Bank for International Settlements

**B-ISDN** COMPUTING broadband ISDN

**BITC** COMPUTING a time code that is transmitted with a video signal and appears on the screen. Full form **burned in time code**

**bitmp** /'bɪtmæp/ COMPUTING a representation of a graphics image in computer memory consisting of rows and columns of dots, each corresponding to a pixel. Full form **bitmap**

**BITNET** /'bɪtnet/ COMPUTING a network similar to the Internet, used to connect mainly academic sites. Full form **Because It's Time Network**

**BIX** COMPUTING a commercial online system founded by Byte magazine. Full form **Byte Information Exchange**

**biz** /bɪz/ ONLINE business (NOTE: The abbreviation **biz** is seen at the end of Internet addresses, preceded by a dot.)

**BJP** POLITICS the political party currently in power in India. Full form **Bharatiya Janata Party**

**BJT** ELECTRICITY bipolar junction transistor

**bk 1.** BANKING bank **2.** book

**Bk** CHEMICAL ELEMENTS berkelium

**bks 1.** MILITARY barracks **2.** books

**bl** barrel

**BL 1.** EDUCATION Bachelor of Law **2.** EDUCATION Bachelor of Letters **3.** *US* LAW Barrister-at-Law **4.** FREIGHT bill of lading **5.** LIBRARIES British Library

**bldg** building

**BLit** EDUCATION Bachelor of Literature

**BLitt** Bachelor of Letters (or Literature) (NOTE: From the Latin *Baccalaureus Litterarum*.)

**blk 1.** block **2.** bulk

**BLL** EDUCATION Bachelor of Laws

**blob** /blɒb/ COMPUTING a field in a database record that can contain a large amount of binary data. Full form **binary large object**

**BLT** FOOD bacon, lettuce, and tomato (sandwich)

**Blvd** ROADS Boulevard

**bm 1.** MEASUREMENTS, CONSTRUCTION a system for measuring timber volume based on the board foot (bd ft). Full form **board measure 2.** PHYSIOLOGY bowel movement

**BM 1.** EDUCATION Bachelor of Medicine **2.** bench mark **3.** ARTS British Museum

**BMA** MEDICINE British Medical Association

**BMI** HEALTH a measure of body fat content, found by dividing a person's weight in kgs by their height in metres squared. Full form **body mass index**

**BMJ** MEDICINE British Medical Journal

**BMP** COMPUTING a filename extension indicating that the file contains a bitmapped graphics image. Full form **bitmap**

**BMR** BIOLOGY the rate at which an organism consumes oxygen while awake but at rest. Full form **basal metabolic rate**

**BMus** EDUCATION Bachelor of Music

**BMX** CYCLING the riding or racing of bicycles designed for use on rough terrain or open country. Full form **bicycle motocross** (NOTE: The abbreviation **BMX** is often used before a noun, as in *a BMX bike*.)

**bn 1.** MILITARY battalion **2.** billion **3.** ONLINE Brunei (NOTE: The abbreviation **bn** is seen at the end of Internet addresses, preceded by a dot.)

**Bn 1.** baron **2.** MILITARY battalion

**BNF 1.** COMPUTING a system of writing and expressing the syntax of a programming language. Full form **Backus-Naur-Form 2.** PHARMACOLOGY British National Formulary

**BNFL** INDUST British Nuclear Fuels Ltd

**bo** ONLINE Bolivia (NOTE: The abbreviation **bo** is seen at the end of Internet addresses, preceded by a dot.)

**BO 1.** PHYSIOLOGY body odour **2.** PERFORMING ARTS box office **3.** COMMERCE branch office

The abbreviation **BO** is used as a noun with reference to the condition of people who smell unpleasant because of excessive sweating or poor personal hygiene, as in *He has BO*. The term was originally coined by a deodorant advertiser in 1919.

**b.o. 1.** COMMERCE branch office **2.** STOCK EXCHANGE broker's order **3.** STOCK EXCHANGE buyer's option

**B/O** ACCOUNTING brought over

**BOD** ENVIRONMENT a measure of the pollution present in water, obtained by measuring the amount of oxygen absorbed from the water by the microorganisms present in it. Full form **biochemical oxygen demand**

**BOF** COMPUTING beginning of file

**BOGOF** /ˈbɒgɒf/ COMMERCE buy one, get one free (NOTE: The abbreviation **BOGOF** is used as a noun to denote such promotions, but advertisements and in-store signs usually bear the full form.)

**BOJ** BANKING Bank of Japan

**Bol. 1.** Bolivia **2.** Bolivian

**BOP** ECONOMICS balance of payments

**BOSS** /bɒs/ POLITICS a South African intelligence organization during the apartheid era. Full form **Bureau of State Security**

**BoT** COMMERCE Board of Trade

**BOT 1.** ECONOMICS balance of trade **2.** COMPUTING beginning of tape **3.** COMMERCE Board of Trade

**bot. 1.** botanical **2.** botany

**bp 1.** baptized **2.** GENETICS a chemical unit linking complementary strands of DNA or RNA. Full form **base pair 3.** FINANCE bills payable **4.** birthplace **5.** CHESS bishop **6.** CHEMISTRY boiling point

**BP 1.** ARCHAEOLOGY a calendar system used in chronological dating. Full form **before the present 2.** FINANCE bills payable **3.** MEDICINE blood pressure **4.** PHARMACEUTICAL INDUSTRY British Pharmacopoeia (NOTE: The abbreviation **BP** is used on product labels to indicate compliance with the specified quality standards.)

**B/P** FINANCE bills payable

**BPC** PHARMACOLOGY British Pharmaceutical Codex

**BPH** MEDICINE benign prostatic hypertrophy

**BPharm** /ˌbiː ˈfɑːm/ EDUCATION Bachelor of Pharmacy

**BPhil** /ˌbiː ˈfɪl/ EDUCATION Bachelor of Philosophy

**bpi** MEASUREMENTS, COMPUTING **1.** bits per inch **2.** bytes per inch

**bpp** COMPUTING bits per pixel

**BPR** BUSINESS the analysis of business practices and redesign of these to improve efficiency. Full form **business process re-engineering**

**bps** MEASUREMENTS, COMPUTING a measurement of data transfer speed, e.g. in modems and serial ports. Full form **bits per second**

**Bq** MEASUREMENTS, PHYSICS becquerel

**br 1.** FINANCE bills receivable **2.** ONLINE Brazil (NOTE: The abbreviation **br** is seen at the end of Internet addresses, preceded by a dot.)

**Br** CHEMICAL ELEMENTS bromine

**BR 1.** *US* ONLINE bathroom (*used in e-mails and text messages*) **2.** bedroom (*used in property advertisements*) **3.** RAIL British Rail

**br. 1.** branch **2.** METALLURGY brass **3.** LAW brief **4.** METALLURGY bronze **5.** brother **6.** brown

**Br. 1.** Britain **2.** British **3.** RELIGION Brother

**B/R** FINANCE bills receivable

**BRAD** BUSINESS British Rate and Data

**Braz. 1.** Brazil **2.** Brazilian

**BRCS** HEALTH British Red Cross Society

**BRE 1.** EDUCATION Bachelor of Religious Education **2.** CONSTRUCTION Building Research Establishment

**Brig.** MILITARY **1.** brigade **2.** Brigadier

**Brig. Gen.** /ˌbrɪg 'dʒen/ *N Am* MILITARY Brigadier General

**Brit. 1.** Britain **2.** British

**bro.** brother

**Bros.** COMMERCE brothers

**bs** ONLINE Bahamas (NOTE: The abbreviation **bs** is seen at the end of Internet addresses, preceded by a dot.)

**BS 1.** *US* EDUCATION Bachelor of Surgery **2.** COMPUTING backspace **3.** COMMERCE bill of sale **4.** PUBLISHING British Standard (NOTE: The abbreviation **BS** is used as part of the number of a BSI publication: *BS EN 771–1*.) **5.** *N Am* bullshit

**b.s. 1.** ACCOUNTING balance sheet **2.** COMMERCE bill of sale

**B/S** ACCOUNTING balance sheet

**BSA** FINANCE Building Societies Association

**BSAM** COMPUTING a method of storing and retrieving blocks of data in a continuous sequence. Full form **basic sequential access method**

**BSB** MEASUREMENTS, MECHANICAL ENGINEERING British Standard brass (NOTE: The abbreviation **BSB** is used to identify a type of screw thread.)

**BSc** EDUCATION Bachelor of Science

**BSD** COMPUTING Berkeley Software Distribution

**BSE** VETERINARY MEDICINE a disease that affects the nervous system of cattle, believed to be caused by a prion (an abnormal transmissible protein) and related to CJD in humans. Full form **bovine spongiform encephalopathy**

The abbreviation **BSE** is used as a noun, and the full form is rarely encountered in general usage. BSE caused major problems for the British meat industry in the late 20th century and became informally known as 'mad cow disease'.

**BSF** MEASUREMENTS, MECHANICAL ENGINEERING British Standard fine (NOTE: The abbreviation **BSF** is used to identify a type of screw thread.)

**bsh.** MEASUREMENTS bushel

**BSI** COMMERCE British Standards Institution

**BSL** LANGUAGE British Sign Language

**Bs/L** FREIGHT bills of lading

**BSN** EDUCATION Bachelor of Science in Nursing

**BSP** MEASUREMENTS, MECHANICAL ENGINEERING British Standard pipe (NOTE: The abbreviation **BSP** is used to identify a type of screw thread.)

**BSS** COMMERCE British Standards Specification

**BST 1.** AGRICULTURE a hormone in cattle that regulates growth and milk production. Full form **bovine somatotrophin 2.** TIME British Summer Time

**BSW** MEASUREMENTS, MECHANICAL ENGINEERING British Standard Whitworth (NOTE: The abbreviation **BSW** is used to identify a type of screw thread.)

**bt** ONLINE Bhutan (NOTE: The abbreviation **bt** is seen at the end of Internet addresses, preceded by a dot.)

**Bt** baronet

**BT** TELECOMMUNICATIONS British Telecommunications plc

**BTEC** /'biːtek/ EDUCATION Business and Technology Education Council

**BTG** BUSINESS British Technology Group

**BThU** MEASUREMENTS, PHYSICS British thermal unit

**BTI** FINANCE Business Times Industrial index

**btry** MILITARY battery

**btu** MEASUREMENTS, PHYSICS British thermal unit

**BTU** MEASUREMENTS, ELECTRICITY a unit for measuring electrical energy, equal to 1 kilowatt-hour. Full form **Board of Trade Unit**

**BTW** ONLINE by the way (*used in e-mails and text messages*)

**bty** MILITARY battery

**bu.** MEASUREMENTS bushel

**BUAV** British Union for the Abolition of Vivisection

**Bucks.** Buckinghamshire

**Bur. 1.** Burma **2.** Burmese

**bus.** business

**b.v.** ACCOUNTING book value

**BVM** CHRISTIANITY Blessed Virgin Mary

**bw** ONLINE Botswana (NOTE: The abbreviation **bw** is seen at the end of Internet addresses, preceded by a dot.)

**BW 1.** MILITARY bacteriological warfare **2.** MILITARY biological warfare **3.** PHOTOGRAPHY, TV black-and-white

**BWG** MEASUREMENTS, MECHANICAL ENGINEERING a numerical system for specifying the diameter of metal rods. Full form **Birmingham Wire Gauge**

**BWI 1.** AVIAT Baltimore-Washington International Airport **2.** British West Indies

**BWR** INDUST boiling-water reactor

**BWV** MUSIC Bach Werke-Verzeichnis (NOTE: The abbreviation **BWV**, from the German, 'catalogue of Bach's works', is used before numbers identifying the works of J. S. Bach: *BWV402*.)

**by** ONLINE Belarus (NOTE: The abbreviation **by** is seen at the end of Internet addresses, preceded by a dot.)

**BYAM** ONLINE between you and me (*used in e-mails*)

**BYO** *ANZ* LEISURE a restaurant, party, or event to which guests bring their own alcoholic beverages. Full form **bring your own**

**BYOB** LEISURE bring your own bottle (NOTE: The abbreviation **BOYB** is used on party invitations to indicate that guests should bring their own alcoholic beverages.)

**bz** ONLINE Belize (*used in Internet addresses*) (NOTE: The abbreviation **bz** is seen at the end of Internet addresses, preceded by a dot.)

# C

**c 1.** cancelled **2.** canine **3.** MEASUREMENTS carat **4.** BUSINESS carbon (paper) **5.** carton **6.** case **7.** SPORTS catcher **8.** SPORTS caught by **9.** MONEY cedi **10.** MONEY cent **11.** MONEY centavo **12.** MEASUREMENTS centi- **13.** MONEY centime **14.** MEASUREMENTS centimetre **15.** centre **16.** HISTORY century **17.** PUBLISHING chapter **18.** PHYSICS a quantum characteristic of elementary particles. Full form **charm 19.** VIDEO the part of a video signal that carries colour information. Symbol for **chrominance 20.** CHRISTIANITY church **21.** CALENDAR circa (NOTE: The abbreviation **c** is chiefly used before dates that are approximate or estimated.) **22.** ELECTRICITY circuit **23.** MATHEMATICS circumference **24.** clockwise **25.** METEOROLOGY cloudy **26.** SCIENCE coefficient **27.** cold **28.** ANATOMY colon **29.** colour **30.** ZOOLOGY colt **31.** CHEMISTRY concentration **32.** MATHEMATICS constant **33.** INTERNATIONAL RELATIONS consul **34.** MUSIC contralto **35.** BUSINESS copy **36.** LAW copyright (NOTE: The abbreviation **c** usually appears in the form of the symbol ©, before the name of the copyright-holder.) **37.** MILITARY corps **38.** FINANCE cost **39.** MEASUREMENTS cubic **40.** MEASUREMENTS, NUCLEAR PHYSICS curie **41.** PHYSICS the speed of light in a vacuum

**C 1.** ELECTRICAL ENGINEERING capacitance **2.** MAPS cape **3.** CHEMICAL ELEMENTS carbon **4.** BUILDINGS castle **5.** CHRISTIANITY Catholic **6.** MEASUREMENTS, PHYSICS Celsius **7.** MEASUREMENTS centi- **8.** MEASUREMENTS, PHYSICS centigrade **9.** HISTORY century **10.** POLITICS Chancellor **11.** PHYSICS a quantum characteristic of elementary particles. Full form **charm 12.** MANAGEMENT chief **13.** city **14.** EDUCATION college **15.** MILITARY Companion **16.** POLITICS Congress **17.** POLITICS Conservative **18.** MILITARY corps **19.** MEASUREMENTS, ELECTRICITY coulomb **20.** court **21.** BIOCHEMISTRY cytosine **22.** PHYSICS heat capacity **23.** ONLINE see

> The abbreviation **C** used after a temperature can stand for Celsius or centigrade, as both scales are based on a range of 100 degrees between the freezing and boiling points of water. However, Celsius is now the preferred term in most contexts.

**C2B** E-COMMERCE consumer-to-business

**C2C** E-COMMERCE consumer-to-consumer

**ca 1.** ONLINE Canada (NOTE: The abbreviation **ca** is seen at the end of Internet addresses, preceded by a dot.) **2.** CALENDAR circa (NOTE: The abbreviation **ca** (or **ca.**) is chiefly used before dates that are approximate or estimated.)

**Ca** CHEMICAL ELEMENTS calcium

**CA 1.** MAIL California (NOTE: The abbreviation **CA** is part of the US sorting code on the last line of a California address.) **2.** GEOGRAPHY Central America **3.** GEOGRAPHY Central American **4.** E-COMMERCE an independent server or authority on the internet that issues certificates guaranteeing the authenticity of a company. Full form **certificate authority 5.** ACCOUNTING certified accountant **6.** ACCOUNTING chartered accountant **7.** ACCOUNTING chief accountant **8.** MEDICINE somebody's real age, as opposed to the age suggested by mental or physical development. Full form **chronological age 9.** INTERNATIONAL RELATIONS consular agent **10.** COMMERCE Consumers' Association

**c/a** BANKING current account

**C/A 1.** FINANCE capital account **2.** FINANCE credit account **3.** BANKING current account

**CAA** AVIAT Civil Aviation Authority

**CAAT** E-COMMERCE a web-based manager that allows a certificate authority to issue digital certificates. Full form **certificate authority administration tool**

**Cab** WINE Cabernet Sauvignon

**CAB 1.** Citizens Advice Bureau **2.** AVIAT an organisation responsible for promoting and regulating the civil air transport industry. Full form **Civil Aeronautics Board**

**CABG** MEDICINE coronary artery bypass graft

**CAC** COMMERCE Central Arbitration Committee

**CAD 1.** COMMERCE cash against documents **2.** /kæd/ COMPUTING computer-aided (or -assisted) design

**CADCAM** /'kædkæm/ COMPUTING computer-aided (or -assisted) design and manufacturing (or manufacture)

**CAE** COMPUTING computer-aided (or -assisted) engineering

**CAF** FREIGHT cost and freight

**CAI** COMPUTING computer-assisted (or -aided) instruction

**cal** MEASUREMENTS, PHYSICS calorie

**Cal** MEASUREMENTS, PHYSICS large calorie

**CAL 1.** calendar **2.** MEASUREMENTS calibre **3.** /kæl/ COMPUTING computer-assisted (or -aided) learning

**Cal.** GEOGRAPHY California

**Calif.** GEOGRAPHY California

**CAM 1.** MEDICINE complementary and alternative medicine **2.** COMPUTING computer-aided (or -assisted) manufacturing (or manufacture) **3.** COMPUTING a method of storing data so that it can be searched for using part of the data, rather than an address. Full form **content-addressable memory**

**Camb.** GEOGRAPHY Cambridge

**Cambs.** GEOGRAPHY Cambridgeshire

**CAMRA** /'kæmrə/ BEVERAGES Campaign for Real Ale

**can. 1.** cancellation **2.** cancelled **3.** MILITARY cannon **4.** MUSIC canon **5.** POETRY canto

**Can.** GEOGRAPHY **1.** Canadian **2.** Canada

**canc. 1.** cancellation **2.** cancelled

**C and F** FREIGHT cost and freight

**C and G** EDUCATION a technical or craft qualification awarded by the City and Guilds Institute. Full form **City and Guilds**

**C & I** FREIGHT cost and insurance

**C and M** INDUSTRY the condition in which a site such as a factory, shipyard, or machinery is kept when it is ready for immediate use at any time. Full form **care and maintenance**

**CANDU** /'kændu:/ INDUST Canada deuterium-uranium (reactor)

**C and W** MUSIC country and western

**cannot** /'kænɒt/ the usual way of writing 'can not'

**can't** /kɑ:nt/ cannot

**Cant. 1.** GEOGRAPHY Canterbury **2.** BIBLE Canticle of Canticles

**CAP 1.** POLITICS Common Agricultural Policy **2.** /kæp/ COMPUTING computer-aided (or -assisted) production **3.** /kæp/ COMPUTING computer-aided (or -assisted) publishing

**cap. 1.** MEASUREMENTS capacity **2.** capital **3.** PRINTING capital letter **4.** capitalize **5.** ANATOMY caput

**CAPD** MEDICINE a type of dialysis in which the patient can manually control the flow of dialysing fluid through their abdomen from a portable belt-attached bag. Full form **continuous ambulatory peritoneal dialysis**

**CAPEX** FINANCE capital expenditure

**CAPM** FINANCE capital asset pricing model

**caps. 1.** PRINTING capital letters **2.** PHARMACOLOGY capsule

**Capt.** MILITARY Captain

**car.** MEASUREMENTS carat

**Card.** CHRISTIANITY Cardinal

**CARE** /keə/ SOCIAL WELFARE Cooperative for American Relief Everywhere

**Carib.** GEOGRAPHY Caribbean

**CARICOM** /'kærɪkɒm/ ECONOMICS Caribbean Community and Common Market

**CARIFTA** /'kærɪftə/ ECONOMICS Caribbean Free Trade Association

**CAS** AEROSPACE calibrated airspeed

**CASE** /keɪs/ COMPUTING **1.** computer-aided (or -assisted) software engineering **2.** computer-aided (or -assisted) systems engineering

**CAT 1.** AVIAT clear-air turbulence **2.** EDUCATION College of Advanced Technology **3.** COMPUTING computer-aided (or -assisted) testing **4.** STOCK EXCHANGE computer-assisted (or -aided) trading **5.** COMPUTING computer-assisted (or -aided) training **6.** MEDICINE a former name for computed tomography (CT) ○ *CAT scan* Full form **computerized axial tomography 7.** ECOLOGY the population density of a species at which control measures must be put into place before it can become a pest. Full form **control action threshold**

**cath.** ELECTRONICS cathode

**Cath. 1.** BUILDINGS cathedral **2.** CHRISTIANITY Catholic

**CATV** *US* TV another name for cable television. Full form **community antenna television**

**CAV** COMPUTING a CD-ROM that spins at a constant speed. Full form **constant angular velocity**

**cav.** MILITARY cavalry

**CB 1.** ONLINE call back (*used in e-mails and text messages*) **2.** BUSINESS cash book **3.** WINE chateau-bottled **4.** RADIO radio frequencies used by the general public to talk to one another over short distances. Full form **Citizens Band 5.** MILITARY Companion of the (Order of the) Bath (NOTE: The abbreviation **CB** is used as a title: *Major General James Wokingham CB.*) **6.** METEOROLOGY cumulonimbus

**CBC** BROADCASTING Canadian Broadcasting Corporation

**cbd** FREIGHT cash before delivery

**CBD 1.** FREIGHT cash before delivery **2.** BUSINESS central business district

**CBE** MILITARY Commander of the (Order of the) British Empire (NOTE: The abbreviation **CBE** is used as a title: *Harvey Weinstein CBE.*)

**CBI 1.** COMPUTING computer-based instruction **2.** INDUSTRY Confederation of British Industry

**CBOT** BUSINESS Chicago Board of Trade

**CBR** COMPUTING constant bit rate

**CBS** BROADCASTING Columbia Broadcasting System

**CBT** COMPUTING computer-based training

**CBW** MILITARY chemical and biological warfare

**cc 1.** BUSINESS carbon copy (NOTE: The abbreviation **cc** also refers to a copy of an e-mail sent to a person other than the primary addressee.) **2.** LITERATURE chapters **3.** ONLINE Cocos Islands (NOTE: The abbreviation **cc** is seen at the end of Internet addresses, preceded by a dot.) **4.** MEASUREMENTS cubic capacity **5.** MEASUREMENTS cubic centimetre ○ *a 600cc motorbike* (NOTE: The abbreviation **cc** is perhaps most frequently encountered with reference to the power of an internal-combustion engine.)

**CC 1.** PUBLIC ADMINISTRATION City Council **2.** BUSINESS a corporation which is owned and controlled by a small number of people and whose shares are not available to the general public. Full form **close corporation 3.** PUBLIC ADMINISTRATION County Council **4.** CRICKET Cricket Club

**CCA 1.** E-COMMERCE cardholder certificate authority **2.** ACCOUNTING current-cost accounting

**CCAB** ACCOUNTING Consultative Committee of Accountancy Bodies

**CCD** COMPUTING a semiconductor device that converts light patterns into digital signals for a computer, especially in digital cameras and optical scanners. Full form **charge-coupled device**

**CCF** MILITARY Combined Cadet Force

**CCITT** COMPUTING an international committee that defines communications protocols and standards. Full form **Comité Consultatif International Téléphonique et Télégraphique**

**CCTV** TV a television system in which cameras transmit pictures by cable to connected monitors, frequently used for the deterrence or detection of crime. Full form **closed-circuit television**

**CCU** HEALTH SERVICES coronary care unit

**cd** MEASUREMENTS, PHYSICS candela

**Cd 1.** CHEMICAL ELEMENTS cadmium **2.** POLITICS command (paper) (NOTE: The abbreviation **Cd**, followed by a serial number, identifies a government document presented to Parliament, historically by royal command.)

**CD 1.** COMPUTING a signal generated by a modem to inform the local computer that it has detected a remote modem. Full form **carrier detect 2.** BANKING certificate of deposit **3.** MILITARY Civil Defence **4.** RECORDING compact disc (NOTE: The abbreviation **CD** is used as a noun in its own right, referring both to pre-recorded audio CDs and to those used in computing to copy or transfer data files.) **5.** INTERNATIONAL RELATIONS Corps Diplomatique (NOTE: The abbreviation **CD** is often displayed on the backs of cars belonging to embassies.)

**c/d 1.** ACCOUNTING carried down **2.** STOCK EXCHANGE with a right to the current dividend when buying a security. Full form **cum dividend**

**CD-E** COMPUTING a compact disc that can have its contents erased and replaced with something else. Full form **compact disc erasable**

**cdf** STATISTICS a procedure that assigns to each possible value of a random variable the probability that this value will be found. Full form **cumulative distribution function**

**CD+G** COMPUTING a compact disc for karaoke use which contains the music to sing to and graphics that appear on a video screen at the same time. Full form **compact disc and graphics**

**CDH** MEDICINE congenital dislocation of the hip

**CD-I** COMPUTING an interactive compact disc containing text, video, and audio, and accessed using a self-contained player plugged into a television set. Full form **compact disc interactive**

**CDM** ENVIRONMENT an international agreement (part of the Kyoto Protocol) to work towards reducing greenhouse gas emissions and to help developing countries to do the same. Full form **Clean Development Mechanism**

**cDNA** GENETICS synthetically-produced single-strand DNA. Full form **complementary DNA**

**Cdr** MILITARY Commander

**CDR** MILITARY Commander

**CD-R** COMPUTING a compact disc that can have its contents erased and replaced with something else. Full form **compact disc recordable**

**Cdre** MILITARY Commodore

**CD-ROM** /ˌsiː diː 'rɒm/ COMPUTING a compact disc containing a large amount of data, including text and images, that can be viewed using a computer but cannot be altered or erased. Full form **compact disc read-only memory**

**CD-ROM/XA** COMPUTING a compact disc with reduced error-detection coding allowing more data storage space. Full form **CD-ROM Extended Architecture**

**CDRTOS** COMPUTING an operating system used to run a CD-I hardware platform. Full form **compact disc real-time operating system**

**CD-RW** COMPUTING a compact disc that can have its contents erased and replaced with something else many times. Full form **compact disc rewritable**

**CDSC** FINANCE a fee that must be paid when selling an investment under certain circumstances. Full form **contingent deferred sales charge**

**CDT** EDUCATION a subject that can be studied to GCSE level. Full form **Craft, Design, and Technology**

**CDTV** COMPUTING a CD-ROM standard combining audio, graphics, and text that is mainly intended as an interactive system for home use, with the player connected to a television and also able to play audio CDs. Full form **Commodore Dynamic Total Vision**

**CDV** VIDEO a compact disc used to store and play back video images, or a player for such discs. Full form **compact disc video**

**CD-WO** COMPUTING a compact disc that can have its contents written only once. Full form **compact disc write once**

**Ce** CHEMICAL ELEMENTS cerium

**CE 1.** CHRISTIANITY Church of England **2.** CHEMICAL ENGINEERING chemical engineer **3.** ENGINEERING chief engineer **4.** CIVIL ENGINEERING civil engineer **5.** CALENDAR Common Era (NOTE: The abbreviation **CE** is sometimes used after a date as a non-Christian alternative for AD.) **6.** ECOLOGY consumption efficiency **7.** ONLINE creative editing (*used in e-mails*) **8.** ECONOMICS Communaute Européenne

**CEGEP** /'seɪʒep/ in Quebec, a post-secondary education institution that offers two-year programmes leading to university and three-year programmes qualifying students in a variety of professions and trades. Full form **Collège d'Enseignement Général et Professionnel** (NOTE: From the French, 'College of General and Professional Education'.)

**CEIC** COMMERCE in the United States, a corporation whose capitalization is fixed, whose capital is invested in other companies, and whose own shares are traded by outside investors. Full form **closed-end investment company**

**cen. 1.** central **2.** TIME century

**CENELEC** /'senɪlek/ ELECTRICITY an EU organization that controls the standard of electrical goods. Full form **Comité Européen de Normalisation Electrotechnique** (NOTE: From the French, 'European Committee for Electrotechnical Standardization'.)

**CEng** ENGINEERING chartered engineer

**cent. 1.** MEASUREMENTS centigrade **2.** central **3.** TIME century

**CEO** MANAGEMENT chief executive officer

**CERN** /sɜːn/ NUCLEAR PHYSICS an EU organization that carries out research into high-energy particle physics, now called the European Laboratory for Particle Physics. Full form **Conseil Européen pour la Recherche Nucléaire** (NOTE: From the French, 'European Organization for Nuclear Research'.)

**CERT** /sɜːt/ ONLINE an organisation that monitors and investigates global network security threats. Full form **computer emergency response team**

**cert. 1.** certificate **2.** certification **3.** certified

**CET 1.** TIME Central European Time **2.** COMMERCE a tariff rate applied by members of a customs union to exports from nonmember countries. Full form **common external tariff**

**cf** ONLINE Central African Republic (NOTE: The abbreviation **cf** is seen at the end of Internet addresses, preceded by a dot.)

**Cf** CHEMICAL ELEMENTS californium

**CF 1.** MILITARY Chaplain to the Forces **2.** COMPUTING a small memory module that can be removed from the parent system. Full form **Compact Flash 3.** FREIGHT cost and freight **4.** MEDICINE cystic fibrosis

**cf.** compare (NOTE: From the Latin *confer*.)

**c/f** ACCOUNTING carried forward

**CFA** FINANCE Communauté financière africaine (NOTE: The *CFA franc*, from the French, 'African financial community', is a unit of currency used in several French-speaking African countries.)

**CFC** CHEMISTRY a gas containing carbon, hydrogen, chlorine, and fluorine, some forms of which have been found to damage the ozone layer. Their use has been almost phased out throughout the world. ○ *aerosols containing CFCs* Full form **chlorofluorocarbon** (NOTE: The abbreviation **CFC** is used as a noun in its own right.)

**CFE 1.** EDUCATION College of Further Education **2.** MILITARY Conventional Forces in Europe

**cfi** FREIGHT cost, freight, and insurance

**CFM** CHEMISTRY chlorofluoromethane

**CFO** COMMERCE chief financial officer

**CFP 1.** FISHERIES Common Fisheries Policy **2.** FINANCE Colonies françaises du Pacifique (NOTE: The *franc CFP* is a unit of currency used in French overseas territories of the Pacific.)

**CFR** BUSINESS cost and freight

**cfs** MEASUREMENTS cubic feet per second

**CFS** MEDICINE an illness without a known cause that is characterized by long-term exhaustion, muscle weakness, depression, and sleep disturbances. Also known as myalgic encephalomyelitis (ME) or postviral syndrome (PVS), it may occur as a reaction to a viral infection. Full form **chronic fatigue syndrome**

**CFT** MEDICINE a blood test to determine the presence of antibodies to Coxiella burnetii bacteria. Full form **complement fixation test**

**cg 1.** MEASUREMENTS centigram **2.** ONLINE Congo (NOTE: The abbreviation **cg** is seen at the end of Internet addresses, preceded by a dot.)

**CG 1.** MILITARY captain general **2.** PHYSICS centre of gravity **3.** EMERGENCIES coastguard **4.** INTERNATIONAL RELATIONS Consul General

**CGA** COMPUTING an early colour video system for the pc. Full form **colour graphics adapter**

**CGBR** FINANCE Central Government Borrowing Requirement. Former name for **Central Government Net Cash Requirement**

**cge 1.** FREIGHT carriage **2.** BANKING charge

**CGI** COMPUTING **1.** a standard that defines how a webpage can call programs or scripts stored on an internet server to carry out functions and exchange information with the program. Full form **common gateway interface 2.** computer-generated image **3.** computer-generated imagery

**cgm** MEASUREMENTS centigram

**CGM** MILITARY Conspicuous Gallantry Medal

**CGNCR** FINANCE a measurement of the difference between government income and expenditure over a given period. Full form **Central Government Net Cash Requirement**

**cgs** MEASUREMENTS centimetre-gram-second (NOTE: The **cgs system** uses the centimetre, gram, and second as the basic units for length, mass, and time, respectively. It has been largely replaced by the SI system in scientific contexts.)

**CGS** MILITARY Chief of General Staff

**CGT** FINANCE capital gains tax

**ch** ONLINE Switzerland
> The use of **ch** as an abbreviation for Switzerland in this and other contexts comes from French *Confédération Helvétique* or Latin *Confederatio Helvetica*, meaning 'Swiss Confederation'. It is seen at the end of Internet addresses, preceded by a dot.

**CH 1.** BANKING clearing house **2.** COMMERCE Companies House **3.** MILITARY Companion of Honour **4.** BUILDINGS custom house

**ch. 1.** MEASUREMENTS chain **2.** LITERATURE chapter **3.** BANKING charge **4.** CHESS check **5.** CHRISTIANITY church

**Ch. 1.** BROADCASTING channel **2.** CONSTRUCTION central heating **3.** GEOGRAPHY China

**C/H** INDUST central heating

**CHAI** HEALTH SERVICES Commission for Healthcare Audit and Improvement

**Chanc.** POLITICS **1.** chancellor **2.** chancery

**chap. 1.** CHRISTIANITY chaplain **2.** LITERATURE chapter

**CHAPS** /tʃæps/ BUSINESS Clearing House Automated Payments System

**ChB** MEDICINE Bachelor of Surgery (NOTE: From the Latin *Chirurgiae Baccalaureus*.)

**CHC** HEALTH SERVICES **1.** child health clinic **2.** community health council

**CHCP** COMPUTING a system command that selects which codepage to use. Full form **change codepage**

**CHD** MEDICINE coronary heart disease

**CHDIR** COMPUTING a system command that moves you around a directory structure. Full form **change directory**

**chem. 1.** chemical **2.** chemist **3.** chemistry

**Ches.** GEOGRAPHY Cheshire

**CHESS** /tʃes/ BANKING Clearing House Electronic Subregister System

**chg. 1.** FINANCE change **2.** BANKING charge

**CHI** HEALTH SERVICES Commission for Health Improvement

**CHIPS** /tʃɪps/ BANKING Clearing House Interbank Payments System

**CHKDSK** /'tʃekdɪsk/ COMPUTING a system command that runs a check on the status of a disc drive. Full form **check disk**

**ChM** MEDICINE Master of Surgery (NOTE: From the Latin *Chirurgiae Magister*.)

**CHP** INDUST energy systems that produce heat and power simultaneously by burning fuel. Full form **combined heat and power**

**Chr. 1.** CHRISTIANITY Christ **2.** CHRISTIANITY Christian **3.** BIBLE Chronicles

**chron. 1.** LITERATURE chronicle **2.** chronological **3.** HISTORY chronology

**Chron.** BIBLE Chronicles

**chronol. 1.** chronological **2.** HISTORY chronology

**ci** ONLINE Côte d'Ivoire (NOTE: The abbreviation **ci** is seen at the end of Internet addresses, preceded by a dot.)

**Ci 1.** METEOROLOGY cirrus **2.** MEASUREMENTS, PHYSICS curie

**CI** GEOGRAPHY **1.** Cayman Islands **2.** Channel Islands

**CIA** a US federal bureau responsible for intelligence and counterintelligence activities outside the United States. In conjunction with the FBI, it is also involved in domestic counterintelligence. Full form **Central Intelligence Agency**

**CIB 1.** BANKING Chartered Institute of Bankers **2.** POLICE Criminal Investigation Branch

**CICA** ACCOUNTING Canadian Institute of Chartered Accountants

**CID 1.** VETERINARY MEDICINE cattle identification document **2.** ONLINE consider it done (*used in e-mails*) **3.** POLICE the detective branch of the UK police force. Full form **Criminal Investigation Department 4.** ONLINE crying in disgrace (*used in Internet chat rooms and text messages*)

**CIDR** COMPUTING a system of organising IP addresses that is more compact and efficient, using a prefix number to separate them into smaller groups. Full form **classless inter-domain routing**

**CIF 1.** COMPUTING a linking format used to interface different video formats during videoconferencing. Full form **common intermediate format 2.** FREIGHT cost, insurance, and freight **3.** BUSINESS customer identification file

**c.i.f.c.i.** FREIGHT cost, insurance, freight, commission, and interest (NOTE: The abbreviation **c.i.f.c.i.** is used in quotes to indicate what is included in the price.)

**CIFE** EDUCATION colleges and institutes for further education

**CII** INSURANCE Chartered Insurance Institute

**CIM** COMPUTING **1.** computer input microfilm **2.** computer-integrated manufacturing

**CIN** MEDICINE a condition in which cells on the surface of the cervix change, a possible precursor to cancer. Full form **cervical intraepithelial neoplasia**

**C in C** MILITARY Commander in Chief

**CIO** MANAGEMENT chief information officer

**CIPD** HUMAN RESOURCES Chartered Institute of Personnel and Development

**CIR** COMPUTING a CPU register that stores the instruction that is currently being executed. Full form **current instruction register**

**cir. 1.** CALENDAR circa (NOTE: From the Latin, 'about'.) **2.** MATHEMATICS circle **3.** ELECTRICITY circuit **4.** PRESS circulation **5.** MATHEMATICS circumference

**CIRO** BUSINESS a model used in evaluating the effectiveness of training. Full form **context, input, reaction, outcome**

**CIS 1.** POLITICS an association formed in 1991 by most of the republics of the former Soviet Union. Full form **Commonwealth of Independent States 2.** COMPUTING contact image sensor

**CISC** /sɪsk/ COMPUTING complex instruction set computer

**CIT** COMPUTING, TELECOMMUNICATIONS computer-integrated telephony

**cit. 1.** cited **2.** citizen

**CITES** ECOLOGY Convention on International Trade in Endangered Species (of Wild Fauna and Flora)

**CIVC** WINE an international joint trade association for companies producing Champagne wine. Full form **Comité Interprofessionel du Vin de Champagne**

**CIX** /kɪks/ E-COMMERCE commercial Internet exchange

**CJ** LAW **1.** Chief Judge **2.** Chief Justice

**CJD** MEDICINE a fatal brain disease, a form of spongiform encephalopathy, that develops slowly, causing dementia and loss of muscle control. Full form **Creutzfeldt-Jakob disease**

**ck** ONLINE Cook Islands (NOTE: The abbreviation **ck** is seen at the end of Internet addresses, preceded by a dot.)

**CKD** COMMERCE used to describe goods that are sold in parts to be assembled later. Full form **completely knocked down** (NOTE: The abbreviation **CKD** is used to describe goods that are sold in parts to be assembled later.)

**CKO** BUSINESS Chief Knowledge Officer

**cl 1.** TRANSPORT carload **2.** MEASUREMENTS centilitre **3.** ONLINE Chile (NOTE: The abbreviation **cl** is seen at the end of Internet addresses, preceded by a dot.)

**Cl** CHEMICAL ELEMENTS chlorine

**cl. 1.** class **2.** classification **3.** RELIGION clergy **4.** FURNITURE closet **5.** TEXTILES cloth

**class. 1.** ARTS classic **2.** ARTS classical **3.** classification **4.** classified

**cld** STOCK EXCHANGE called

**CLI** TELECOMMUNICATIONS calling line identification

**Cllr** PUBLIC ADMINISTRATION Councillor

**clm** ARCHITECTURE column

**CLM** ONLINE career limiting move (*used in e-mails*)

**CLNP** COMPUTING connectionless network protocol

**CLS** COMPUTING a system command to clear the screen. Full form **clear screen**

**CLV** COMPUTING a disk technology in which the disk spins at different speeds according to the track being accessed. Full form **constant linear velocity**

**cm 1.** ONLINE Cameroon (NOTE: The abbreviation **cm** is seen at the end of Internet addresses, preceded by a dot.) **2.** MEASUREMENTS centimetre

**Cm** CHEMICAL ELEMENTS curium

**CM 1.** BUSINESS a marketing strategy grouping products together into categories so that these can be more efficiently targeted at consumers. Full form **category management 2.** COMPUTING central memory **3.** BUSINESS compounding method

**c.m. 1.** PHYSICS centre of mass **2.** MILITARY court martial

**CMA** MEDICINE **1.** Canadian Medical Association **2.** certified medical assistant

**CMBS** FINANCE commercial mortgage-backed securities

**Cmdr** MILITARY Commander

**CME** BUSINESS Chicago Mercantile Exchange

**CMEA** INTERNATIONAL RELATIONS Council for Mutual Economic Assistance

**CMG** MILITARY Companion of the Order of St Michael and St George

**CMI** COMPUTING computer-managed instruction

**CMIP** COMPUTING common management information protocol

**cml** commercial

**CML 1.** COMPUTING computer-managed learning **2.** FINANCE Council of Mortgage Lenders

**CMO** MEDICINE Chief Medical Officer

**c'mon** /kəˈmɒn/ come on

**CMOS** /ˈsiːmɒs/ COMPUTING an integrated circuit design that uses a pair of complementary p- and n-type transistors. Full form **complementary metal oxide semiconductor**

**CMV** MEDICINE a virus that causes enlargement of epithelial cells, usually resulting in mild infections but causing more serious disorders in Aids patients and in newborn babies. Full form **cytomegalovirus**

**CMYK** PRINTING the standard model for printing in which all colours are described in terms of the quantity of cyan, magenta, yellow, and black they contain. Display devices use the RGB (red, green, blue) model. ○ *The letter 'K' stands for 'key', as black was traditionally the standard colour used in printing against which others were defined* Full form **cyan, magenta, yellow, black**

**cn** ONLINE China (NOTE: The abbreviation **cn** is seen at the end of Internet addresses, preceded by a dot.)

**C/N 1.** MEDICINE charge nurse **2.** INSURANCE cover note **3.** COMMERCE credit note

**CNAA** EDUCATION Council for National Academic Awards

**CNAR** FINANCE compound net annual rate

**CNC 1.** COMPUTING computer numeric control **2.** ACCOUNTING the National Council for Accountancy in France. Full form **Conseil National de la Comptabilité**

**CNCC** ACCOUNTING the National Audit Office of France. Full form **Compagnie Nationale des Commissaires aux Comptes**

**CND** POLITICS Campaign for Nuclear Disarmament

**CNN** *US* BROADCASTING an international news and information broadcast network based in the USA. Full form **Cable News Network**

**CNS** ANATOMY central nervous system

**co** ONLINE Colombia (NOTE: The abbreviation **co** is seen at the end of Internet addresses, preceded by a dot.)

**Co** CHEMICAL ELEMENTS cobalt

**CO 1.** CHEMISTRY carbon monoxide **2.** MAIL Colorado (NOTE: The abbreviation **CO** is part of the US sorting code on the last line of a Colorado address.) **3.** MILITARY commanding officer **4.** POLITICS Commonwealth Office **5.** MILITARY conscientious objector

**Co. 1.** GEOGRAPHY Colorado **2.** COMMERCE Company (NOTE: The abbreviation **Co.** is used in the names of businesses.) **3.** GEOGRAPHY County ○ *Co. Kildare* (NOTE: The abbreviation **Co.** is used in place names, especially the names of Irish counties.)

**c/o 1.** MAIL care of (NOTE: The abbreviation **c/o** is used in addresses, typically when the intended recipient of the item is not a permanent resident at the address.) **2.** ACCOUNTING carried over

**CoA** BIOCHEMISTRY a complex compound that combines with a specific protein to form an active enzyme. Full form **coenzyme A**

**COAD** MEDICINE chronic obstructive airways disease

**COAG** GOVERNMENT Council of Australian Governments

**COB** FINANCE an organisation overseeing the operation of the French Stock Exchange. Full form **Commission des Opérations de Bourse**

**COBOL** /ˈkəʊbɒl/ COMPUTING a high-level computer programming language, widely adopted for corporate business applications. Full form **common business-oriented language**

**COD 1.** MAIL cash on delivery **2.** BIOCHEMISTRY chemical oxygen demand

**coef.** MATHEMATICS coefficient

**C of C** COMMERCE chamber of commerce

**C of E** CHRISTIANITY Church of England

**C of S** MILITARY chief of staff

**COGS** COMMERCE cost of goods sold

**COHSE** /ˈkəʊzi/ HUMAN RESOURCES a former trade union, now part of UNISON. Full form **Confederation of Health Service Employees**

**COI** Central Office of Information

**COL** /kɒl/ **1.** COMPUTING computer-oriented language **2.** ECONOMICS cost of living

**col. 1.** EDUCATION college **2.** SOCIAL SCIENCES colony **3.** colour **4.** PRINTING column

**Col. 1.** MILITARY Colonel **2.** GEOGRAPHY Colorado **3.** BIBLE Colossians **4.** GEOGRAPHY Columbia **5.** GEOGRAPHY Columbian

**COLA** /ˈkəʊlə/ **1.** SOCIAL SCIENCES cost-of-living adjustment **2.** BUSINESS cost-of-living allowance

**coll. 1.** COMMERCE collateral **2.** colleague **3.** collect **4.** collection **5.** collector **6.** EDUCATION college **7.** EDUCATION collegiate **8.** LANGUAGE colloquial

**colloq.** LANGUAGE colloquial

**Colo.** GEOGRAPHY Colorado

**com** ONLINE commercial organization

> The abbreviation **com** is seen at the end of Internet addresses, preceded by a dot. It has given rise to the noun *dot.com*, a generic name for Internet-based businesses (whether or not their Internet address ends in .com).

**COM** COMPUTING **1.** a framework devised by Microsoft to standardise the way an application can access an object. Full form **Component Object Model, Common Object Model 2.** the process of converting computer output directly to microfilm. Full form **computer output microfilm**

**com. 1.** ARTS comedy **2.** PRESS comic **3.** commerce **4.** commercial **5.** committee **6.** SOCIAL SCIENCES commune

**Com. 1.** MILITARY Commander **2.** MILITARY Commodore **3.** POLITICS Communist

**comb. 1.** combination **2.** combining **3.** combustion

**Comdr** MILITARY Commander

**Comdt** MILITARY Commandant

**Comecon** /ˈkɒmɪkɒn/ INTERNATIONAL RELATIONS an organization of the former Soviet Union and satellite Communist countries that existed between 1949 and 1991 and was aimed at encouraging economic development. Full form **Council for Mutual Economic Assistance**

**COMEX** /ˈkɒmeks/ STOCK EXCHANGE (New York) Commodity Exchange

**comm. 1.** commerce **2.** commercial **3.** committee **4.** POLITICS commonwealth

**comp. 1.** companion **2.** GRAMMAR comparative **3.** compare **4.** HUMAN RESOURCES compensation **5.** COMPUTING compilation **6.** COMPUTING compiled **7.** complete **8.** MUSIC composer **9.** composite **10.** composition **11.** compound **12.** comprehensive **13.** comprising

**compar.** GRAMMAR comparative

**compd** compound

**CON** COMPUTING console

**con. 1.** MUSIC concerto **2.** LAW conclusion **3.** TELECOMMUNICATIONS, TRANSPORT connection **4.** COMMERCE consolidated **5.** continued **6.** contra

**Con. 1.** CHRISTIANITY Conformist **2.** POLITICS Conservative **3.** INTERNATIONAL RELATIONS Consul

**conc. 1.** CHEMISTRY concentrated **2.** CHEMISTRY concentration **3.** concerning **4.** MUSIC concerto **5.** concession

**conf. 1.** confer **2.** conference **3.** CHRISTIANITY confessor **4.** confidential

**confed.** POLITICS **1.** confederate **2.** confederation

**Cong. 1.** CHRISTIANITY Congregational **2.** POLITICS Congress **3.** POLITICS Congressional

**conj. 1.** GRAMMAR conjugation **2.** ASTRONOMY, GRAMMAR conjunction **3.** GRAMMAR conjunctive

**CONS** COMPUTING connection-oriented network services

**cons. 1.** RELIGION consecrated **2.** MAIL consigned **3.** MAIL consignment **4.** PHONETICS consonant **5.** POLITICS constitution **6.** POLITICS constitutional

**Cons. 1.** POLITICS Conservative **2.** POLICE Constable **3.** POLITICS Constitution **4.** INTERNATIONAL RELATIONS Consul

**const. 1.** MATHEMATICS, PHYSICS constant **2.** POLITICS constitution

**cont. 1.** containing **2.** PUBLISHING contents **3.** GEOGRAPHY continent **4.** GEOGRAPHY continental **5.** continued **6.** continuous **7.** GRAMMAR contraction **8.** control

**contd** continued

**contr. 1.** GRAMMAR contraction **2.** MUSIC contralto **3.** control

**contrib. 1.** contribution **2.** contributor

**Conv.** CHRISTIANITY a member of a branch of a Franciscan order of friars who live a less austere life than in other branches. Full form **Conventual**

**COO** BUSINESS chief operating officer

**coop** ONLINE cooperative

> The abbreviation **coop** is seen in the Internet addresses of nonprofitmaking cooperatives. In other contexts **coop** (or *co-op*) is an informal shortening used to denote any cooperative organization or venture.

**COPD** MEDICINE chronic obstructive pulmonary disease

**cor. 1.** corner **2.** MUSIC cornet **3.** correction **4.** COMMUNICATION correspondence **5.** PRESS correspondent

**Cor.** BIBLE Corinthians

**CORBA** /'kɔːbə/ COMPUTING a framework devised by the Object Management Group to standardise the way an application can access an object. Full form **common object request broker architecture**

**CORE** /kɔː/ US LAW Congress of Racial Equality

**CORGI** /'kɔːgi/ INDUST Council for Registered Gas Installers

**Corn.** GEOGRAPHY Cornwall

**corp.** BUSINESS, PUBLIC ADMINISTRATION corporation

**Corp. 1.** MILITARY Corporal **2.** BUSINESS Corporation

**corr. 1.** correct **2.** corrected **3.** correction **4.** COMMUNICATION correspondence **5.** PRESS correspondent

**cos** MATHEMATICS cosine

**COS 1.** FREIGHT cash on shipment **2.** MILITARY chief of staff

**COSATU** /kəʊ'saːtuː/ HUMAN RESOURCES Congress of South African Trades Unions

**cosec** /kəʊsek/ MATHEMATICS cosecant

**cot** MATHEMATICS cotangent

**CoT** EDUCATION college of technology

**cotan** MATHEMATICS cotangent

**co.uk** ONLINE UK commercial organization

> The abbreviation **co.uk** is seen at the end of Internet addresses, preceded by a dot. Some of these websites are UK branches of businesses whose Internet addresses end in .com (although some UK companies have Internet addresses ending in .com in their own right).

**couldn't** /'kʊd(ə)nt/ could not

**could've** /'kʊd(ə)v/ could have

**cov** STATISTICS covariance

**Coy.** MILITARY company

**CP 1.** PRESS Canadian Press **2.** GEOGRAPHY Cape Province **3.** COMPUTING card punch **4.** ONLINE chat post (*another term for a message board*) **5.** CHEMISTRY chemically pure **6.** MILITARY command post **7.** BUSINESS commercial paper **8.** POLITICS Communist Party **9.** *Aus* POLITICS former name for the National Party of Australia. Full form **Country Party**

**cp.** compare

**CPA 1.** ACCOUNTING certified public accountant **2.** BUSINESS cost per acquisition **3.** COMPUTING the definition of tasks or jobs and the time each requires in order to achieve certain goals. Full form **critical path analysis 4.** BUSINESS customer profitability analysis

**CPAP** MEDICINE a condition in which the airways are constricted, a possible cause of snoring. Full form **continuous positive airways pressure**

**cpd** compound

**CPF** HUMAN RESOURCES a Government-run pensions scheme in Singapore. Full form **Central Provident Fund**

**cpi** COMPUTING characters per inch

**CPI** ECONOMICS consumer price index

**CPIX** *Can* ECONOMICS a measure of the pace of inflation in Canada

**Cpl** MILITARY Corporal

**CPM 1.** BUSINESS cost per thousand (NOTE: The 'M' is from Latin *mille* 'thousand' and the Roman numeral for 1000.) **2.** COMPUTING the use of analysis and the projection of each critical step in a large project to help a management team. Full form **critical path method**

**CPN** HEALTH SERVICES community psychiatric nurse

**CPO 1.** MILITARY Chief Petty Officer **2.** BUSINESS cost per order

**CPP** BUSINESS the amount of goods that can be purchased at a particular time with the resources available to a person or company. Full form **current purchasing power**

**CPR 1.** RAIL Canadian Pacific Railway **2.** MEDICINE an emergency technique that involves clearing the patient's airways and then alternating heart compression with mouth-to-mouth respiration. Full form **cardiopulmonary resuscitation**

**CPRE** ENVIRONMENT Council for the Protection of Rural England

**cps 1.** COMPUTING characters per second **2.** MEASUREMENTS, PHYSICS cycles per second

**CPS** LAW Crown Prosecution Service

**CPSA** HUMAN RESOURCES Civil and Public Services Association

**CPSU** *Aus* HUMAN RESOURCES Community and Public Service Union

**CPT** BUSINESS cost per thousand

**Cpt.** MILITARY Captain

**CPU** COMPUTING central processing unit

**CQ** MILITARY charge of quarters

**cr** ONLINE Costa Rica (NOTE: The abbreviation **cr** is seen at the end of Internet addresses, preceded by a dot.)

**Cr 1.** CHEMICAL ELEMENTS chromium **2.** PUBLIC ADMINISTRATION Councillor

**CR 1.** COMPUTING a special code, character or key that causes the cursor to move to the beginning of a new line, named after the key or lever on a typewriter that physically performs the same function by sending the carriage back and rotating the paper upward. Full form **carriage return 2.** RELIGION a religious group that undertakes charitable work in the UK and abroad. Full form **Community of the Resurrection 3.** PSYCHOLOGY conditioned reflex **4.** PSYCHOLOGY conditioned response **5.** GEOGRAPHY Costa Rica **6.** FINANCE credit **7.** ECOLOGY critically endangered

**cr. 1.** FINANCE credit **2.** FINANCE creditor **3.** creek (*used on maps*)

**CRB** GOVERNMENT Criminal Records Bureau

**CRC** COMPUTING an error-detection system that checks one bit in a group of a given number against the original to see whether that group contains errors. Full form **cyclic redundancy check**

**CRE** LAW Commission for Racial Equality

**Cres.** ROADS Crescent (NOTE: The abbreviation **Cres.** is used in addresses.)

**cresc.** MUSIC crescendo

**CREST** /krest/ FINANCE the Central Securities Depository for the UK and Ireland

**criminol.** criminology

**crit. 1.** ARTS critic **2.** MEDICINE critical **3.** ARTS criticism

**CR/LF** COMPUTING a special code, character or key that causes the cursor to move down and to the beginning of a new line. Full form **carriage return/line feed**

**CRM** BUSINESS **1.** customer relationship management **2.** customer relations management

**CRNA** MEDICINE certified registered nurse anaesthetist

**CRO 1.** PHYSICS cathode-ray oscilloscope **2.** SOCIAL SCIENCES Community Relations Officer **3.** COMMERCE Companies Registration Office **4.** CRIME Criminal Records Office

**CRP** *S Asia* POLICE Central Reserve Police

**CRT** ELECTRONICS cathode-ray tube

**cryst. 1.** crystalline **2.** crystallography

**Cs** CHEMICAL ELEMENTS caesium

**CS 1.** FINANCE capital stock **2.** CIVIL ENGINEERING chartered surveyor **3.** MILITARY chief of staff **4.** COMPUTING a single line on a chip that will enable it to function when a signal is present. Full form **chip select 5.** CHRISTIANITY Christian Science **6.** CHRISTIANITY Christian Scientist **7.** GOVERNMENT civil service **8.** LAW Court of Session

**CSA** SOCIAL WELFARE Child Support Agency

**CSB** MEDICINE chemical stimulation of the brain

**CSC** MATHEMATICS cosecant

**CSC** GOVERNMENT Civil Service Commission

**CSE** EDUCATION a former examination primarily for 16-year-olds in England and Wales that was replaced (along with the Ordinary level of the General Certificate of Education) by the General Certificate of Secondary Education (GCSE). A high-grade CSE pass was considered equivalent to a pass at GCE O level. ○ *His father left school with three CSEs.* Full form **Certificate of Secondary Education**

**CSEU** HUMAN RESOURCES Confederation of Shipbuilding and Engineering Unions

**CSF** MEDICINE cerebrospinal fluid

**CS gas** CHEMISTRY a gas that causes tears, salivation, and painful breathing, used in riot control and warfare (NOTE: The gas is named after the US chemists B. B. Corson and R. W. Stoughton, who invented it in 1928.)

**CSIRO** TECHNOLOGY Commonwealth Scientific and Industrial Research Organization

**CSLIP** ONLINE a version of the SLIP protocol that compresses data before it is transmitted, resulting in greater data transfer rate. Full form **compressed serial line Internet protocol**

**CSM 1.** COMPUTING an efficient optical character recognition system. Full form **combined symbol matching 2.** MILITARY Company Sergeant-Major

**CSMA-CD** COMPUTING a method of controlling access to a network. Full form **carrier sense multiple access-collision detection**

**CSO** STATISTICS Central Statistical Office

**CSP** E-COMMERCE commerce service provider

**C-SPAN** /'siː spæn/ TV a US cable television channel that focuses chiefly on public affairs such as Congressional hearings and cultural and social issues. Full form **Cable Satellite Public Affairs Network**

**CSS 1.** COMPUTING a method of describing and storing the font, spacing and colour of the text in a webpage so that it can reapplied to other bodies of text. Full form **cascading style sheet 2.** SOCIAL WELFARE Certificate in Social Service

**CST 1.** TIME Central Standard Time **2.** PSYCHIATRY convulsive shock treatment

**CSU** HUMAN RESOURCES Civil Service Union

**CSYS** *Scotland* EDUCATION Certificate of Sixth Year Studies

**ct** MONEY cent

**Ct** Count (NOTE: The abbreviation **Ct** is used in titles: *Ct von Wittenberg*.)

**CT 1.** TIME Central Time **2.** MEDICINE a technique for producing images of cross-sections of the body, used in medical diagnosis (*CT scanning*). A computer processes data from X-rays penetrating the body from many directions and projects the results on a screen. Full form **computed (or computerized) tomography 3.** MAIL Connecticut (NOTE: The abbreviation **CT** is part of the US sorting code on the last line of a Connecticut address.)

**ct.** EDUCATION certificate

**CTC 1.** EDUCATION City Technology College **2.** CYCLING Cyclists' Touring Club

**CTD** MEDICINE the US name for repetitive strain injury (RSI). Full form **cumulative trauma disorder**

**CTI** COMPUTING, TELECOMMUNICATIONS computer-telephony integration

**ctn 1.** carton **2.** MATHEMATICS cotangent

**CTO** MANAGEMENT chief technical officer

**CTR** COMPUTING the number of visitors to a website per hour who click on a banner ad and are sent to the advertiser's own website. Full form **clickthrough rate**

**Ctrl** COMPUTING a computer key that is held down while another other key is pressed, to perform a particular function or produce a particular character. Full form **control (key)**

**CTS** COMPUTING indicating that a line or device is ready for data transmission. Full form **clear to send**

**CTT** FINANCE capital transfer tax

**CTV** TV Canadian Television Network Limited

**cu** ONLINE Cuba (NOTE: The abbreviation **cu** is seen at the end of Internet addresses, preceded by a dot.)

**Cu** CHEMICAL ELEMENTS copper

**CU** COMPUTING control unit

**cu.** MEASUREMENTS cubic

**CUL** ONLINE see you later (*used in e-mails and text messages*)

**Cumb.** GEOGRAPHY Cumbria

**cum div.** STOCK EXCHANGE with a right to the current dividend when buying a security. Full form **cum dividend**

**CUTS** /kʌts/ COMPUTING a device that adapts a computer to be able to read data from a cassette. Full form **Computer Users' Tape System**

**cv** ONLINE Cape Verde (NOTE: The abbreviation **cv** is seen at the end of Internet addresses, preceded by a dot.)

**CV 1.** GEOGRAPHY Cape Verde **2.** MILITARY Cross of Valour **3.** HUMAN RESOURCES a summary of a person's educational qualifications, skills, and professional history. Full form **curriculum vitae**

> The abbreviation **CV** is one of several that are typically found in job advertisements: because advertising is charged by the length of the advert, saving space is important. Other standard abbreviations you will see in job ads are *a.a.e* ('according to age and experience'); *c.* ('about'); *IRO* ('in the region of'); *K* ('thousand', as in *Salary 20K*); *p.a* ('per annum, annually'); *OTE* ('on-target earnings'); and *SAE* ('self-addressed envelope').

**CVA** MEDICINE the technical name for a stroke. Full form **cerebrovascular accident**

**CVE** EDUCATION Certificate of Vocational Education

**CVO** MILITARY Commander of the Royal Victorian Order

**CVS 1.** MEDICINE a prenatal test for birth defects carried out by examining cells from the tiny hairy outgrowths (villi) of the outer membrane (chorion) surrounding an embryo, which have the same DNA as the foetus. Full form **chorionic villus sampling 2.** SOCIAL SCIENCES Council of Voluntary Service

**CW 1.** MILITARY chemical warfare **2.** ARMS chemical weapons **3.** PHYSICS continuous wave

**CWO 1.** COMMERCE cash with order **2.** MILITARY Chief Warrant Officer **3.** ONLINE chief Web officer

**CWP** COMPUTING communicating word processor

**CWS** COMMERCE a former consumer-owned business that now forms part of the Cooperative Group. Full form **Cooperative Wholesale Society**

**cwt** MEASUREMENTS hundredweight (NOTE: The 'c' is from Latin *centum* 'hundred' and the Roman numeral for 100.)

**cx** ONLINE Christmas Island (NOTE: The abbreviation **cx** is seen at the end of Internet addresses, preceded by a dot.)

**cXML** E-COMMERCE a feature of the XML webpage markup language that that provides a standard way of offering products for sale in an online shop. Full form **commerce XML (Extensible Markup Language)**

**cy** ONLINE Cyprus (NOTE: The abbreviation **cy** is seen at the end of Internet addresses, preceded by a dot.)

**CYA** ONLINE see ya (*used in e-mails and text messages*)

**CYL** ONLINE see you later (*used in e-mails and text messages*)

**cyl. 1.** cylinder **2.** cylindrical

# D

**d 1.** ZOOLOGY the female parent of an animal. Full form **dam 2.** CALENDAR date **3.** daughter **4.** TIME day **5.** MEASUREMENTS deci- **6.** MEASUREMENTS degree **7.** TRANSPORT departs **8.** depth **9.** PHYSICS deuteron **10.** MATHEMATICS diameter **11.** died **12.** MONEY dollar **13.** MONEY drachma **14.** MONEY penny (or pence) (NOTE: The abbreviation **d** was used in the old-style system of UK currency, in which there were 240 pence to the pound, which was replaced by the decimal system in 1971.) **15.** PHYSICS relative density

**'d 1.** did **2.** had **3.** should **4.** would

**D 1.** CALENDAR December **2.** Department **3.** JUDAEO-CHRISTIAN Deus **4.** CHEMISTRY deuterium **5.** MATHEMATICS diameter **6.** MONEY dinar **7.** OPTICS dioptre **8.** MANAGEMENT Director **9.** PHYSICS dispersion **10.** JUDAEO-CHRISTIAN Dominus **11.** a title used before a man's name in Spain and other Spanish-speaking countries. Full form **Don 12.** AEROSPACE drag **13.** AUTOMOTIVE drive (NOTE: The abbreviation **D** is used on the gear lever of a car with automatic transmission.) **14.** Duchess **15.** Duke

**da** MEASUREMENTS deca-

**DA 1.** HAIRDRESSING a man's hairstyle, popular in the 1950s, in which the hair is slicked back and drawn into a point at the back of the neck. Full form **duck's arse** (NOTE: The hairstyle is said to resemble a duck's tail, hence its name.) **2.** COMMERCE deed of arrangement **3.** ARMS delayed action **4.** BANKING deposit account **5.** COMPUTING desk accessory **6.** ELECTRONICS digital-to-analogue **7.** LAW district attorney

**D/A 1.** COMMERCE a measure of the length of time between a client accepting some delivery and the supplier issuing a bill for this. Full form **days after acceptance 2.** COMMERCE delivery on acceptance **3.** BANKING deposit account **4.** ELECTRONICS digital-to-analogue **5.** COMMERCE instructions to a bank not to release purchase documents until the drawer has accepted a bill of exchange from the seller. Full form **documents against acceptance**

**DAC** ELECTRONICS digital-to-analogue converter

**DAH** MEDICINE disordered action of the heart

**dal** MEASUREMENTS decalitre

**DAL** COMPUTING data access language

**dam** MEASUREMENTS decametre

**DAMA** COMPUTING demand assigned multiple access

**Dan. 1.** BIBLE Daniel **2.** LANGUAGE Danish

**D & B** FINANCE a major international market research and management consultancy company. Full form **Dun and Bradstreet**

**D and C** MEDICINE a surgical procedure in which the cervix is widened and some of the womb lining is scraped out for diagnostic or treatment purposes. Full form **dilatation and curettage** (NOTE: The abbreviation **D and C** has entered the language as a noun, and the full form is rarely encountered in general usage.)

**D and V** MEDICINE diarrhoea and vomiting

**DAR** BUSINESS a method of testing the performance of an advert by assessing how many people who were exposed to it remember the key details the following day. Full form **day after recall (test)**

**DAS** COMPUTING a station that connects to both rings in an FDDI network. Full form **dual attachment (or attached) station**

**DASD** COMPUTING direct access storage device

**DAT** /dæt/ RECORDING a magnetic tape used in the digital recording of music. Full form **digital audio tape**

**DATV** /ˌdeɪ tiː ˈviː/ TV digitally assisted television

**DAX** /dæks/ STOCK EXCHANGE a share index on the Frankfurt Stock Exchange. Full form **Deutsche Aktienindex** (NOTE: From the German, 'German share price index'.)

**dB** MEASUREMENTS, ACOUSTICS decibel

**Db** CHEMICAL ELEMENTS dubnium

**DB** ACCOUNTING daybook

**DBA 1.** COMPUTING database administrator **2.** COMMERCE Doctor of Business Administration

**DB connector** COMPUTING a connector that facilitates serial and parallel input and output. Full form **data bus connector**

**DBE** MILITARY Dame Commander of the (Order of the) British Empire (NOTE: The abbreviation **DBE** is used as a title: *Peter Blakeney DBE*.)

**DBMS** COMPUTING database management system

**DBS** BROADCASTING **1.** direct broadcast (or broadcasting) by satellite **2.** direct broadcasting satellite

**DC 1.** MUSIC da capo (NOTE: The abbreviation **DC**, from the Italian, 'from the head', is used on sheet music to indicate that a passage or piece is to be played or sung again from the beginning.) **2.** POLICE Detective Constable **3.** ELECTRICITY direct current **4.** PUBLIC ADMINISTRATION District Commissioner **5.** GEOGRAPHY a federal district of the United States that is coextensive with the city of Washington. Full form **District of Columbia** (NOTE: Washington, capital city of the United States, is known as Washington, DC or Washington, D.C.)

**DCA 1.** GOVERNMENT Department for Constitutional Affairs **2.** COMPUTING a document format defined by IBM that allows documents to be exchanged between computer systems. Full form **document content architecture**

**DCB** MILITARY Dame Commander of the Order of the Bath

**DCC** RECORDING digital compact cassette

**DCD 1.** COMPUTING a signal from a modem to a computer indicating that a carrier is being received. Full form **data carrier detect 2.** RECORDING digital compact disc

**DCE 1.** COMPUTING data communications equipment **2.** FINANCE domestic credit expansion

**DCF** ACCOUNTING discounted cash flow

**DCL** LAW Doctor of Civil Law

**DCM 1.** FINANCE Development Capital Market **2.** MILITARY Distinguished Conduct Medal

**DCMG** MILITARY Dame Commander of the Order of St Michael and St George

**DCR** MEDICINE a medical procedure to remove blockages in the tear ducts. Full form **dacryocystorhinostomy**

**DCT** COMPUTING an algorithm used to encode and compress images. Full form **discrete cosine transform**

**DCVO** MILITARY Dame Commander of the Royal Victorian Order

**dd** COMMERCE **1.** dated **2.** delivered

**DD 1.** BANKING demand draft **2.** BANKING direct debit **3.** MILITARY dishonourable discharge **4.** CHRISTIANITY Doctor of Divinity **5.** COMPUTING used to describe a disk that can hold twice the amount of information that a standard disk can hold. Full form **double-density 6.** COMMERCE the degree of care that a prudent person would exercise, a legally relevant standard for establishing liability. Full form **due diligence**

**D/D** BANKING direct debit

**DDC** COMPUTING direct digital control

**DDE** COMPUTING **1.** direct data entry **2.** dynamic data exchange

**DDL** COMPUTING data description language

**DDP** COMPUTING distributed data processing

**DDR** GEOGRAPHY the former republic of East Germany. Full form **Deutsche Demokratische Republik** (NOTE: From the German, 'German Democratic Republic'.)

**DDR SDRAM** COMPUTING RAM that is designed to increase efficiency by synchronising output with a preset clock speed. Full form **double data rate synchronous dynamic random-access memory**

**DDS 1.** LIBRARIES a system of classifying library books in ten main classes divided into categories with three-digit numbers and subcategories with numbers after a decimal point. Full form **Dewey Decimal System 2.** DENTISTRY Doctor of Dental Science **3.** DENTISTRY Doctor of Dental Surgery

**DDSc** DENTISTRY Doctor of Dental Science

**DDT** CHEMISTRY an insecticide effective especially against malaria-carrying mosquitoes. It has been banned in many countries since 1974 because of its toxicity, its persistence in the environment, and its ability to accumulate in living tissue. Full form **dichlorodiphenyltrichloroethane** (NOTE: The abbreviation **DDT** is used as a noun in its own right, and the full form is rarely encountered.)

**de** ONLINE Germany (NOTE: The abbreviation **de**, from the German *Deutschland*, is seen at the end of Internet addresses, preceded by a dot.)

**DE** MAIL Delaware (NOTE: The abbreviation **DE** is part of the US sorting code on the last line of a Delaware address.)

**deb. 1.** FINANCE debenture **2.** BANKING debit

**dec. 1.** deceased **2.** declaration **3.** GRAMMAR declension **4.** ASTRONOMY declination **5.** decrease

**Dec.** CALENDAR December

**decresc.** MUSIC decrescendo

**DED** FUNGI Dutch elm disease

**def. 1.** defence **2.** LAW defendant **3.** FINANCE deferred **4.** GRAMMAR definite **5.** LINGUISTICS definition

**DEFRA** /'defrə/ GOVERNMENT Department of the Environment, Food, and Rural Affairs

**deg** MATHEMATICS, MEASUREMENTS degree

**Del** COMPUTING delete

**del. 1.** POLITICS delegate **2.** POLITICS delegation **3.** PRINTING delete

**dem.** GRAMMAR demonstrative

**Dem.** POLITICS **1.** Democrat **2.** Democratic

**DEN** HEALTH SERVICES District Enrolled Nurse

**denom.** RELIGION denomination

**dent. 1.** dental **2.** dentistry

**dep. 1.** department **2.** TRANSPORT departs **3.** TRANSPORT departure **4.** GRAMMAR used to describe a verb that inflects like a passive verb but is active in meaning. Full form **deponent 5.** LAW deposed **6.** FINANCE deposit **7.** TRANSPORT depot **8.** deputy

**dept** department

**deriv. 1.** derivation **2.** derivative

**DES 1.** E-COMMERCE data encryption standard **2.** PHARMACOLOGY a synthetic oestrogen used in hormone replacement therapy. Full form **diethylstilboestrol**

**det.** GRAMMAR determiner

**DETR** GOVERNMENT Department of the Environment, Transport and the Regions

**Deut.** BIBLE Deuteronomy

**DF 1.** RELIGION a title held by English and British monarchs since 1521, when it was given by Pope Leo X to King Henry VIII. Full form **Defender of the Faith 2.** COMMUNICATION a device used to determine the direction of a transmitted radio signal. Full form **direction finder**

**DFC** MILITARY Distinguished Flying Cross

**DfEE** GOVERNMENT Department for Education and Employment

**DfES** GOVERNMENT Department for Education and Skills. Former name **Department for Education and Employment**

**DFID** /ˈdɪfɪd/ GOVERNMENT Department for International Development

**DFM 1.** MILITARY Distinguished Flying Medal **2.** ONLINE don't flame me (NOTE: The abbreviation **DFM** is used in Internet chat rooms and text messages, meaning 'don't criticise or disparage me'.)

**DfT** GOVERNMENT Department for Transport

**dg** MEASUREMENTS decigram

**DG 1.** CHRISTIANITY Deo gratias (NOTE: From the Latin, 'thanks be to God'.) **2.** MANAGEMENT director-general

**d/g** double glazing

**DGO** WINE a declaration that a wine has come from a single, approved growing region. Full form **Declared Geographical Origin**

**DH 1.** GOVERNMENT Department of Health **2.** BASEBALL designated hitter

**DHA 1.** HEALTH SERVICES District Health Authority **2.** BIOCHEMISTRY a polyunsaturated essential fatty acid found in cold-water fish and some algae that has been linked to the reduction of cardiovascular disease and other health benefits. Full form **docosahexaenoic acid**

**DHSS** GOVERNMENT a former UK government department, now split into the Department of Health (DH) and the Department of Social Security (DSS). Full form **Department of Health and Social Security**

**DHW** UTILITIES domestic hot water

**DI** MEDICINE a method of assisted conception using sperm from a man who is not the woman's sexual partner. Full form **donor insemination**

**DIA** COMPUTING document interchange architecture

**dia.** MATHEMATICS diameter

**diag. 1.** MATHEMATICS diagonal **2.** diagram

**dial.** LANGUAGE **1.** dialect **2.** dialectal

**DIANE** /daɪˈæn/ COMPUTING direct information access network for Europe

**DIB** COMPUTING a bus used when transferring data from section of a computer to another. Full form **data input bus**

**DIC** MEDICINE a condition in which blood clotting occurs in diverse sites around the body other than that at a site of injury, causing inefficient wound healing and clots to form in the blood stream. Full form **disseminated intravascular coagulation**

**dict. 1.** dictation **2.** POLITICS dictator **3.** PUBLISHING dictionary

**didn't** /ˈdɪd(ə)nt/ did not

**DIF** COMPUTING data interchange format

**diff. 1.** difference **2.** different

**DIG** SOCIAL WELFARE income support available to people with disabilities in the UK. Full form **disability income guarantee**

**DIM 1.** ONLINE do it myself (*used in e-mails and text messages*) **2.** COMPUTING document image management

**dim. 1.** dimension **2.** MUSIC diminuendo **3.** GRAMMAR diminutive

**dimin. 1.** MUSIC diminuendo **2.** GRAMMAR diminutive

**DIMM** /dɪm/ COMPUTING a plug-in module that adds random-access memory to a computer. Full form **dual in-line memory module**

**din** MONEY dinar

**DIN** /dɪn/ a system of numbers used to indicate the speed of a photographic film, or a system of standard electrical connections used in television and audio equipment. Full form **Deutsche Industrie-Norm** (NOTE: From the German, 'German industry standard'.)

**dinky** /'dɪŋki/ SOCIAL SCIENCES either member of a couple who both have careers, usually in well-paid jobs, and who have no children. Full form **dual (or double) income, no kids (yet)**

> The acronym **dinky** or *DINKY*, one of a number coined in the late 20th century to denote various socioeconomic groups, has entered the language as a noun in its own right. Of the other coinages, only *yuppie* (young urban [or upwardly mobile] professional) has stood the test of time; those that have fallen by the wayside include *pippie* (person inheriting parents' property), *woopy* (well-off older person), *yappy* (young affluent parent), *LOMBARD* (loads of money but a right dickhead), *SINBAD* (single income, no boyfriend, absolutely desperate), *OINK* (one income, no kids), and *SINK* (single, independent, no kids), and *SWELL* (single woman earning lots in London).

**DIP 1.** MEDICINE distal interphalangeal (joint) (NOTE: The *DIP joint* is the finger joint furthest from the knuckle, at the fingertip.) **2.** COMPUTING document image processing **3.** COMPUTING dual in-line package (NOTE: A *DIP switch* is a switch that turns optional settings on or off on a computer component.)

**dip.** EDUCATION diploma

**DipEd** /dɪp'ed/ EDUCATION Diploma in Education

**dipl.** INTERNATIONAL RELATIONS **1.** diplomat **2.** diplomatic

**disc. 1.** COMMERCE discount **2.** discovered

**dist. 1.** distance **2.** district

**distr. 1.** distribution **2.** distributor

**div. 1.** diversion **2.** MATHEMATICS divide **3.** FINANCE dividend **4.** MATHEMATICS division **5.** SOCIAL SCIENCES divorced

**DIY 1.** ONLINE do it yourself (NOTE: The abbreviation **DIY** is used in e-mails, typically in response to a request to do something.) **2.** DOMESTIC the activity of doing repairs and alterations in the home yourself, especially as a hobby, instead of employing tradespeople to do the work. Full form **do-it-yourself** (NOTE: The abbreviation **DIY** has entered the language as a noun in its own right, used interchangeably with the full form.)

**dj** ONLINE Djibouti (NOTE: The abbreviation **dj** is seen at the end of Internet addresses, preceded by a dot.)

**DJ 1.** CLOTHING a man's jacket without tails that is worn on formal occasions, especially in the evening. Full form **dinner jacket 2.** MUSIC somebody who plays records or other recorded music, either for people to dance to (e.g. at a club or disco) or on a radio show. Full form **disc jockey**

**DJIA** FINANCE Dow Jones Industrial Average

**dk 1.** dark **2.** NAUTICAL deck **3.** ONLINE Denmark (NOTE: The abbreviation **dk** is seen at the end of Internet addresses, preceded by a dot.) **4.** SHIPPING dock

**DK** ONLINE (I) don't know (*used in e-mails*)

**dl** MEASUREMENTS decilitre

**DL** ONLINE download (*used in e-mails*)

**D/L** BANKING demand loan

**DLE** MEDICINE **1.** a disease of connective tissue resulting in skin lesions on the face and nose. Full form **discoid lupus erythematosus 2.** a disease of connective tissue causing inflammation, weakness and skin lesions. Full form **disseminated lupus erythematosus**

**DLit** /diːˈlɪt/ EDUCATION Doctor of Literature

**DLitt** /diːˈlɪt/ EDUCATION Doctor of Letters (or Literature) (NOTE: From the Latin *Doctor Litterarum.*)

**DLL** COMPUTING a library of utility programs that can be called from a main program. Full form **dynamic link library**

**dm 1.** MEASUREMENTS decimetre **2.** ONLINE Dominica (NOTE: The abbreviation **dm** is seen at the end of Internet addresses, preceded by a dot.)

**DM 1.** MONEY the former unit of currency in Germany, replaced by the euro in 2002. Full form **Deutschmark 2.** MARKETING direct marketing

**DMA 1.** MARKETING designated market area **2.** COMPUTING direct memory access

**DMAC** /ˈdiːmæk/ TV a coding system used for broadcasting colour television programmes via satellite. Full form **duobinary multiplexed analogue component**

**DMD** DENTISTRY Doctor of Dental Medicine (NOTE: From the Latin *Dentariae Medicinae Doctor.*)

**DMK** POLITICS a political party in the Indian state of Tamil Nadu. Full form **Dravida Munnetra Kazagham**

**DML** COMPUTING data manipulation language

**DMS 1.** COMPUTING data management system **2.** MANAGEMENT Diploma in Management Studies

**DMSO** a clear odourless liquid compound used as a solvent in medicine, to enable drugs to penetrate the skin. Full form **dimethylsulphoxide**

**DMU** BUSINESS decision-making unit

**DMus** MUSIC Doctor of Music

**DMZ** MILITARY demilitarized zone

**D/N** FINANCE debit note

**DNA 1.** GENETICS a nucleic acid molecule in the form of a double helix (a twisted double strand) that is the major component of chromosomes and carries genetic information. **DNA**, which is found in all living organisms except some viruses, is self-replicating and is responsible for passing on hereditary characteristics from one generation to the next. Full form **deoxyribonucleic acid** (NOTE: In this context, the abbreviation **DNA** refers to a patient who failed to attend an appointment with a doctor or at a clinic.) **2.** ONLINE did not answer (*used in e-mails and text messages*) **3.** HEALTH SERVICES did not attend

**DNase** /ˌdiː en ˈeɪz/ BIOCHEMISTRY an enzyme that aids the breakdown of DNA into smaller molecules. Full form **deoxyribonuclease**

**DNOC** CHEMISTRY a chemical compound used as a pesticide spray on fruit trees, found to have a poisoning effect on humans over time. Full form **dinitro-ortho-cresol**

**DNR** MEDICINE do not resuscitate (NOTE: If a patient undergoing a serious medical procedure does not wish to be resuscitated in the event of an arrest, or if this would be futile, a **DNR** order is given and written on their charts.)

**DNS** COMPUTING **1.** domain name server **2.** domain name system

**do** ONLINE Dominican Republic (NOTE: The abbreviation **do** is seen at the end of Internet addresses, preceded by a dot.)

**DO 1.** OPHTHALMOLOGY Doctor of Optometry **2.** MEDICINE Doctor of Osteopathy

**D/O** COMMERCE **1.** delivery order **2.** direct order

**DOA 1.** MEDICINE dead on arrival **2.** DRUGS drug of abuse

**DOB** date of birth

**DOC** WINE **1.** a certification for Portuguese wine that guarantees its origin. Full form **Denominação de Origem Controlada** (NOTE: From the Portuguese, 'name of origin controlled'.) **2.** a certification for Italian wine that guarantees its origin. Full form **Denominazione di Origine Controllata**

**doc.** LAW document

**DOCa** WINE a certification for Spanish wine that guarantees its origin. Full form **Denominación de Origen Calificada** (NOTE: From the Spanish, 'name of origin controlled'.)

**DOCG** WINE a strict certification for Italian wine that guarantees its origin, awarded by the Government. Full form **Denominazione di Origine Controllata e Garantita** (NOTE: From the Italian, 'name of origin controlled and guaranteed'.)

**DoE** *US* GOVERNMENT Department of Employment

**DOE 1.** *US* INDUST Department of Energy **2.** GOVERNMENT Department of the Environment. Former name for **Department of the Environment, Transport and the Regions**

**doesn't** /ˈdʌz(ə)nt/ does not

**dol.** MONEY dollar

**DOM 1.** CHRISTIANITY Deo Optimo Maximo (NOTE: From the Latin, 'to God, the best, the greatest'.) **2.** ENVIRONMENT the amount of an animal's-feed that it actually absorbs and so gains nutrition from. Full form **digestible organic matter 3.** ENVIRONMENT the matter that an animal eats. Full form **dry organic matter** (NOTE: The abbreviation **DOM** is used when measuring the nutritional value of a foodstuff or particular diet.)

**dom. 1.** domestic **2.** MUSIC dominant

**don't** /dəʊnt/ do not

**Dors.** GEOGRAPHY Dorset

**DOS** /dɒs/ COMPUTING **1.** an incident in which a system is deliberately bombarded with information and is overwhelmed, so that authorised users cannot use it. Full form **denial-of-service 2.** disk operating system

**DOVAP** /ˈdəʊvæp/ AEROSPACE a system for measuring the speed and position of objects in flight that is based on the frequency of sound waves. Full form **Doppler velocity and position**

**doz.** dozen

**DP 1.** COMPUTING data processing **2.** PHYSICS the temperature at which the air cannot hold all the moisture in it and dew begins to form. Full form **dew point 3.** SOCIAL SCIENCES a refugee from war or political oppression. Full form **displaced person**

**D/P** COMMERCE **1.** documents against payment **2.** a situation in which documents are held at a bank and a buyer must pay a balance for them in order to claim possession of goods shipped to them. Full form **documents against presentation**

**DPA** COMPUTING a technique of loading protocol stacks in memory only if they are required for a particular session. Full form **demand protocol architecture**

**DPB** *NZ* SOCIAL WELFARE a state benefit payable to those with family responsibilities who have little or no other income. Full form **domestic purposes benefit**

**DPCM** COMPUTING a method of encoding an analogue signal into a digital form. Full form **differential pulse coded modulation**

**DPhil** /ˈdiːfɪl/ EDUCATION Doctor of Philosophy

**dpi** COMPUTING, PRINTING a measure of the density of the image produced by a computer screen or printer. Full form **dots per inch**

**DPM** COMPUTING data processing manager

**DPP** LAW Director of Public Prosecutions

**DPS** STOCK EXCHANGE dividends per share

**dpt 1.** department **2.** GRAMMAR used to describe a verb that inflects like a passive verb but is active in meaning. Full form **deponent**

**DPT** IMMUNOLOGY diphtheria, pertussis, tetanus (vaccine) (NOTE: *Pertussis* is the technical name for whooping cough.)

**dr 1.** FINANCE debit (NOTE: The use of **dr** as an abbreviation for 'debit' is an extension of its use as an abbreviation for 'debtor'.) **2.** FINANCE debtor **3.** drawer

**Dr** Doctor

**DR 1.** NAVIGATION dead reckoning **2.** dining room (*used in property advertisements*) **3.** MONEY the former unit of currency in Greece, replaced by the euro in 2002. Full form **drachma 4.** CONSTRUCTION a waterless pipe that runs vertically, with connections on different levels of a building to which a firefighter's hose can be attached in case of fire. Full form **dry riser**

**dr. 1.** MONEY the former unit of currency in Greece, replaced by the euro in 2002. Full form **drachma 2.** MEASUREMENTS dram

**Dr.** ROADS Drive (NOTE: The abbreviation **Dr.** is used in addresses.)

**DRAM** /'di: ræm/ COMPUTING the most common type of RAM which needs constant electronic refreshing. Full form **dynamic random access memory**

**dram.** THEATRE dramatic

**DRIP** FINANCE dividend reinvestment plan

**DRP** COMMERCE the action of planning supply and replenishment of goods logistically in response to demand, including transport and stock requirements. Full form **distribution resource planning**

**DRV** HEALTH dietary reference values

**Ds** CHEMICAL ELEMENTS darmstadtium

**DS** MUSIC to be played or sung again from the point marked with a sign to the point marked *fine*. Full form **dal segno**

**d.s.** BUSINESS **1.** days after sight **2.** document signed

**DSc** EDUCATION Doctor of Science

**DSC** MILITARY Distinguished Service Cross

**DSL** TELECOMMUNICATIONS a high-speed telephone line supplying telephony, television, and Internet access. Full form **digital subscriber line**

**DSM** MILITARY Distinguished Service Medal

**DSO 1.** FINANCE days' sales outstanding **2.** MILITARY Distinguished Service Order

**DSP** COMPUTING digital signal processing

**d.s.p.** decessit sine prole (NOTE: From the Latin, 'died without issue (i.e. childless)'.)

**DSR** COMPUTING data set ready

**DSS 1.** GOVERNMENT Department of Social Security **2.** SOCIAL WELFARE Director of Social Services

**DST** TIME daylight-saving time

**DSTP** COMPUTING data space transfer protocol

**DSW** COMPUTING a data word transmitted from a device that contains information about its current status. Full form **device status word**

**DT** TIME daylight time

**DTC** HEALTH SERVICES diagnostic and treatment centre

**DTE** COMPUTING data terminal equipment

**DTF** FINANCE Derivative Trading Facility

**DTI** GOVERNMENT Department of Trade and Industry

**DTLGR** GOVERNMENT Department of Transport, Local Government, and the Regions

**DTMF** COMPUTING a method of dialling in a telephone system where two tones are generated according to the row and column position on the keypad of the number pressed. Full form **dual tone multi frequency**

**DTP** COMPUTING desktop publishing

**DTR** COMPUTING data terminal ready

**DTs** MEDICINE agitation, tremors, and hallucinations caused by alcohol dependence and withdrawal. Full form **delirium tremens** (NOTE: **DTs** (usually *the DTs* or *the DT's*) is an informal abbreviation for this condition, used in everyday language rather than medical terminology.)

**DTV** BROADCASTING digital television

**DTW** WINE Deutscher Tafelwein (NOTE: From the German, 'German table wine'.)

**DU** CHEMISTRY depleted uranium

**dunno** /dʌ'nəʊ/ (I) don't know

**DV** CHRISTIANITY Deo volente (NOTE: From the Latin, 'God willing'.)

**DVD** COMPUTING a high-capacity optical disc that can store a large quantity of video, audio, or other information. Full form **digital video disc, digital versatile disc**

**DVD-A** RECORDING digital video disc audio

**DVD-R** COMPUTING a DVD that can have its contents erased and replaced with something else. Full form **digital video disc recordable**

**DVD-RAM** /,di: vi: di: 'ræm/ COMPUTING a DVD drive that allows a user to write, erase, and rewrite data on a DVD. Full form **digital video disc random-access memory**

**DVD-ROM** /,di: vi: di: 'rɒm/ a DVD on which data can be stored but not altered. Full form **digital video disc read-only memory**

**DVD-RW** a DVD that can have it contents erased and replaced with something else many times. Full form **digital video disc rewritable**

**DVI** COMPUTING digital video imaging

**DV-I** COMPUTING digital video interactive

**DVLA** PUBLIC ADMINISTRATION Driving and Vehicle Licensing Agency

**DVM** VETERINARY MEDICINE Doctor of Veterinary Medicine

**DVR** TV digital video recorder

**DVT** MEDICINE a blood clot in a deep vein, particularly in the leg, that may be caused by being in a confined space such as an aeroplane seat for some time without moving. Full form **deep-vein thrombosis**

**D/W** LAW a customhouse licence or authority. Full form **dock warrant**

**DWA** SOCIAL WELFARE disability working allowance

**DWP** GOVERNMENT Department for Work and Pensions

**dwt** MEASUREMENTS dead weight tonnage

**DX** TELECOMMUNICATIONS long-distance

**Dy** CHEMICAL ELEMENTS dysprosium

**dyn** MEASUREMENTS, PHYSICS dyne

**dz** ONLINE Algeria

The use of **dz** as an abbreviation for Algeria in this and other contexts comes from the Arabic name for the country, *Al Djazair*. It is seen at the end of Internet addresses, preceded by a dot.

# E

**e 1.** PHYSICS electron **2.** ONLINE electronic (NOTE: The abbreviation **e** is used as a prefix in words such as *e-mail*, *e-commerce*, and *e-learning*, referring to electronic data transfer via the Internet.) **3.** ENGINEERING engineer **4.** ENGINEERING engineering

**E 1.** Earl **2.** ELECTRICITY earth **3.** east **4.** eastern **5.** PHYSICS electric field strength **6.** PHYSICS electromotive force **7.** TELECOMMUNICATIONS e-mail (address) (NOTE: The abbreviation **E** is used to contrast with T (telephone number) and F (fax number).) **8.** PHYSICS energy **9.** LANGUAGE English **10.** MEASUREMENTS exa- **11.** PHYSICS internal energy **12.** LOGIC a negative categorical proposition

**E2E** E-COMMERCE exchange

**EA** ENVIRONMENT Environment Agency

**ea.** each

**EAA** ACCOUNTING European Accounting Association

**EAC** ECONOMICS East African Community

**EAI** E-COMMERCE enterprise application integration

**E & O** COMMERCE errors and omissions

**E & OE** COMMERCE errors and omissions excepted

**e. & o.e.** COMMERCE errors and omissions excepted

**EAN-UCC** BUSINESS a system of barcoding used on all products sold internationally, introduced in Belgium in 1977 and regulated in the US by the Uniform Code Council. Full form **European Article Numbering – Uniform Code Council**

**EAP** HUMAN RESOURCES employee assistance programme

**EAPROM** /ˌiː eɪ ˈpiː ˌrɒm/ COMPUTING electrically alterable, programmable read-only memory

**EAROM** /ˌiː eɪ ˈrɒm/ COMPUTING electrically alterable read-only memory

**EASDAQ** STOCK EXCHANGE an independent European stock market, based in Brussels and London, trading in companies with European-wide interests. Full form **European Association of Securities Dealers Automated Quotation**

**EAT** BUSINESS employment appeal tribunal

**EBA** BANKING Euro Banking Association

**EBCDIC** /ˈeb siː dɪk/ a binary computer character code representing 256 standard letters, numbers, symbols, and control characters by means of eight binary digits. Full form **extended binary coded decimal interchange code**

**EBIT** FINANCE earnings before interest and taxes

**EBITDA** FINANCE earnings before interest, taxes, depreciation, and amortization

**EbN** east by north

**EBNF** COMPUTING extended BNF

**EBR** COMPUTING electron beam recording

**EBRD** BANKING European Bank for Reconstruction and Development

**EbS** east by south

**EBV** MEDICINE a virus believed to cause glandular fever and associated with some cancers. Full form **Epstein-Barr virus**

**ec** Ecuador (NOTE: The abbreviation **ec** is seen at the end of Internet addresses, preceded by a dot.)

**EC 1.** POLITICS the executive arm of the European Union, which formulates community policy and drafts community legislation. Full form **European Commission 2.** ECONOMICS a political and economic union of European countries that developed from the European Economic Community (EEC) and was replaced by the European Union (EU). Full form **European Community**

**ECB** BANKING European Central Bank

**ECG** MEDICINE **1.** an ultrasound device used to examine the working heart and display moving images of its action. Full form **echocardiograph 2.** a visual record of the heart's electrical activity produced by an electrocardiograph. Full form **electrocardiogram 3.** a device that records the electrical activity of the heart muscle via electrodes placed on the chest. Full form **electrocardiograph**

**ECGD** COMMERCE Export Credits Guarantee Department

**ECL** COMPUTING a high-speed logic circuit design using the transistor emitters as output connectors. Full form **emitter-coupled logic**

**ECMA** COMPUTING European Computer Manufacturers Association

**ECML** E-COMMERCE electronic commerce modelling language

**ecol. 1.** ecological **2.** ecology

**E. coli** /ˌiː ˈkəʊlaɪ/ MEDICINE a bacterium found in the colon of human beings and animals that becomes a serious contaminant when it enters the food or water supply. Full form **Escherichia coli**

**econ. 1.** economics **2.** economist **3.** economy

**ECOWAS** ECONOMICS Economic Community of West African States

**ECP** COMMERCE an IOU issued by a company for a short-term loan in a Euro currency. Full form **European Commercial Paper**

**ECS** TELECOMMUNICATIONS European Communications Satellite

**ECSC** INDUSTRY European Coal and Steel Community

**ECT** PSYCHIATRY electroconvulsive therapy

**ECU** /ˈaɪkjuː/ MONEY the official monetary unit of the European Union from 1979 to 1999. Full form **European Currency Unit**

**ed. 1.** PUBLISHING edited **2.** PUBLISHING edition **3.** PUBLISHING editor **4.** education

**EDAC** COMPUTING error detection and correction

**EDB** ECONOMICS Economic Development Board

**EDC 1.** E-COMMERCE electronic data capture **2.** MILITARY European Defence Community

**EDD** MEDICINE expected date of delivery

**EDI** COMPUTING electronic data interchange

**EDIFACT** E-COMMERCE electronic data interchange for administration, commerce, and transport (or trade)

**edit.** PUBLISHING **1.** edited **2.** edition **3.** editor

**EDLIN** COMPUTING an MS-DOS system utility that allows a user to make changes to a file on a line-by-line basis. Full form **edit line**

**EDMA** COMMERCE European Direct Marketing Association

**EDP** COMPUTING electronic data processing

**EDT 1.** TIME Eastern Daylight Time **2.** E-COMMERCE electronic depository transfer

**EDTA** CHEMISTRY a colourless compound that reacts with metals, used as a food preservative, as an anticoagulant, and in the treatment of lead poisoning. Full form **ethylene diamine tetra-acetate**

**edu** ONLINE US educational organization (NOTE: The abbreviation **edu** is used in Internet addresses.)

**educ. 1.** education **2.** educational

**ee** ONLINE Estonia (NOTE: The abbreviation **ee** is seen at the end of Internet addresses, preceded by a dot.)

**EE 1.** LANGUAGE Early English **2.** ELECTRICAL ENGINEERING electrical engineer **3.** ELECTRICAL ENGINEERING electrical engineering

**EEA** ECONOMICS European Economic Area

**EEC** ECONOMICS an alliance of European countries that ultimately expanded and developed into the European Union (EU). Full form **European Economic Community**

**EECA** E-COMMERCE a certificate authority that issues certificates for merchants and payment gateways. Full form **end entity certificate authority**

**EEG** MEDICINE **1.** an ultrasound device used to examine the structures of the brain. Full form **echoencephalograph 2.** the record of the electrical activity of the brain that is produced by an electrocardiograph. Full form **electroencephalogram 3.** a machine that uses electrodes placed on the scalp to monitor the electrical activity of different parts of the brain. Full form **electroencephalograph**

**EEOC** BUSINESS Equal Employment Opportunity Commission

**EEPROM** COMPUTING electrically erasable programmable read-only memory

**EER** MEASUREMENTS energy efficiency ratio

**EEROM** COMPUTING electrically erasable read-only memory

**EFA** HEALTH essential fatty acid

**EFL** EDUCATION English taught to people who live in a non-English-speaking country. Full form **English as a foreign language**

**EFRA** /'efrə/ E-COMMERCE electronic forms routing and approval

**EFT** BANKING electronic funds transfer

**EFTA** /'eftə/ COMMERCE European Free Trade Association

**EFTPOS** /'eftpɒs/ COMMERCE electronic funds transfer at a point of sale

**EFTS** /efts/ BANKING electronic funds transfer system

**eg** ONLINE Egypt (NOTE: The abbreviation **eg** is seen at the end of Internet addresses, preceded by a dot.)

**e.g.** for example

The abbreviations **e.g.** and **i.e.** are often confused, but use **e.g.** (from the Latin expression *exempli gratia*, 'for example') when you want to list a few typical examples of the thing mentioned: *I have the laboratory equipment, e.g.* [not i.e.] *beakers, thermometers, and test tubes, that we need*. Use **i.e.**, meaning 'that is, that is to say' (from the Latin expression *id est* 'that is') when you want to be more precise about the thing mentioned: *The tribunal, i.e.* [not e.g.] *the industrial tribunal, is set for noon on Friday*.

**EGA** COMPUTING enhanced graphics adapter

**EGM** BUSINESS extraordinary general meeting

**eh** ONLINE Western Sahara (NOTE: The abbreviation **eh** is seen at the end of Internet addresses, preceded by a dot.)

**EHO** HEALTH Environmental Health Officer

**EIA 1.** COMPUTING Electronics Industry Association **2.** ENVIRONMENT environmental impact assessment **3.** MEDICINE exercise-induced asthma

**EIB** BANKING European Investment Bank

**EIL** ECOLOGY the point at which a pest species is causing such damage that it becomes worth the time and expense of controlling them. Full form **economic injury level**

**EIRIS** BUSINESS Ethical Investment Research Service

**EIS 1.** BUSINESS Enterprise Investment Scheme **2.** ENVIRONMENT environmental impact statement **3.** ENVIRONMENT environmental impact study **4.** COMPUTING executive information system

**EISA** COMPUTING extended industry standard architecture

**EKG** MEDICINE electrocardiogram (NOTE: From Dutch or German *Electrokardiogram*.)

**el.** elevation

**ELDO** /'eldəʊ/ AEROSPACE European Launch Development Organization

**elec. 1.** electric **2.** electrical **3.** electricity

**elev.** elevation

**ELF 1.** LANGUAGE English as a Lingua Franca **2.** RADIO extremely low frequency

**ELINT** /'iːlɪnt/ MILITARY the gathering of information by electronic means, e.g. from aircraft or ships, or the section of the military intelligence service involved in this. Full form **electronic intelligence**

**ELISA** /ɪ'laɪzə/ IMMUNOLOGY a technique for determining the presence or amount of protein in a biological sample, using an enzyme that bonds to an antibody or antigen and causes a colour change. Full form **enzyme-linked immunosorbent assay**

**ELT** EDUCATION the teaching of English to non-native speakers of English. Full form **English language teaching** (NOTE: The abbreviation **ELT** is used as a noun in its own right.)

**'em** /əm/ them

**EM 1.** PHYSICS electromagnetic **2.** PHYSICS electron microscope **3.** COMPUTING a code that indicates the end of usable physical medium. Full form **end of medium**

**EmA** MEDICINE igA antiendomysial antibody

**EMAS** /'iːmæs/ ENVIRONMENT a voluntary scheme of the European Union in which commercial and other organizations are encouraged to assess their approach to environmental matters against a given set of criteria. Full form **Eco-Management and Audit Scheme**

**emf** PHYSICS electromotive force

**EMF 1.** PHYSICS electromotive force **2.** ECONOMICS European Monetary Fund

**EMG** MEDICINE **1.** a graphical tracing of the electrical activity in a muscle at rest or during contraction, used to diagnose nerve and muscle disorders. Full form **electromyogram 2.** a machine for producing an electromyogram from electrical activity picked up via electrodes inserted into muscle tissue. Full form **electromyograph**

**EMH** FINANCE efficient markets hypothesis

**EMI** FINANCE European Monetary Institute

**Emp. 1.** Emperor **2.** Empire **3.** Empress

**EMS 1.** E-COMMERCE electronics manufacturing services **2.** HEALTH SERVICES emergency medical services **3.** BUSINESS environmental management system **4.** FINANCE European Monetary System

**EMT** HEALTH SERVICES emergency medical technician

**EMU 1.** MEASUREMENTS, PHYSICS electromagnetic unit **2.** ECONOMICS European Monetary Union

**EN 1.** ECOLOGY endangered (species) **2.** ECOLOGY English Nature **3.** HEALTH SERVICES enrolled nurse

**EN(G)** *Aus, NZ, N Am* HEALTH SERVICES enrolled nurse (general)

**EN(M)** *Aus, NZ, N Am* HEALTH SERVICES enrolled nurse (mental)

**EN(MH)** *Aus, NZ, N Am* HEALTH SERVICES enrolled nurse (mental handicap)

**enc.** BUSINESS **1.** enclosed **2.** enclosure

**encl.** BUSINESS **1.** enclosed **2.** enclosure

**ENE** east-northeast

**ENEA** INDUST European Nuclear Energy Agency

**ENG** BROADCASTING electronic newsgathering

**eng. 1.** engine **2.** engineer **3.** engineering

**Eng. 1.** GEOGRAPHY England **2.** LANGUAGE English

**engr.** PRINTING **1.** engraved **2.** engraver **3.** engraving

**enl. 1.** PHOTOGRAPHY enlarged **2.** MILITARY enlisted

**ENO** MUSIC English National Opera

**ENQ** COMPUTING enquiry

**Ens.** MILITARY Ensign

**ENSA** /'ensə/ MILITARY a British organization formed to provide entertainment for Allied forces during World War II. Full form **Entertainments National Service Association**

**ENSO** OCEANOGRAPHY an environmental phenomenon whereby strong winds cause the movement of warm Pacific waters westwards into cooler water areas, disrupting their ecosystems. It happens ever 2–7 years and is usually accompanied by heavy rainstorms. Full form **El Niño Southern Oscillation**

**ENT** MEDICINE ear, nose, and throat

**E number** /'iː ˌnʌmbə/ FOOD INDUSTRY a code by which a given additive is identified on food labels, consisting of the letter E followed by a number. Contrary to popular belief, E numbers can denote natural substances (e.g. lactic acid and pectin) as well as artificial additives. (NOTE: The E stands for 'European': such additives have been approved for use throughout the European Union.)

**EOA** COMPUTING end of address

**EOB** COMPUTING end of block

**EOC** LAW Equal Opportunities Commission

**EOD** COMPUTING end of data

**EOF** COMPUTING end of file

**EOJ** COMPUTING end of job

**EOL** COMPUTING end of line

**EOM** COMPUTING end of message

**e.o.m.** COMMERCE end of the month

**EOQ** COMMERCE economic order quantity

**EOR** COMPUTING end of record

**EOT** COMPUTING **1.** end of text **2.** end of transmission

**Ep.** BIBLE Epistle

**e.p.** CHESS used when a pawn that has moved two squares is captured by an enemy pawn as if it had only moved one square. Full form **en passant** (NOTE: From the French, 'in passing'.)

**EPA 1.** BIOCHEMISTRY a polyunsaturated essential fatty acid found in some fish that has been linked to various health benefits. Full form **eicosapentaenoic acid 2.** ENVIRONMENT Environmental Protection Agency

**EPAC** /'iːpæk/ ECONOMICS an independent organization made up of leading politicians and business figures that advises the Australian federal government on economic policy. Full form **Economic Planning and Advisory Committee**

**Eph.** BIBLE Ephesians

**Epis. 1.** CHRISTIANITY Episcopal **2.** CHRISTIANITY Episcopalian **3.** BIBLE Epistle

**Epist.** BIBLE Epistle

**EPNS** METALLURGY electroplated nickel silver

**EPOS** /'iːpɒs/ COMMERCE electronic point of sale

**EPROM** /ˌiː ˈpiː ˌrɒm/ COMPUTING an integrated circuit that can be reprogrammed by a user to correct an error in the program or to add a function. Full form **erasable-programmable read-only memory**

**eps** FINANCE earnings per share

**EPS 1.** FINANCE earnings per share **2.** COMPUTING PostScript commands contained in a file that can be placed within a graphics or DTP program. Full form **encapsulated PostScript**

**EPSF** COMPUTING encapsulated PostScript file

**EQ** EDUCATION the ratio of educational attainment to chronological age. Full form **educational quotient**

**eq. 1.** equal **2.** equation **3.** equivalent

**equiv.** equivalent

**er** ONLINE Eritrea (NOTE: The abbreviation **er** is seen at the end of Internet addresses, preceded by a dot.)

**Er** CHEMICAL ELEMENTS erbium

**ER 1.** Eduardus Rex (NOTE: From the Latin, 'King Edward'.) **2.** Elizabetha Regina **3.** HEALTH SERVICES the US equivalent of A & E (the accident and emergency department, traditionally known as casualty). Full form **emergency room** (NOTE: The abbreviation **ER** is used as a noun in its own right.) **4.** MEDICINE an intricate system of tubular membranes in the cytoplasm of a cell. Full form **endoplasmic reticulum**

**ERA 1.** EDUCATION a law passed in 1988 covering the publication of information on schools, open enrolment, and grant-maintained schools. Full form **Education Reform Act 2.** *US* LAW Equal Rights Amendment

**ERCP** MEDICINE a medical procedure to diagnose problems with the liver, bile duct and pancreas, consisting of an endoscopic procedure to inject dye followed by an x-ray. Full form **endoscopic retrograde cholangiopancreatography**

**ERDF** COMMERCE European Regional Development Fund

**ERG** OPHTHALMOLOGY a record of the electrical activity of the retina obtained via electrodes placed on the eye. Full form **electroretinogram**

**ERID** ECOLOGY disease which can be controlled but not eradicated, whose incidence in humans has increased and continues to do so. Full form **emerging and re-emerging infectious disease**

**ERM** ECONOMICS a system of controlling the exchange rate between some countries in the European Union. Full form **Exchange Rate Mechanism** (NOTE: The **ERM** has become redundant with the advent of the single European currency.)

**Ernie** /ˈɜːniː/ FINANCE in the United Kingdom, the machine used for drawing winning premium bond numbers. Full form **electronic random number indicating equipment** (NOTE: The abbreviation **Ernie**, which bestows a 'human' identity on the machine, is used in preference to the full form.)

**EROM** /ˈiː rɒm/ COMPUTING electrically alterable read-only memory

**ERP** FINANCE extra return on an equity in preference to a bond, because of the extra risk involving in investing in these. Full form **equity risk premium**

**ERPC** MEDICINE evacuation of retained products of conception

**ERR** FINANCE expected rate of return

**es** ONLINE Spain (NOTE: The abbreviation **es**, from the Spanish *España*, is seen at the end of Internet addresses, preceded by a dot.)

**Es** CHEMICAL ELEMENTS einsteinium

**ES** GEOGRAPHY Eastern States

**ESA 1.** ENVIRONMENT environmentally sensitive area **2.** AEROSPACE European Space Agency

**Esc** COMPUTING the key on a computer keyboard that allows a user to exit a program, cancel a command, or return to a previous menu. Full form **escape (key)**

**ESCB** BANKING European System of Central Banks

**Esd.** BIBLE Esdras

**ESDI** COMPUTING enhanced small device interface

**ESE** east-southeast

**ESF** SOCIAL WELFARE a fund which provides support to programs in the European Union which help people find employment or train in new skills. Full form **European Social Fund**

**ES-IS** COMPUTING end system to intermediate system

**ESL** EDUCATION English taught to people who live in an English-speaking country but whose first language is not English. Full form **English as a second language**

**ESOL** /ˈiːsɒl/ EDUCATION English for speakers of other languages

**ESOP** /ˈiːsɒp/ COMMERCE an investment plan in which employees acquire shares in the company they work for by making tax-deductible contributions. Full form **employee share ownership plan**

**ESP 1.** ENVIRONMENT a device that removes small particles of smoke, dust, or oil from air by electrostatically charging them and then attracting them to an oppositely charged collector plate or surface. Full form **electrostatic precipitator 2.** COMMERCE the period of employment that an employee's benefits from a superannuation scheme are calculated on. Full form **eligible service period 3.** EDUCATION English for special purposes **4.** PARAPSYCHOLOGY extrasensory perception

**esp.** especially

**Esq.** Esquire (NOTE: The abbreviation **Esq.** is used as a courtesy title in correspondence, placed after a man's full name.)

**ESR 1.** PHYSICS a method of dating minerals by testing their reaction to magnetic fields. Full form **electron spin resonance 2.** MEDICINE an outdated method of diagnosing illness by testing the sedimentation rate of blood cells in a solution. Full form **erythrocyte sedimentation rate**

**ESRC** SOCIAL SCIENCES Economic and Social Research Council

**ESRD** MEDICINE complete failure of the kidneys, requiring substitute treatment such as dialysis. Full form **end-stage renal disease**

**EST** TIME Eastern Standard Time

**estd** established

**Esth.** BIBLE Esther

**esu** MEASUREMENTS, PHYSICS electrostatic unit

**et** ONLINE Ethiopia (NOTE: The abbreviation **et** is seen at the end of Internet addresses, preceded by a dot.)

**ET** SCIENCE FICTION extraterrestrial (NOTE: The abbreviation **ET** was popularized by the blockbusting 1982 film of this name and its endearing eponymous hero.)

**ETA 1.** TRAVEL estimated time of arrival **2.** /ˈetə/ POLITICS a Basque nationalist guerrilla group that seeks separation and independence from Spain for the Basque region. Full form **Euzkadi ta Askatsuna**

**etc.** et cetera

**ETD** TRAVEL estimated time of departure

**ETF** BANKING electronic transfer of funds

**ETLLD** GOVERNMENT Enterprise, Transport and Lifelong Learning Department

**ETP** FINANCE a lump sum from a superannuation fund payable to an employee on termination of their employment. Full form **eligible termination payment**

**ETX** COMPUTING end of text

**ety.** LINGUISTICS **1.** etymological **2.** etymology

**etymol.** LINGUISTICS **1.** etymological **2.** etymology

**Eu** CHEMICAL ELEMENTS europium

**EU** POLITICS an economic and political union of European nations. Full form **European Union**

**Eur.** GEOGRAPHY **1.** Europe **2.** European

**EURIBOR** /'juːrɪbɔː/ BANKING European Interbank Offered Rate

**eV** MEASUREMENTS, PHYSICS electron volt

**EVA 1.** COMMERCE the difference between a company's profit and the cost of its capital. Full form **economic value added 2.** AEROSPACE extravehicular activity

**evan.** CHRISTIANITY **1.** evangelical **2.** evangelist

**evang.** CHRISTIANITY **1.** evangelical **2.** evangelist

**EW** MILITARY enlisted woman

**EWO** EDUCATION Educational Welfare Officer

**Ex.** BIBLE Exodus

**exch. 1.** exchange **2.** POLITICS exchequer

**Exch.** POLITICS Exchequer

**excl. 1.** GRAMMAR exclamation **2.** exclusive

**EXE** COMPUTING a filename extension for a program file. Full form **executable**

**EXNOR** /eks'nɔː/ MATHEMATICS a logical function whose output is true if all inputs are at the same level, and false if they are not. Full form **exclusive NOR**

**exor** LAW executor

**EXOR** /eks'ɔː/ MATHEMATICS a logical function whose output is true if any input is true, and false if all the inputs are the same. Full form **exclusive OR**

**exp. 1.** experiment **2.** experimental **3.** expired **4.** expires **5.** MATHEMATICS exponential function **6.** COMMERCE export **7.** COMMERCE exported **8.** TRANSPORT express

**ext. 1.** TELECOMMUNICATIONS extension **2.** exterior **3.** external **4.** PHARMACOLOGY extract

**EZ** BUSINESS enterprise zone

**Ez.** BIBLE Ezra

**Ezek.** BIBLE Ezekiel

**Ezr.** BIBLE Ezra

# F

**f 1.** MEASUREMENTS femto- **2.** PHOTOGRAPHY the ratio of the focal length to the effective diameter of a camera lens. Symbol for **f-number 3.** PHYSICS the distance from the centre of a lens or the surface of a mirror to the point at which light passing through the lens or reflected from the mirror is focused. Symbol for **focal length 4.** MUSIC forte (NOTE: The abbreviation **f**, usually italicized, is used on sheet music at a passage that is to be played or sung loudly.) **5.** PHYSICS frequency **6.** MATHEMATICS function **7.** MONEY guilder (NOTE: The guilder is also called a *florin*, hence the abbreviation.) **8.** PUBLISHING folio (NOTE: The abbreviation **F**, followed by a number, is used in publishing to refer to a particular sheet of a manuscript or page of a book.) **9.** following (line or page)

**F 1.** MEASUREMENTS, PHYSICS Fahrenheit **2.** false (NOTE: The abbreviation **F** is usually contrasted with **T** meaning 'true', as possible answers to a question.) **3.** MEASUREMENTS, ELECTRICITY farad **4.** MEASUREMENTS, ELECTRICITY faraday (NOTE: As an abbreviation for *faraday*, **F** is usually italicized.) **5.** MEASUREMENTS fathom **6.** TELECOMMUNICATIONS fax (number) (NOTE: The abbreviation **F** is used to contrast with E (e-mail address) and T (telephone number).) **7.** CALENDAR February **8.** Fellow **9.** female **10.** GRAMMAR feminine **11.** METALLURGY with all or most impurities removed. Full form **fine 12.** CHEMICAL ELEMENTS fluorine **13.** PHYSICS force **14.** SPORTS foul **15.** MONEY franc **16.** CALENDAR Friday

**F2F** ONLINE face-to-face (*used in e-mails and text messages*)

**F2T** ONLINE free to talk (*used in e-mails, text messages and Internet chat rooms*)

**FA 1.** MILITARY field artillery **2.** FINANCE financial adviser **3.** ARTS fine art **4.** SOCCER Football Association **5.** FREIGHT freight agent

**FAA** NAVY Fleet Air Arm

**FAB** BEVERAGES flavoured alcoholic beverage

**Fahr.** MEASUREMENTS, PHYSICS Fahrenheit

**FAM** COMPUTING fast access memory

**fam. 1.** familiar **2.** family

**FAO** AGRICULTURE Food and Agriculture Organization (of the United Nations)

**f.a.o.** BUSINESS for the attention of (NOTE: The abbreviation **f.a.o.** is used before the name of the intended recipient of a letter, memorandum, or other communication.)

**FAP** MEDICINE a pre-cancerous condition resulting in the development of polyps on the colon, caused by a genetic mutation. Full form **familial adenomatous polyposis**

**FAQ 1.** SHIPPING free alongside quay **2.** /fæk, ˌef eɪ ˈkjuː/ COMPUTING frequently asked question(s)

**FAQs** /fæks/ COMPUTING frequently asked questions

**FARC** /fɑːk/ POLITICS Revolutionary Armed Forces of Colombia (NOTE: From the Spanish, 'Fuerzas Armadas Revolucionarias de Colombia'.)

**FAS 1.** *US* FINANCE Federal Accounting Standards **2.** MEDICINE a condition affecting babies born to women who drank excessive amounts of alcohol during pregnancy, characterized by a range of effects including facial abnormalities and learning difficulties. Full form **foetal alcohol syndrome 3.** SHIPPING with the cost of delivery to the quayside included, but not the cost of loading onto a ship, as opposed to *free on board* (FOB). Full form **free alongside ship**

**FASB** FINANCE Financial Accounting Standards Board

**FASIT** FINANCE Financial Asset Securitisation Investment Trust

**FASTER** STOCK EXCHANGE Fully Automated Screen Trading and Electronic Registration

**Fast-SCSI** /ˌfɑːst ˈskʌzi/ COMPUTING a development that allows data to be transferred at a higher rate than with the original SCSI specification

**FAT** /fæt/ COMPUTING in MS-DOS, an internal store of information about the structure of files on a disk. Full form **file allocation table**

**FBA** Fellow of the British Academy

**FBC** INDUSTRY a technique to improve the efficiency of fuel combustion in power plants by mixing the fuel with jets of air during the combustion process. Full form **fluidized-bed combustion**

**FBI** CRIME a bureau of the US Department of Justice that deals with matters of national security, interstate crime, and crimes against the government. Full form **Federal Bureau of Investigation**

**FBR** INDUST fast-breeder reactor

**FC 1.** INDUSTRY fibre-concrete **2.** SOCCER Football Club **3.** TREES Forestry Commission

**FCA 1.** ACCOUNTING Fellow of the Institute of Chartered Accountants (in England and Wales) **2.** BUSINESS, ENVIRONMENT the practice of including the indirect costs and benefits of a product or activity, e.g. its social and environmental effects on health and the economy, along with its direct costs when making business decisions. Full form **full cost accounting**

**FCB** COMPUTING file control block

**FCCA** ACCOUNTING Fellow of the Association of Chartered Certified Accountants

**FCI** BUSINESS Finance Corporation for Industry

**FCII** INSURANCE Fellow of the Chartered Insurance Institute

**FCM** STOCK EXCHANGE futures commission merchant

**FCMA** ACCOUNTING Fellow of the Chartered Institute of Management Accountants

**FCO** GOVERNMENT Foreign and Commonwealth Office

**FCSD** GOVERNMENT Financial and Central Services Department

**FD 1.** CHRISTIANITY Fidei Defensor. ◊ **DF** (NOTE: The abbreviation **FD**, from the Latin, 'Defender of the Faith', is used on British coins, after the name of the monarch.) **2.** BUSINESS financial director **3.** COMPUTING floppy disk **4.** COMMERCE free delivery **5.** COMPUTING data transmission down a channel in two directions simultaneously. Full form **full duplex**

**f/d** COMMERCE free delivery

**FDA** HEALTH the US federal agency that oversees trade in and the safety of food and drugs. Full form **Food and Drug Administration**

**FDC** COMPUTING floppy disk controller

**FDD** COMPUTING floppy disk drive

**FDDI** COMPUTING a standard for high-speed networks which use fibreoptic cable in a dual-ring topology. Full form **fibre distributed data interface**

**FDI** BUSINESS foreign direct investment

**FDIC** BUSINESS Federal Deposit Insurance Corporation

**FDISK** /ˈef dɪsk/ COMPUTING an MS-DOS system utility that configures the partitions on a hard disk (NOTE: 'Fixed disk' is an older term for 'hard disk'.)

**FDM** COMPUTING a system of assigning different signals to different frequencies so that they can be sent simultaneously. Full form **frequency division multiplexing**

**FDR** 32nd president of the United States (1933–45). Full form **Franklin Delano Roosevelt**

**FDX** COMPUTING full duplex. ◊ **FD**

**Fe** CHEMICAL ELEMENTS iron (NOTE: From the Latin *ferrum*.)

**FE** EDUCATION further education

**Feb.** CALENDAR February

**fec.** ARTS he or she made it (NOTE: The abbreviation **fec.**, from the Latin *fecit*, follows the artist's name on a piece of work.)

**FED** COMPUTING a method of producing thin, flat displays for laptop computers. Full form **field emission display**

**fed.** POLITICS **1.** federal **2.** federated **3.** federation

**Fed.** POLITICS **1.** Federal **2.** Federated **3.** Federation

**FEDUSA** HUMAN RESOURCES Federation of Unions of South Africa

**fem. 1.** BIOLOGY female **2.** GRAMMAR feminine

**FEMA** /ˈfiːmə/ US GOVERNMENT Federal Emergency Management Agency

**FEP** COMPUTING a computer that carries out preliminary processing on data before passing it to another computer for further processing. Full form **front-end processor**

**FES** SOCIAL SCIENCES Family Expenditure Survey

**FESS** MEDICINE functional endoscopic sinus surgery

**FET** ELECTRONICS field-effect transistor

**FEV** MEDICINE the amount of air that can be expelled in one breath, a measure of lung capacity and function. Full form **forced expiratory volume**

**ff** MUSIC fortissimo (NOTE: The abbreviation **ff**, usually italicized, is used on sheet music at a passage that is to be played or sung very loudly.)

**FF 1.** ELECTRONICS an electronic circuit or mechanical device that has two stable states and can be switched between the two. Full form **flip-flop 2.** COMPUTING a command to start a new page on a printer. Full form **form feed**

**ff. 1.** PUBLISHING folios (NOTE: The abbreviation **ff.**, followed by a series or range of numbers, is used in publishing to refer to particular sheets of a manuscript or pages of a book.) **2.** following (lines or pages) (NOTE: The abbreviation **ff.** is used after a line or page number.)

**FGD** ENVIRONMENT flue gas desulphurization

**FH** EMERGENCIES fire hydrant

**f/h** COMMERCIAL LAW freehold

**FHFB** US FINANCE Federal Housing Finance Board

**FHLBB** US BANKING Federal Home Loan Bank Board

**FHLBS** US BANKING Federal Home Loan Bank System

**FHLMC** US FINANCE Federal Home Loan Mortgage Corporation

**fhp** MECHANICAL ENGINEERING friction horsepower

**FHSA** HEALTH SERVICES Family Health Services Authority

**FIBOR** /ˈfaɪbɔː/ BANKING Frankfurt Interbank Offered Rate

**FID** Aus FINANCE Financial Institutions Duty

**Fid. Def.** CHRISTIANITY Fidei Defensor. ◊ **DF** (NOTE: Formerly seen on British coins, the preferred abbreviation now used is **FD**. From the Latin, 'Defender of the Faith'.)

**FIDE** CHESS World Chess Federation (NOTE: From the French, *Fédération Internationale des Échecs*.)

**FIF** FINANCE Foreign Investment Funds (Tax)

**FIFA** /ˈfiːfə/ SOCCER the governing organization of international football. Full form **Fédération Internationale de Football Association** (NOTE: From the French, 'International Federation of Association Football'.)

**FIFO** /ˈfaɪfəʊ/ first in, first out

**fig. 1.** figurative **2.** figure (NOTE: The abbreviation **fig.** is most frequently used in the captions of (or textual references to) illustrations, diagrams, or tables in a book.)

**FIM** MEDICINE a test to evaluate the amount of assistance that a person with a disability needs to carry out basic activities. Full form **functional independence measure**

**FIMBRA** /'fɪmbrə/ FINANCE Financial Intermediaries, Managers, and Brokers Regulatory Association

**fin. 1.** finance **2.** financial **3.** finish

**Fin. 1.** GEOGRAPHY Finland **2.** LANGUAGE Finnish

**FIO** COMMERCE for information only

**f.i.o.** COMMERCE for information only

**FIRB** BUSINESS Foreign Investment Review Board

**fj** ONLINE Fiji (NOTE: The abbreviation **fj** is seen at the end of Internet addresses, preceded by a dot.)

**Fkr** MONEY Faroese krona

**FL 1.** MILITARY Flight Lieutenant **2.** MAIL Florida (NOTE: The abbreviation **FL** is part of the US sorting code on the last line of a Florida address.)

**fl. 1.** floor **2.** MONEY florin **3.** floruit (NOTE: The abbreviation **fl.** is used before the name or number of the period in which a particular person or movement was most active, especially when the exact dates are unknown.) **4.** MUSIC flute **5.** MONEY guilder (NOTE: The guilder is also called a *florin*, hence the abbreviation.)

**Fl. 1.** GEOGRAPHY Flanders **2.** LANGUAGE Flemish

**FLA** BUSINESS Finance and Leasing Association

**flak** /flæk/ ◊ see note at **Aids**

**FLOP** /flɒp/ MATHEMATICS a mathematical operation carried out on a number expressed in floating point (standardising) notation. Full form **floating-point operation**

**flops** /flɒps/ COMPUTING floating-point operations per second (NOTE: The acronym **flops** is used to indicate the speed of a computer.)

**flor.** floruit (NOTE: From the Latin, 'flourished'.)

**fl oz** MEASUREMENTS fluid ounce

**FLQ** POLITICS a terrorist organization seeking the secession of Quebec from Canada. Full form **Front de Libération du Québec** (NOTE: From the French, 'Quebec Liberation Front'.)

**F/Lt** MILITARY Flight Lieutenant

**Flt Lt** MILITARY Flight Lieutenant

**Flt Sgt** MILITARY Flight Sergeant

**fm 1.** MEASUREMENTS fathom **2.** RADIO frequency modulation **3.** ONLINE (Federated States of) Micronesia (NOTE: The abbreviation **fm** is seen at the end of Internet addresses, preceded by a dot.)

**Fm** CHEMICAL ELEMENTS fermium

**FM 1.** ARMY field manual **2.** ENGINEERING a parameter or characteristic of a machine, component, or instrument that is used as a measure of its performance. Full form **figure of merit 3.** RADIO frequency modulation **4.** GEOGRAPHY (Federated States of) Micronesia

**FMA** FINANCE Fund Managers' Association

**FMCG** COMMERCE fast-moving consumer goods

**fml** formal

**FMS 1.** PSYCHOLOGY a situation in which examination, therapy, or hypnosis has elicited apparent memories, especially of childhood abuse, that are disputed by family members and often traumatic to the patient. Full form **false memory syndrome 2.** MANUFACTURING flexible manufacturing system **3.** AVIAT flight management system

**FNMA** *US* FINANCE Federal National Mortgage Association

**FNQ** GEOGRAPHY Far North Queensland

**fo** ONLINE Faroe Islands (NOTE: The abbreviation **fo** is seen at the end of Internet addresses, preceded by a dot.)

**FO 1.** FINANCE finance officer **2.** GOVERNMENT Foreign Office

**fo.** PUBLISHING folio (NOTE: The abbreviation **fo.**, followed by a number, is used in publishing to refer to a particular sheet of a manuscript or page of a book.)

**FOB** SHIPPING with the cost of delivery to a port and loading onto a ship included, as opposed to *free alongside ship* (FAS). Full form **free on board**

**FoC** HUMAN RESOURCES a shop steward representing members of a trade union in a printing office or publishing house. Full form **father of the chapel**

**FOD** TELECOMMUNICATIONS fax-on-demand

**FoE** ENVIRONMENT Friends of the Earth

**FOK** FINANCE an order to either execute a transaction immediately and in full, or, if not possible, to cancel it. Full form **fill or kill**

**FOL** *ANZ* POLITICS Federation of Labour

**FOR** COMMERCE with the cost of delivery to a railway station and loading onto a train included. Full form **free on rail**

**for. 1.** foreign **2.** forestry

**forex** /'fɔːreks/ FINANCE foreign exchange

**FORTRAN** /'fɔːtræn/ COMPUTING the earliest high-level computer programming language. Full form **formula translation**

**4GL** COMPUTING fourth-generation language

**4WD** AUTOMOTIVE four-wheel drive

**FOX** /fɒks/ FINANCE Futures and Options Exchange

**FPA** FINANCE Financial Planning Association of Australia

**fps 1.** MEASUREMENTS feet per second **2.** MEASUREMENTS foot-pound-second (NOTE: The **fps system** uses the foot, pound, and second as the basic units for length, mass, and time, respectively. It has been largely replaced by the SI system in scientific contexts.) **3.** PHOTOGRAPHY a measure of camera shutter speed. Full form **frames per second**

**FPS** COMPUTER GAMES **1.** first person shooter **2.** a measure of the rate of screen refreshment in a real-time computer game. Full form **frames per second**

**FPU** COMPUTING a CPU unit that can process numbers expressed in floating-point notation very quickly. Full form **floating-point unit**

**fr** ONLINE France (NOTE: The abbreviation **fr** is seen at the end of Internet addresses, preceded by a dot.)

**Fr 1.** CHRISTIANITY Father **2.** CHEMICAL ELEMENTS francium

**FR** BUILDINGS family room (*used in property advertisements*)

**fr. 1.** fragment **2.** from

**Fr. 1.** MONEY franc **2.** GEOGRAPHY France **3.** the German equivalent of Mrs. Full form **Frau 4.** LANGUAGE French **5.** CHRISTIANITY Friar **6.** CALENDAR Friday

**f.r.** PUBLISHING folio recto (NOTE: From the Latin, 'on the right-hand page'.)

**FRB** *US* **1.** BANKING Federal Reserve Bank **2.** FINANCE Federal Reserve Board

**FRCS** SURGERY Fellow of the Royal College of Surgeons

**freq. 1.** frequency **2.** GRAMMAR used to describe a verb or affix that expresses repeated action. Full form **frequentative 3.** frequently

**FRG** GEOGRAPHY the full official name for Germany. Full form **Federal Republic of Germany**

**Fri.** CALENDAR Friday

**Frl.** the German equivalent of Miss. Full form **Fräulein**

**FRN** FINANCE loans arranged by a bank which are not at a fixed rate of interest. Full form **floating rate note**

**FROM** /'ef rɒm/ COMPUTING fusible read-only memory

**FRS** SCIENCE Fellow of the Royal Society

**FRSB** FINANCE Financial Reporting Standards Board

**FRY** GEOGRAPHY the full official name for the former state of Yugoslavia (now in two separate states, Macedonia, and Serbia and Montenegro). Full form **Federal Republic of Yugoslavia**

**FSA 1.** ARTS Fellow of the Society of Antiquaries **2.** FINANCE Financial Services Authority **3.** FOOD INDUSTRY Food Standards Agency

**FSAVC** PENSIONS an **AVC** which is run by an independent pension fund company and not by the investor's employer. Full form **free-standing additional voluntary contribution**

**FSB** BUSINESS Federation of Small Businesses

**FSH 1.** BIOCHEMISTRY a hormone that stimulates the growth of egg follicles in the ovaries and the making of sperm in the testes. Full form **follicle-stimulating hormone 2.** AUTOMOTIVE full service history (NOTE: The abbreviation **FSH** is seen in used-car advertisements, indicating that documentary evidence of routine maintenance on the vehicle is available.)

**FSI** MARKETING a separate piece of advertising matter inserted into a newspaper or similar for wide distribution. Full form **free-standing insert**

**ft 1.** MEASUREMENTS foot **2.** MILITARY fort

**FT** PRESS Financial Times

**FTC** *US* BUSINESS Federal Trade Commission

**fth.** MEASUREMENTS fathom

**FTP** COMPUTING a standard procedure that allows one computer to transfer files to and from another over a network such as the Internet. Full form **file transfer protocol**

**FTSE** STOCK EXCHANGE Financial Times Stock Exchange 100 Index

> The abbreviation **FTSE** (informally called *Footsie*) is used for a number of share indexes, including the FTSE 100 (a measure of the 100 largest companies in Britain), the 250 (concerned with medium-sized companies) and the TMT (technology, media and telecoms companies).

**fur.** MEASUREMENTS furlong

**furn.** furnished (*used in property advertisements*)

**fut. 1.** future **2.** FINANCE futures

**f.v.** PUBLISHING folio verso (NOTE: From the Latin, 'on the left-hand page'.)

**fwd** forward

**FWD** AUTOMOTIVE **1.** four-wheel drive **2.** front-wheel drive

**FWIW** ONLINE for what it's worth (*used in e-mails*)

**fx** ONLINE France, Metropolitan (NOTE: The abbreviation **fx** is seen at the end of Internet addresses, preceded by a dot. The term distinguishes European France from its overseas departments.)

**FX 1.** CINEMA (special) effects (NOTE: The abbreviation **FX** reflects the sound, rather than the spelling, of the full form.) **2.** FINANCE foreign exchange

**FY** FINANCE financial year

**FYI** ONLINE for your information (*used in e-mails and office memos*)

**FYM** AGRICULTURE farmyard manure

**FYROM** GEOGRAPHY Former Yugoslav Republic of Macedonia (NOTE: FYR Macedonia became independent from Yugoslavia in 1991.)

# G

**g 1.** PHYSICS acceleration of free fall as a result of gravity **2.** gauge **3.** GRAMMAR gender **4.** MEASUREMENTS gram **5.** MONEY guilder **6.** MONEY guinea

**G 1.** ELECTRICITY conductance **2.** MEASUREMENTS, PHYSICS gauss **3.** SOCIAL SCIENCE gay (NOTE: The abbreviation **G** is used in personal advertisements.) **4.** SCIENCE Gibbs free energy (NOTE: The abbreviation **G** is italicized in this sense.) **5.** MEASUREMENTS, COMPUTING giga- **6.** EDUCATION good (NOTE: The abbreviation **G** is italicized in this sense.) **7.** MEASUREMENTS gram **8.** PHYSICS gravitational constant (NOTE: The abbreviation **G** is used in marking students' work.) **9.** ONLINE grin(ning) (*used in Internet chat rooms and text messages*) **10.** BIOCHEMISTRY guanine **11.** MONEY guilder **12.** MONEY guinea **13.** GEOGRAPHY Gulf

**G5** FINANCE a group of 5 leading countries that agree to cooperate on economic and monetary issues. Full form **Group of Five** (NOTE: The five countries are Japan, France, Germany, the UK and the U.S.A.)

**G7** INTERNATIONAL RELATIONS the group of the seven most industrialized nations in the world that met to discuss and draw up global economic policies before they were joined by Russia to form the Group of Eight (G8). The seven were Canada, France, (West) Germany, Italy, Japan, the United Kingdom, and the United States. Full form **Group of Seven**

**G8** INTERNATIONAL RELATIONS the group of the eight most industrialized nations in the world, comprising Canada, France, Germany, Italy, Japan, Russia, the United Kingdom, and the United States. Representatives from these countries meet regularly to discuss and draw up global economic policies. Full form **Group of Eight**

**G10** FINANCE a group of 10 major world banks linked to the Bank for International Settlement (BIS). Full form **Group of Ten**

**ga** ONLINE Gabon (NOTE: The abbreviation **ga** is seen at the end of Internet addresses, preceded by a dot.)

**Ga** CHEMICAL ELEMENTS gallium

**GA 1.** LAW general agent **2.** General Assembly (of the United Nations) **3.** SHIPPING, INSURANCE general average **4.** MAIL Georgia (NOTE: The abbreviation **GA** is part of the US sorting code on the last line of a Georgia address.) **5.** ONLINE go ahead (*used in e-mails, text messages and Internet chat rooms*)

**GAAP** /gæp/ ACCOUNTING a summary of best practice in accountancy, with no legal status. Full form **generally accepted accounting principles**

**GAB** FINANCE general arrangements to borrow

**GABA** /'gæbə/ BIOCHEMISTRY gamma-aminobutyric acid

**GAFIA** ONLINE get away from it all (*used in e-mails*)

**GAL** ONLINE get a life (*used in e-mails, text messages and Internet chat rooms*)

**gal.** MEASUREMENTS gallon

**Gal.** BIBLE Galatians

**gall.** MEASUREMENTS gallon

**galv. 1.** ELECTRICAL ENGINEERING galvanic **2.** galvanized

**G & T** BEVERAGES gin and tonic (NOTE: The abbreviation **G & T** is chiefly used in informal conversation.)

**GAS** ACCOUNTING Government Accountancy Service

**GATT** /gæt/ COMMERCE General Agreement on Tariffs and Trade

**gaz. 1.** PRESS gazette **2.** PUBLISHING gazetteer

**Gb** MEASUREMENTS, COMPUTING gigabyte

**GB 1.** MEASUREMENTS, PHYSICS gilbert **2.** GEOGRAPHY Great Britain

**GBE 1.** MILITARY Knight or Dame Grand Cross of the (Order of the) British Empire (NOTE: The abbreviation **GBE** is used as a title: *Christina Massey GBE*.) **2.** BUSINESS Government Business Enterprise

**GBH** CRIME grievous bodily harm

The abbreviation **GBH** has entered the language as a noun in its own right. It is sometimes used figuratively to denote any serious attack, not necessarily physical, especially in the slang phrase *GBH of the earhole*, which denotes incessant talking, nagging, or complaining.

**GBLT** SOCIAL SCIENCE gay, bisexual, lesbian, or transgender

**Gbyte** MEASUREMENTS, COMPUTING gigabyte

**Gc** MEASUREMENTS, PHYSICS gigacycle

**GC** MILITARY George Cross

**GCB** MILITARY Knight or Dame Grand Cross of the Order of the Bath (NOTE: The abbreviation **GCB** is used as a title: *Sir William Harpole, CGB*.)

**GCE** EDUCATION an examination for secondary-school pupils in England and Wales at Advanced level (A level) and formerly at Ordinary level (O level), set and marked by various independent examination boards. At Ordinary level it has been replaced by the GCSE. Full form **General Certificate of Education**

**GCH** INDUST gas central heating (*used in property advertisements*)

**GCHQ** GOVERNMENT Government Communications Headquarters

**GCM** ECOLOGY general circulation model

**GCMG** MILITARY Grand Cross of the Order of St Michael and St George

The honours **CMG**, **KCMG**, and **GCMG**, awarded in that order, are facetiously said to stand for 'call me God', 'kindly call me God', and 'God calls me God'. These alternative meanings were popularised by an episode of the series 'Yes, Minister' televised in 1981.

**GCS** MEDICINE a system for assessing the severity of brain impairment in somebody with a brain injury using the sum of scores given for eye opening, verbal, and motor responses. A high score of fifteen indicates no impairment and a score of eight or less indicates severe impairment. Full form **Glasgow coma scale**

**GCSE** EDUCATION an examination for 16-year-olds in England and Wales that includes assessment of work completed during the course. It replaced the General Certificate of Education (GCE) O level and the Certificate of Secondary Education (CSE). ○ *She left school with five GCSEs.* Full form **General Certificate of Secondary Education** (NOTE: The abbreviation **GCSE** is used as a noun in its own right, referring to an examination or qualification at this level in a single subject.)

**GCV** PHYSICS gross calorific value

**GCVO** MILITARY Grand Cross of the Victorian Order (NOTE: The abbreviation **GCVO** is used as a title.)

**gd** ONLINE Grenada (NOTE: The abbreviation **gd** is seen at the end of Internet addresses, preceded by a dot.)

**Gd** CHEMICAL ELEMENTS gadolinium

**GD&RF** ONLINE grinning, ducking, and running fast (*used in e-mails, text messages and Internet chat rooms*)

**GD&WVVF** ONLINE grinning, ducking, and walking very very fast (*used in e-mails, text messages and Internet chat rooms*)

**GDC** DENTISTRY General Dental Council

**GDI** COMPUTING graphics device interface

**Gdns** ROADS Gardens (NOTE: The abbreviation **Gdns** is used in addresses.)

**GDP** ECONOMICS the total value of all goods and services produced within a country in a year, minus net income from investments in other countries. Full form **gross domestic product**

**GDR 1.** GEOGRAPHY the former republic of East Germany. Full form **German Democratic Republic 2.** ONLINE grinning, ducking, and running (*used in e-mails, text messages and Internet chat rooms*)

**ge** ONLINE Georgia (NOTE: The abbreviation **ge** is seen at the end of Internet addresses, preceded by a dot.)

**Ge** CHEMICAL ELEMENTS germanium

**GEB** FINANCE an investment that guarantees not to fall below the original amount invested. Full form **Guaranteed Equity Bond**

**gen. 1.** gender **2.** general **3.** GRAMMAR genitive **4.** BIOLOGY genus

**Gen. 1.** MILITARY General **2.** BIBLE Genesis

**geog. 1.** geographic **2.** geographical **3.** geography

**geol. 1.** geologic **2.** geological **3.** geology

**geom. 1.** geometric **2.** geometrical **3.** geometry

**GERD** MEDICINE a condition in which stomach acids repeatedly reflux over the oesophagus, damaging its surface. Full form **gastroesophageal reflux disease** (NOTE: The UK spelling is *gastro-oesophageal reflux disease* (GORD).)

**GeV** MEASUREMENTS, PHYSICS giga-electron volt

**gf** ONLINE French Guiana (NOTE: The abbreviation **gf** is seen at the end of Internet addresses, preceded by a dot.)

**GF** ONLINE girlfriend (*used in e-mails and text messages*)

**GFN** ONLINE gone for now (*used in e-mails and Internet chat rooms*)

**GFR 1.** glomerular filtration rate **2.** COMPUTING a file-removal utility designed to reclaim hard drive storage space. Full form **grim file reaper**

**gg** ONLINE Guernsey (NOTE: The abbreviation **gg** is seen at the end of Internet addresses, preceded by a dot.)

**GG 1.** YOUTH ORG Girl Guides **2.** ONLINE got game (*used in Internet chat rooms and text messages*) **3.** ONLINE gotta go (*used in Internet chat rooms and text messages*) **4.** POLITICS Governor General

**gge** BUILDINGS garage (*used in property advertisements*)

**gh** ONLINE Ghana (NOTE: The abbreviation **gh** is seen at the end of Internet addresses, preceded by a dot.)

**GH** BIOCHEMISTRY growth hormone

**GHB** DRUGS a chemical compound that occurs naturally in animals, used for treating anxiety and as an anaesthetic. Full form **gammahydroxybutyrate**

**GHI** MARKETING the number of viewers that a television advertising spot is guaranteed by the seller of the airtime to reach. Full form **guaranteed homes impressions**

**GHQ** MILITARY the headquarters of an organization, especially a military headquarters commanded by a general. Full form **general headquarters**

**GHR** MARKETING guaranteed homes ratings. ◊ **GHI**

**GHz** MEASUREMENTS, PHYSICS gigahertz

**gi** ONLINE Gibraltar (NOTE: The abbreviation **gi** is seen at the end of Internet addresses, preceded by a dot.)

**GI 1.** METALLURGY galvanized iron **2.** ANATOMY gastrointestinal

The abbreviation **GI**, stamped on various items of US military equipment made of galvanized iron and subsequently reinterpreted as an abbreviation of 'government issue', gave rise to the nickname **GI** for a soldier in the US armed forces.

**GIB** FINANCE Guaranteed Income Bond

**GIFT** /gɪft/ MEDICINE a method of assisted conception in which eggs are removed from a woman's ovary, mixed with sperm, and placed in one of her fallopian tubes. Full form **gamete intrafallopian transfer**

**GIGO** /ˈgaɪgəʊ/ COMPUTING the principle that a computer program or process is only as good as the ideas or data put into it. Full form **garbage in, garbage out**

**gimme** /ˈgɪmi/ give me

**GINO** COMPUTING graphical input/output

**GIS** GEOGRAPHY geographic information system

**GIV** LAW a gift made by one living person to another, as opposed to money or property left in a will. Full form **gift inter vivos** (NOTE: From the Latin, '(gift) between living people'.)

**GLA** BIOCHEMISTRY an essential fatty acid required to form prostaglandins, found in high concentrations in evening primrose oil and borage oil. It can be taken as a dietary supplement for menstrual disorders and for the pain of arthritis. Full form **gamma linolenic acid**

**GLBT** gay, lesbian, bisexual, or transgender

**GLC 1.** CHEMISTRY gas-liquid chromatography **2.** PUBLIC ADMINISTRATION the local government administrative body for Greater London between 1965 and 1986. Full form **Greater London Council** (NOTE: The *Greater London Authority* currently administers the region.)

**Glos.** Gloucestershire

**gm 1.** ONLINE Gambia (NOTE: The abbreviation **gm** is seen at the end of Internet addresses, preceded by a dot.) **2.** GENETICS genetically modified **3.** MEASUREMENTS gram

**GM 1.** MANAGEMENT general manager **2.** GENETICS genetically modified **3.** GENETICS genetic modification **4.** MILITARY George Medal **5.** CHESS grand master **6.** EDUCATION grant-maintained **7.** COMMERCE gross margin **8.** ARMS guided missile

**GmbH** COMMERCE Gesellschaft mit beschrankter Haftung (NOTE: From the German, 'company with restricted liability'.)

**GMC** MEDICINE General Medical Council

**GMO** GENETICS genetically modified organism

**GMP** PENSIONS guaranteed minimum pension

**GMS** EDUCATION grant-maintained status

**GMT** TIME Greenwich Mean Time

**GMTA** ONLINE great minds think alike (*used in e-mails*)

**GMW** CHEMISTRY gram-molecular weight

**gn** ONLINE Guinea (NOTE: The abbreviation **gn** is seen at the end of Internet addresses, preceded by a dot.)

**GND** ELECTRICITY the US equivalent of earth (an electrical connection intended to carry current safely away from a circuit in the event of a fault). Full form **ground**

**GNMA** FINANCE government national mortgage association

**GNP** ECONOMICS the total value of all goods and services produced within a country in a year, including net income from investments in other countries. Full form **gross national product**

**GNVQ** EDUCATION a qualification designed to provide vocationally oriented skills and knowledge for progression from school to employment or university. Full form **General National Vocational Qualification** (NOTE: The abbreviation **GNVQ** is used as a noun in its own right.)

**GOC** OPHTHALMOLOGY General Optical Council

**gonna** /ˈgʌnə/ going to

**GOQ** BUSINESS circumstances under which a person could be lawfully employed or dismissed on the grounds of their gender, age or similar, i.e. that being of the correct gender or age is a GOQ of the position. For example, a man could be lawfully denied employment on a chat line which advertises its employees as female. Full form **genuine occupational qualification**

**GORD** MEDICINE a condition in which stomach acids repeatedly reflux over the oesophagus, damaging its surface. Full form **gastro-oesophageal reflux disease** (NOTE: The US spelling is *gastresophageal reflux disease* (GERD).)

**GOSUB** /'gəʊsʌb/ COMPUTING a programming command that executes a routine then returns to the following instruction. Full form **go to subroutine**

**GOTO** /'gəʊtuː/ COMPUTING a programming command that instructs a jump to another point or routine in the program (NOTE: **GOTO** is not an abbreviation, it simply means 'go to'.)

**GOTS** MARKETING the total number of people exposed to a particular advert or insert. Full form **gross opportunity to see**

**gov** ONLINE government organization (NOTE: The abbreviation **gov** is seen at the end of Internet addresses, preceded by a dot.)

**gov. 1.** government **2.** governor

**govt** government

**gp** ONLINE Guadeloupe (NOTE: The abbreviation **gp** is seen at the end of Internet addresses, preceded by a dot.)

**GP 1.** MUSIC general pause **2.** HEALTH SERVICES general practice **3.** HEALTH SERVICES a doctor who deals with patients' general medical problems, either at a surgery or (sometimes) at their homes. Full form **general practitioner** (NOTE: The abbreviation **GP** is used as a noun in its own right in this sense and has largely replaced the full form in everyday usage.) **4.** SPORTS Grand Prix

**GPI** MEDICINE a condition that occurs in the late stages of syphilis and is characterized by dementia, speech difficulty, and inability to move. Full form **general paralysis of the insane**

**GPIA** COMPUTING general purpose interface adapter

**GPIB** COMPUTING general purpose interface bus

**GPM** FINANCE graduated payment mortgage

**GPMU** HUMAN RESOURCES Graphical, Paper, and Media Union

**GPO** MAIL the former name for the organization now know as the post office (PO) in the United Kingdom. Full form **General Post Office**

**GPP** ECOLOGY gross primary productivity

**GPRS** ONLINE a system that provides immediate and continuous access to the Internet from wireless devices such as mobile phones. Full form **general packet radio service**

**gps** MEASUREMENTS gallons per second

**GPS 1.** NAVIGATION a worldwide navigation system that uses information received from orbiting satellites. Full form **Global Positioning System** (NOTE: The abbreviation **GPS** is used as a noun to refer to the system itself or to a navigational device using this system.) **2.** *Aus* EDUCATION Great Public Schools

**GPU** POLITICS the Soviet secret police, from 1922 to 1923. Full form **Gosudarstvennoe politicheskoe upravlenie** (NOTE: From the Russian, 'State Political Directorate'.)

**gq** ONLINE Equatorial Guinea (NOTE: The abbreviation **gq** is seen at the end of Internet addresses, preceded by a dot.)

**gr 1.** MEASUREMENTS grain **2.** ONLINE Greece (NOTE: The abbreviation **gr** is seen at the end of Internet addresses, preceded by a dot.)

**gr. 1.** grade **2.** MEASUREMENTS grain **3.** MEASUREMENTS gram **4.** MEASUREMENTS gross

**Gr. 1.** GEOGRAPHY Greece **2.** LANGUAGE Greek

**GR8** ONLINE great (NOTE: The abbreviation **GR8**, used in e-mails and text messages, is one of many that use the number 8 to represent its sound.)

**grad. 1.** gradient **2.** graduated

**gram. 1.** grammar **2.** grammatical

**GRP 1.** INDUSTRY glass-reinforced plastic **2.** MARKETING a measure of the total number of exposures to advertising during a particular media schedule. Full form **gross rating point**

**gr. wt** COMMERCE gross weight

**gs** ONLINE South Georgia (NOTE: The abbreviation **gs** is seen at the end of Internet addresses, preceded by a dot.)

**GS 1.** POLITICS General Secretary **2.** MILITARY general staff

**GSA** US POLITICS General Services Administration

**GSM** TELECOMMUNICATIONS an international wireless communications network for mobile phones. Full form **Global System for Mobile Communications**

**GSOH** good sense of humour (NOTE: The abbreviation **GSOH** is used in personal advertisements.)

**GSP** BUSINESS legislation allowing industrialised countries to charge preferential import tariffs to selected other countries in order to encourage their industrialisation. Full form **Generalized System of Preferences**

**GSR 1.** PHYSIOLOGY a change in the electrical conductivity of the skin caused by sweating and increased blood flow and linked to a strong emotion such as fear. Full form **galvanic skin response 2.** ASTRONOMY global solar radiation

**GST** FINANCE in Canada and New Zealand, a value-added tax charged on all goods and services. Full form **goods and services tax**

**GSTT** FINANCE generation-skipping transfer tax

**gt** ONLINE Guatemala (NOTE: The abbreviation **gt** is seen at the end of Internet addresses, preceded by a dot.)

**GT** AUTOMOTIVE Gran Turismo (NOTE: The abbreviation **GT**, from the Italian, 'grand touring', is used as part of the name of a high-performance car.)

**GTC** BUSINESS good till cancelled

**GTG** ONLINE got to go (*used in e-mails, text messages and Internet chat rooms*)

**GTi** AUTOMOTIVE Gran Turismo injection (NOTE: The abbreviation **GTi**, from the Italian, 'grand touring (injection)', is used as part of the name of a high-performance car.)

**gTLD** ONLINE the portion of an Internet address that identifies it as belonging to a specific generic domain class (e.g. com, edu, or gov). Full form **generic top-level domain**

**GTT** MEDICINE glucose tolerance test

**gu** ONLINE Guam (NOTE: The abbreviation **gu** is seen at the end of Internet addresses, preceded by a dot.)

**GU 1.** MEDICINE gastric ulcer **2.** PHYSIOLOGY genitourinary **3.** GEOGRAPHY Guam

**GUI** /'guːi/ COMPUTING a user interface on a computer that relies on icons, menus, and a mouse rather than typed commands. Full form **graphical user interface**

**GUM** MEDICINE genitourinary medicine

**GUT** /gʌt/ PHYSICS the theory that all known processes in the universe are caused by the same original energetic force. Full form **Grand Unified Theory**

**GVW** MEASUREMENTS, AUTOMOTIVE gross vehicle weight

**gw** ONLINE Guinea-Bissau (NOTE: The abbreviation **gw** is seen at the end of Internet addresses, preceded by a dot.)

**GW 1.** E-COMMERCE (payment) gateway **2.** MEASUREMENTS, ELECTRICITY gigawatt

**GWh** MEASUREMENTS, ELECTRICITY gigawatt-hour

**GWI** MILITARY the war of 1991 following the invasion of Kuwait by Iraq. Full form **Gulf War I**

**GWII** MILITARY the war fought in the spring of 2003 against Iraq by a coalition of US, British, Spanish and other forces. Full form **Gulf War II**

**gy** ONLINE Guyana (NOTE: The abbreviation **gy** is seen at the end of Internet addresses, preceded by a dot.)

**Gy** MEASUREMENTS, NUCLEAR PHYSICS gray

**gynaecol. 1.** gynaecological **2.** gynaecologist **3.** gynaecology

**Gy Sgt** MILITARY Gunnery Sergeant

# H

**h 1.** harbour **2.** hard **3.** hardness **4.** MEASUREMENTS hecto- **5.** height **6.** high **7.** BASEBALL hit **8.** horizontal **9.** MUSIC horn **10.** HEALTH SERVICES hospital **11.** hot **12.** MEASUREMENTS, TIME hour **13.** hundred **14.** husband **15.** PHYSICS Planck's constant

**H 1.** PHYSICS enthalpy **2.** harbour **3.** hard (NOTE: The abbreviation **H**, when used on pencils, indicates that the lead is hard.) **4.** hardness **5.** MATHEMATICS Hamiltonian function **6.** height **7.** MEASUREMENTS, ELECTRICITY henry **8.** high **9.** CHEMICAL ELEMENTS hydrogen

**H2** ONLINE how to (*used in e-mails*)

**ha** MEASUREMENTS hectare

**HA** HEALTH SERVICES health authority

**Ha.** GEOGRAPHY **1.** Haiti **2.** Haitian **3.** Hawaiian

**Hab.** BIBLE Habakkuk

**hadn't** /'hæd(ə)nt/ had not

**Hag.** BIBLE Haggai

**HAI** MEDICINE hospital acquired infection

**HAND** ONLINE have a nice day (*used in e-mails*)

**h & c** hot and cold (water)

**Hants.** GEOGRAPHY Hampshire (NOTE: The abbreviation **Hants.** is derived from the Old English *Hantum + Scir* meaning '-shire'.)

**hasn't** /'hæz(ə)nt/ has not

**HAV** MEDICINE hepatitis A virus

**haven't** /'hæv(ə)nt/ have not

**HAZ** MEDICINE health action zone

**HAZMAT** /'hæzmæt/ INDUSTRY hazardous material

**Hb** BIOCHEMISTRY haemoglobin

**HB 1.** hard black (NOTE: The abbreviation **HB**, when used on pencils, indicates that the lead is midway between hard (H) and soft (B).) **2.** ONLINE hurry back (*used in e-mails, text messages and Internet chat rooms*)

**HBM 1.** Her Britannic Majesty **2.** His Britannic Majesty

**HBV** MEDICINE hepatitis B virus

**HC** GOVERNMENT House of Commons

**HCF** MATHEMATICS highest common factor

**HCFC** a gas containing carbon, chlorine, fluorine, and hydrogen that has been identified as being less damaging to the ozone layer than CFCs. Full form **hydrochlorofluorocarbon**

**hCG** BIOCHEMISTRY a hormone that helps to maintain a pregnancy. Full form **human chorionic gonadotrophin**

**HCHS** HEALTH SERVICES Health and Community Health Services

**HCI** COMPUTING **1.** a piece of software enabling different external modules to access Bluetooth hardware in the same uniform way. Full form **host controller interface 2.** human-computer interaction

**HCl** CHEMISTRY hydrochloric acid

**HCN** CHEMISTRY hydrocyanic acid

**hd 1.** hand **2.** head

**HD 1.** COMPUTING half duplex **2.** COMPUTING hard disk **3.** COMPUTING hard drive **4.** INDUSTRY heavy-duty **5.** high-density

**HDD** COMPUTING hard disk drive

**HDL** BIOCHEMISTRY an aggregate of fat and protein that transports cholesterol away from the arteries. Full form **high-density lipoprotein**

**HDLC** COMPUTING high-level data link control

**HDSL** TELECOMMUNICATIONS high-bit-rate (or high-data-rate) digital subscriber line

**HDTV** TV high definition television

**HDX** COMPUTING half duplex

**He** CHEMICAL ELEMENTS helium

**HE 1.** Her Excellency **2.** CHRISTIANITY His Eminence **3.** His Excellency

**Heb. 1.** LANGUAGE Hebrew **2.** BIBLE Hebrews

**Hebr. 1.** LANGUAGE Hebrew **2.** BIBLE Hebrews

**HECS** /heks/ *Aus* EDUCATION Higher Education Contribution Scheme

**he'd** /hiːd/ **1.** he had **2.** he would

**he'll** /hiːl/ **1.** he shall **2.** he will

**her. 1.** heraldic **2.** heraldry

**Herts.** GEOGRAPHY Hertfordshire

**he's** /hiːz/ **1.** he has **2.** he is

**hex** COMPUTING hexadecimal

**HEX** /heks/ STOCK EXCHANGE Helsinki Stock Exchange

**hex. 1.** hexagon **2.** hexagonal

**Hf** CHEMICAL ELEMENTS hafnium

**HF** high frequency

**HFC** CHEMISTRY hydrofluorocarbon

**HFEA** HEALTH SERVICES Human Fertilization and Embryology Authority

**HFS** COMPUTING hierarchical filing system

**hg 1.** BIOCHEMISTRY haemoglobin **2.** MEASUREMENTS hectogram

**Hg** CHEMICAL ELEMENTS mercury

**HG 1.** Her Grace **2.** His Grace

**HGH** BIOCHEMISTRY human growth hormone

**HGPRT** MEDICINE an enzyme that is responsible for controlling the level of uric acid in the body. Full form **hypoxanthine guanine phosphoribosyl transferase** (NOTE: Lesch-Nyhan Syndrome, a rare genetic disorder causing involuntary convulsive movements and impaired kidney function, is caused by a deficiency in **HGPRT**.)

**HGV** VEHICLES heavy goods vehicle (NOTE: Although such a vehicle is now officially known as a *large goods vehicle* (LGV), the abbreviation **HGV** is still in everyday use as a noun in its own right.)

**hh** MEASUREMENTS hands (NOTE: The abbreviation **hh** is used in measuring a horse's height.)

**HH 1.** double hard (NOTE: The abbreviation **HH**, when used on pencils, indicates that the lead is very hard.) **2.** Her Highness **3.** LAW Her Honour **4.** His Highness **5.** CHRISTIANITY His Holiness **6.** LAW His Honour

**HI 1.** MAIL Hawaii (NOTE: The abbreviation **HI** is part of the US sorting code on the last line of a Hawaii address.) **2.** MEDICINE hearing-impaired

**Hib** /hɪb/ MICROBIOLOGY a bacterium that causes meningitis. Full form *Haemophilus influenzae* **type B** (NOTE: The *Hib* vaccine, usually given in the first year of life, protects against the form of meningitis that is caused by this bacterium.)

**HIH 1.** Her Imperial Highness **2.** His Imperial Highness

**HIM 1.** Her Imperial Majesty **2.** His Imperial Majesty

**Hind. 1.** LANGUAGE Hindi **2.** RELIGION Hindu **3.** GEOGRAPHY Hindustan **4.** LANGUAGE Hindustani

**HIS** HEALTH SERVICES Health Information Service

**hist. 1.** MEDICINE histology **2.** historic **3.** historical **4.** history

**HIV** MICROBIOLOGY either of two strains of a retrovirus, HIV-1 or HIV-2, that destroys the immune system's helper T cells, the loss of which causes Aids. Full form **human immunodeficiency virus**

> The abbreviation **HIV** is used as a noun in its own right, and the full form is rarely encountered in general usage. A test for antibodies to **HIV** in the bloodstream can reveal whether a person is infected with the virus (*HIV-positive*).

**hk** ONLINE Hong Kong (NOTE: The abbreviation **hk** is seen at the end of Internet addresses, preceded by a dot.)

**HK 1.** GOVERNMENT the lower house of the legislature of the Isle of Man. Full form **House of Keys 2.** ONLINE hugs and kisses (*used in e-mails*)

**hl** MEASUREMENTS hectolitre

**HL** GOVERNMENT House of Lords

**HLA** IMMUNOLOGY the major antigen compatibility complex in humans that is genetically determined and is involved in cell self-identification and histocompatibility (compatibility of donor tissues and blood with the body's own in transplant and transfusion procedures). Full form **human leucocyte (or lymphocyte) antigen**

**HLDLC** COMPUTING high-level data link control

**HLL** COMPUTING high-level language

**HLS** COMPUTING a method of defining and describing colour in computer displays. Full form **hue, lightness, saturation**

**hm 1.** MEASUREMENTS hectometre **2.** ONLINE Heard & McDonald Islands (NOTE: The abbreviation **hm** is seen at the end of Internet addresses, preceded by a dot.)

**HM 1.** EDUCATION headmaster **2.** EDUCATION headmistress **3.** MUSIC heavy metal **4.** Her Majesty **5.** His Majesty

**HMA** COMPUTING high memory area

**HMAS** NAVY **1.** Her Majesty's Australian Ship **2.** His Majesty's Australian Ship

**HMCE** GOVERNMENT **1.** Her Majesty's Customs and Excise **2.** His Majesty's Customs and Excise

**HMCS** NAVY **1.** Her Majesty's Canadian Ship **2.** His Majesty's Canadian Ship

**HMF** MILITARY **1.** Her Majesty's Forces **2.** His Majesty's Forces

**HMG** GOVERNMENT **1.** Her Majesty's Government **2.** His Majesty's Government

**HMI 1.** EDUCATION Her Majesty's Inspector (of Schools) **2.** EDUCATION His Majesty's Inspector (of Schools) **3.** COMPUTING human-machine interface

**HMIP** ENVIRONMENT **1.** Her Majesty's Inspectorate of Pollution **2.** His Majesty's Inspectorate of Pollution

**HMO 1.** HEALTH SERVICES Health Maintenance Organization **2.** SOCIAL SCIENCES a house in which two or more households share basic facilities. Full form **house in multiple occupation**

**HMS 1.** Her Majesty's Service **2.** NAVY Her Majesty's Ship **3.** His Majesty's Service **4.** NAVY His Majesty's Ship

**HMSO** PUBLISHING **1.** Her Majesty's Stationery Office **2.** His Majesty's Stationery Office

**HMT** FINANCE **1.** Her Majesty's Treasury **2.** His Majesty's Treasury

**hn** ONLINE Honduras (NOTE: The abbreviation **hn** is seen at the end of Internet addresses, preceded by a dot.)

**Hn** CHEMICAL ELEMENTS hahnium

**HNC** EDUCATION a UK qualification in a technical subject that is recognized by many professional and technical establishments. Full form **Higher National Certificate** (NOTE: The abbreviation **HNC** is used as a noun in its own right.)

**HND** EDUCATION a UK post-school vocational award that requires the equivalent of two years' full-time study and is generally regarded as roughly equivalent to a university pass degree. Full form **Higher National Diploma** (NOTE: The abbreviation **HND** is used as a noun in its own right.)

**Ho** CHEMICAL ELEMENTS holmium

**HOAS** ONLINE hold on a second (*used in e-mails, text messages and Internet chat rooms*)

**HOF 1.** ONLINE hall of fame (NOTE: The abbreviation **HOF** is used in IP addresses to denote pages featuring a hall of fame: 'www.baseballplayers.com/hof'.) **2.** COMPUTING head of form

**hon. 1.** honorary **2.** honourable

**Hon. 1.** Honorary **2.** used as a courtesy title for the children of some members of the aristocracy. Full form **Honourable**

**Hons** EDUCATION Honours (NOTE: The abbreviation **Hons** is used to denote an honours degree, as in *BA Hons*.)

**Hon. Sec.** Honorary Secretary

**HOQ** BUSINESS a matrix form assessing customer needs against production requirements for ensuring quality when designing a new service or product. Full form **house of quality**

**hor. 1.** horizon **2.** horizontal **3.** horology

**horol. 1.** horological **2.** horology

**hort.** PLANTS **1.** horticultural **2.** horticulture

**Hos.** BIBLE Hosea

**HOV** VEHICLES high-occupancy vehicle

**howe'er** /haʊˈeə/ however

**hp** MEASUREMENTS horsepower

**HP 1.** PLANTS hardy perennial **2.** high pressure **3.** COMMERCE hire purchase **4.** ONLINE home page **5.** MEASUREMENTS horsepower **6.** GOVERNMENT Houses of Parliament

**HPGL** COMPUTING Hewlett Packard graphics language

**HPIB** COMPUTING Hewlett Packard interface bus

**HP-PCL** COMPUTING Hewlett Packard printer control language

**HPV** MEDICINE a virus that causes warts in the genital area. Full form **human papilloma virus**

**HQ** headquarters (NOTE: The abbreviation **HQ** is used as a noun in its own right.)

**hr 1.** ONLINE Croatia (NOTE: The abbreviation **hr**, from the Croatian, *Hrvatska*, is seen at the end of Internet addresses, preceded by a dot.) **2.** MEASUREMENTS, TIME hour

**HR 1.** POLITICS Home Rule **2.** GOVERNMENT House of Representatives **3.** COMMERCE the field of business concerned with recruiting and managing employees. Full form **human resources**

**HRA** HEALTH health risk assessment

**HRE 1.** Holy Roman Emperor **2.** Holy Roman Empire

**HREOC** LAW Human Rights and Equal Opportunities Commission

**HRH 1.** Her Royal Highness **2.** His Royal Highness

**HRIS** COMMERCE human resource information system

**HRM** COMMERCE human resources management

**HRP** COMMERCE human resource planning

**hrs** MEASUREMENTS, TIME hours

**HRT** MEDICINE hormone replacement therapy

**Hs** CHEMICAL ELEMENTS hassium

**HS 1.** EDUCATION high school **2.** GOVERNMENT Home Secretary

**HSB** COMPUTING a method of defining and describing colour in computer displays. Full form **hue, saturation, brightness**

**HSC 1.** GOVERNMENT Health and Safety Commission **2.** *Aus* EDUCATION a qualification taken by most students when they reach the end of secondary education (aged approximately 16). Full form **Higher School Certificate**

**HSE** GOVERNMENT Health and Safety Executive

**HSH 1.** Her Serene Highness **2.** His Serene Highness

**HSI** COMPUTING a method of defining and describing colour in computer displays. Full form **hue, saturation, intensity**

**HSRC** SCIENCE Human Sciences Research Council

**HST 1.** FINANCE in some Canadian provinces, a tax combining the goods and services tax (GST) and the provincial sales tax (PST). Full form **harmonized sales tax 2.** RAIL high-speed train **3.** ASTRONOMY Hubble Space Telescope **4.** TRANSPORT hypersonic transport

**HSV** COMPUTING a method of defining and describing colour in computer displays. Full form **hue, saturation, value**

**ht 1.** ONLINE Haiti (NOTE: The abbreviation **ht** is seen at the end of Internet addresses, preceded by a dot.) **2.** heat **3.** height

**HT 1.** SPORTS half-time **2.** ELECTRICAL ENGINEERING high tension **3.** OCEANOGRAPHY high tide

**HTH** ONLINE (*used in e-mails*) **1.** happy to help **2.** hope this helps

**HTLV** MICROBIOLOGY human T-cell lymphotropic virus

**HTLV-I** MICROBIOLOGY a virus associated with cancers of the lymphatic system. Full form **human T-cell lymphotropic virus I**

**HTLV-II** MICROBIOLOGY a virus associated with leukaemia. Full form **human T-cell lymphotropic virus II**

**HTML** ONLINE the markup language (i.e. language with coding added for layout and style) used for creating documents on the World Wide Web. Full form **HyperText Markup Language**

**Hts** GEOGRAPHY Heights (*used on maps*)

**HTTP** ONLINE the client/server protocol that defines how messages are formatted and transmitted on the World Wide Web. Full form **HyperText Transfer Protocol**

**hu** ONLINE Hungary (NOTE: The abbreviation **hu** is seen at the end of Internet addresses, preceded by a dot.)

**HUD** /hʌd/ COMPUTING a display of instrument data projected onto a screen at eye level so that a pilot or driver does not have to look down to see it. Full form **head-up display**

**humint** /'hjuːmɪnt/ intelligence information acquired from people in enemy territory. Full form **human intelligence**

**Hung. 1.** LANGUAGE Hungarian **2.** GEOGRAPHY Hungary

**HUT** MARKETING a measure of potential audience used in advertising, referring to the number of households estimated to be watching television at a given time in a particular area. Full form **households using television**

**hv** PHYSICS high velocity

**HV 1.** HEALTH SERVICES health visitor **2.** PHYSICS high velocity **3.** ELECTRICITY high voltage

**HVAC** CIVIL ENGINEERING heating, ventilation (or ventilating), and air conditioning

**HW 1.** ONLINE hardware **2.** ENVIRONMENT hazardous waste **3.** the highest level reached by a stretch of water, e.g. the sea at high tide or a river during a flood. Full form **high water 4.** CRICKET hit wicket **5.** hot water

**h.w.** CRICKET hit wicket

**HWM** high-water mark

**HWR** INDUST heavy water reactor
**hwy** ROADS highway
**HYCOSY** MEDICINE a procedure examining for blockage of the fallopian tubes, used in fertility testing. Full form **hysterosalpingo-contrast sonography**
**hyp.** **1.** MATHEMATICS hypotenuse **2.** hypothesis **3.** hypothetical
**hypoth.** **1.** hypothesis **2.** hypothetical
**HYV** AGRICULTURE high-yielding variety
**Hz** MEASUREMENTS, PHYSICS Hertz

# I

**i 1.** DENTISTRY incisor **2.** BANKING interest **3.** GRAMMAR intransitive **4.** GEOGRAPHY island **5.** GEOGRAPHY isle **6.** MATHEMATICS the imaginary number &#8730;-1

**I 1.** ELECTRICITY electric current **2.** Imperial **3.** PRINTING (single column) inch (*used in advertisements*) **4.** incumbent **5.** independence **6.** Independent **7.** Inspector **8.** Institute **9.** instructor **10.** intelligence **11.** International **12.** interpreter **13.** CHEMICAL ELEMENTS iodine **14.** CHEMISTRY ionization potential **15.** GEOGRAPHY Island **16.** GEOGRAPHY Isle **17.** QUANTUM PHYSICS isospin **18.** issue **19.** PHYSICS moment of inertia **20.** LOGIC a particular affirmative categorical statement **21.** MATHEMATICS unit matrix

**IA** MAIL Iowa (NOTE: The abbreviation **IA** is part of the US sorting code on the last line of an Iowa address.)

**IAA 1.** BIOCHEMISTRY a plant hormone that stimulates growth and root formation in cuttings. Full form **indoleacetic acid 2.** MARKETING International Advertising Association

**IAAF** ATHLETICS International Amateur Athletic Federation

**IAB 1.** INDUSTRY Industrial Advisory Board **2.** INDUSTRY Industrial Arbitration Board **3.** ONLINE Internet Activities Board

**IAC** ONLINE in any case (*used in e-mails*)

**IAE** ONLINE in any event (*used in e-mails*)

**IAEA** INDUST International Atomic Energy Agency

**IAF** AIR FORCE Indian Air Force

**IAM 1.** MANAGEMENT Institute of Administrative Management **2.** AUTOMOTIVE Institute of Advanced Motorists **3.** COMPUTING intermediate-access memory **4.** ANATOMY a passageway through which the auditory nerve carrying sound and balance signals to the brain passes. Full form **internal auditory meatus**

**IANA** ONLINE formerly, the US organisation that oversaw the assignation of Internet protocol numbers to Internet service providers. Full form **Internet Assigned Numbers Authority** (NOTE: The work is now undertaken by the global organisation **ICANN**.)

**IAP** ONLINE Internet access provider

**IAR** COMPUTING a CPU register which contains the address of the next instruction to be processed. Full form **instruction address register**

**IARC** MEDICINE International Agency for Research on Cancer

**IAS 1.** COMPUTING image analysis system **2.** COMPUTING immediate-access store **3.** POLITICS Indian Administrative Service **4.** AVIAT indicated air speed **5.** FINANCE a form issued by the Australian Taxation Office on which businesses report income and calculate related income tax payments. Full form **instalment activity statement**

**IASC** ACCOUNTING International Accounting Standards Committee

**IATA** /iːˈɑːtə/ AVIAT International Air Transport Association

**IAU 1.** EDUCATION International Association of Universities **2.** ASTRONOMY International Astronomical Union

**IAW** ONLINE in accordance with (*used in e-mails*)

**IB 1.** COMMERCE in bond **2.** ARMS incendiary bomb **3.** COMMERCE industrial business **4.** EDUCATION an examination in several subjects, taken by students in various countries, that is approximately equivalent to GCE A level and is accepted as a qualification for university entrance. Full form **International Baccalaureate 5.** BANKING investment bank **6.** COMMERCE invoice book

**ib.** ibidem (NOTE: The abbreviation **ib.**, from the Latin, 'in the same place', is used before a textual reference to a publication, chapter, or page already cited.)

**IBA 1.** BROADCASTING Independent Broadcasting Authority **2.** CHEMISTRY a synthetic plant hormone that stimulates growth in stems. Full form **indolebutyric acid 3.** LAW International Bar Association **4.** BANKING Investment Bankers' Association

**IBD 1.** MEDICINE inflammatory bowel disease **2.** ENGINEERING a method of depositing protective thin film coatings on magnetic elements such as compact disks. Full form **ion-beam deposition**

**IBF** BOXING International Boxing Federation

**IBG** COMPUTING a blank section of magnetic tape inserted between one block of data and the next. Full form **interblock gap**

**ibid.** ibidem (NOTE: The abbreviation **ibid.**, from the Latin, 'in the same place', is used before a textual reference to a publication, chapter, or page already cited.)

**IBO** BUSINESS an incident in which a business is bought wholesale by an outside investor, often without involving the current management. Full form **institutional buyout**

**IBR** BANKING Inter Bank Rate

**IBRD** BANKING the official name for the World Bank, a specialized agency of the United Nations that guarantees loans to member nations for the purpose of reconstruction and development. Full form **International Bank for Reconstruction and Development**

**IBS** MEDICINE irritable bowel syndrome

**IC** ELECTRONICS a tiny complex of electronic components contained on a thin chip or wafer of semiconducting material. Full form **integrated circuit**

**i/c 1.** in charge **2.** in command

**ICA 1.** ACCOUNTING Institute of Chartered Accountants **2.** ARTS Institute of Contemporary Arts **3.** COMMERCE International Coffee Agreement **4.** COMMERCE International Commodity Agreement **5.** INTERNATIONAL RELATIONS International Cooperation Administration

**ICAC** /'aɪkæk/ Aus POLICE in New South Wales, a body set up to investigate corruption in the police force. Full form **Independent Commission Against Corruption**

**ICAEW** ACCOUNTING Institute of Chartered Accountants in England and Wales

**ICAI** ACCOUNTING Institute of Chartered Accountants in Ireland

**ICANZ** ACCOUNTING Institute of Chartered Accountants of New Zealand

**ICAO** AVIAT International Civil Aviation Organization

**ICAS** ACCOUNTING Institute of Chartered Accountants of Scotland

**ICBM** ARMS intercontinental ballistic missile

**ICC 1.** COMMERCE International Chamber of Commerce **2.** INTERNATIONAL LAW International Criminal Court **3.** COMMERCE Interstate Commerce Commission

**ICCH** COMMERCE International Commodities Clearing House

**ICE 1.** MEDICINE ice, compress, elevation (NOTE: The acronym **ICE** refers to first-aid treatment of injuries and bruises.) **2.** CIVIL ENGINEERING Institution of Civil Engineers **3.** ENGINEERING internal-combustion engine **4.** INTERNATIONAL RELATIONS International Cultural Exchange

**ICFC** FINANCE Industrial and Commercial Finance Corporation

**ICFTU** HUMAN RESOURCES International Confederation of Free Trade Unions

**IChemE** CHEMICAL ENGINEERING Institution of Chemical Engineers

**ICJ** INTERNATIONAL LAW International Court of Justice

**ICM 1.** FINANCE Institute of Credit Management **2.** INTERNATIONAL RELATIONS Intergovernmental Committee for Migrations (NOTE: The **ICM** is part of the United Nations.) **3.** HEALTH SERVICES International Confederation of Midwives

**ICN** HEALTH SERVICES **1.** infection control nurse **2.** International Council of Nurses

**ICP** MEDICINE intracranial pressure

**ICQ** ONLINE a computer program that makes contact with a user who is chatting online (NOTE: The abbreviation **ICQ**, representing 'I seek you', comes from the company name ICQ Inc.)

**ICR 1.** MEDICINE Institute for Cancer Research **2.** COMPUTING intelligent character recognition

**ICRC** MEDICINE International Committee of the Red Cross

**ICRP** ECOLOGY International Commission on Radiological Protection

**ICS 1.** FINANCE instalment credit selling **2.** SHIPPING Institute of Chartered Shipbrokers **3.** SHIPPING International Chamber of Shipping **4.** FINANCE investors' compensation scheme

**ICSH** BIOCHEMISTRY another name for luteinizing hormone (LH), a pituitary hormone that causes the ovary to produce one or more eggs, to secrete progesterone, and to form the corpus luteum, and that causes the testes to secrete male sex hormones. Full form **interstitial-cell-stimulating hormone**

**ICSI** MEDICINE a method of assisted conception in which a single sperm is injected directly into the egg. Full form **intracytoplasmic sperm injection**

**ICSID** FINANCE International Centre for Settlement of Investment Disputes

**ICT** COMPUTING information and communications technologies

**ICU** HEALTH SERVICES intensive care unit

**I'd** /aɪd/ **1.** I had **2.** I would or I should

**ID 1.** MAIL Idaho (NOTE: The abbreviation **ID** is part of the US sorting code on the last line of an Idaho address.) **2.** identification **3.** MEDICINE infectious disease(s) **4.** MEASUREMENTS inner diameter **5.** MEASUREMENTS inside diameter **6.** MEASUREMENTS internal diameter **7.** MEDICINE intradermal

> The abbreviation **ID** is used as a noun in its own right in a wide variety of contexts, from personal proof of identity (as in *Do you have any ID?*) to computing. It is also used informally as a verb, meaning 'to identify somebody or check somebody's identity' (as in *ID the suspect*).

**id.** a book, article, or chapter previously referred to. Full form **idem** (NOTE: From the Latin, 'same'.)

**IDA 1.** COMPUTING Infocomm Development Authority **2.** BANKING a specialized agency of the United Nations that provides credit to nations on easier terms than the World Bank. Full form **International Development Association**

**IDB** BANKING Industrial Development Bank

**IDC** BUSINESS industrial development certificate

**IDD 1.** MEDICINE insulin-dependent diabetes **2.** TELECOMMUNICATIONS international direct dialling

**IDE** COMPUTING integrated drive electronics

**IDK 1.** ONLINE I don't know (*used in e-mails, text messages and Internet chat rooms*) **2.** MEDICINE internal derangement of the knee

**IDP 1.** COMPUTING integrated data processing **2.** CHEMISTRY iodine diphosphate

**IDR** BANKING International Depository Receipt

**IDTS** ONLINE I don't think so (*used in e-mails, text messages and Internet chat rooms*)

**IDTT** ONLINE I'll drink to that (*used in e-mails, text messages and Internet chat rooms*)

**ie** ONLINE Ireland (NOTE: The abbreviation **ie** is seen at the end of Internet addresses, preceded by a dot.)

**i.e.** that is (NOTE: From the Latin *id est*.)

**IEE** ELECTRICAL ENGINEERING Institution of Electrical Engineers

**IEEE** /ˌaɪ ˌtrɪp(ə)l ˈiː/ ELECTRICAL ENGINEERING Institute of Electrical and Electronic Engineers

**IEN** ONLINE a series of reports pertinent to the internet. Full form **Internet experiment note**

**IESG** ONLINE Internet Engineering Steering Group

**IETF** ONLINE Internet Engineering Task Force

**IF** ELECTRONICS intermediate frequency

**IFA 1.** FINANCE independent financial adviser **2.** ACCOUNTING Institute of Financial Accountants

**IFC** FINANCE a specialized agency of the United Nations that is affiliated with the World Bank and promotes private enterprise in developing nations by providing risk capital. Full form **International Finance Corporation**

**IFOR** /'aɪfɔː/ MILITARY a NATO-led multinational force sent to maintain peace in the former Yugoslavia after the signing of the Dayton Accords by the presidents of Bosnia, Croatia, and Serbia in 1995. Full form **Implementation Force**

**IFR** AVIAT instrument flying regulations

**Ig** IMMUNOLOGY immunoglobulin

**IgA** IMMUNOLOGY a class of antibodies, found in respiratory and alimentary secretions, saliva, and tears, that help the body to neutralize harmful bacteria and viral antigens. Full form **immunoglobulin A**

**IgD** IMMUNOLOGY a class of antibodies, present on most cell surfaces and predominant in B-cells, that help the body to resist antigens. Full form **immunoglobulin D**

**IgE** IMMUNOLOGY a class of antibodies, abundant in tissues, that help the body to expel intestinal parasites and cause allergic reactions in response to antigens. Full form **immunoglobulin E**

**IgG** IMMUNOLOGY a class of antibodies, predominant in serum, that pass through the placental wall into foetal circulation and help to prepare the immune system for the period of infancy. Full form **immunoglobulin G**

**IgM** IMMUNOLOGY a class of antibodies, circulating in the blood and secretions, that help the body to resist viruses. Full form **immunoglobulin M**

**IGM** CHESS International Grandmaster

**ign. 1.** ignites **2.** ignition **3.** unknown

**IGP** COMPUTING interior gateway protocol

**IGT** WINE a classification of the place of origin of Italian. Full form **Indicazione Geografica Tipica** (NOTE: From the Italian, 'indication of typical geographical origin'.)

**IH** COMPUTING a piece of software that accepts interrupt signals and acts on them. Full form **interrupt handler**

**IHD** MEDICINE ischaemic heart disease

**ihp** MECHANICAL ENGINEERING indicated horsepower

**IHS** CHRISTIANITY Jesus

> *IHS*, a transliteration of the first three letters of the name of Jesus in Greek, is also taken as an abbreviation of Latin *Iesus hominum salvator* 'Jesus saviour of humankind', *in hoc signo* 'in this sign (you shall conquer)', *in hac salus* 'in this (cross) is salvation', and other religious phrases.

**IHT** FINANCE inheritance tax

**iid** STATISTICS independent identically distributed

**IIL** COMPUTING a type of circuit design able to produce very small, low-power components. Full form **integrated injection logic**

**IINM** ONLINE if I'm not mistaken (*used in e-mails*)

**IIRC** ONLINE if I remember (or recall) correctly (*used in e-mails*)

**IJWTK** ONLINE I just want to know (*used in e-mails*)

**IJWTS** ONLINE I just want to say (*used in e-mails*)

**IKBS** COMPUTING intelligent knowledge-based system

**IKWUM** ONLINE I know what you mean (*used in Internet chat rooms and text messages*)

**il** ONLINE Israel (NOTE: The abbreviation **il** is seen at the end of Internet addresses, preceded by a dot.)

**IL** MAIL Illinois (NOTE: The abbreviation **IL** is part of the US sorting code on the last line of an Illinois address.)

**IL-1** BIOCHEMISTRY a protein factor produced by white blood cells that stimulates the production of other factors that activate the immune system. Full form **interleukin-1**

**IL-2** BIOCHEMISTRY a protein factor produced by white blood cells that stimulates T-cells to fight infection. Full form **interleukin-2**

**ILG** FINANCE index-linked gilt

**I'll** /aɪl/ I will or I shall

**ill.** PUBLISHING **1.** illustrated **2.** illustration **3.** illustrator

**illus.** PUBLISHING **1.** illustrated **2.** illustration **3.** illustrator

**ILM** HUMAN RESOURCES internal labour market

**ILO** HUMAN RESOURCES International Labour Organization

**ILS 1.** AEROSPACE instrument landing system **2.** CHEMISTRY ionization-loss spectroscopy

**im** ONLINE Isle of Man (NOTE: The abbreviation **im** is seen at the end of Internet addresses, preceded by a dot.)

**I'm** /aɪm/ I am

**IM 1.** CHESS International Master **2.** ONLINE instant messaging **3.** MEDICINE intramuscular

**IMA 1.** ONLINE I might add (used in e-mails) **2.** COMPUTING Interactive Multimedia Association **3.** COMPUTING International MIDI Association **4.** FINANCE Investment Management Agreement **5.** FINANCE Investment Management Association

**IMarE** ENGINEERING Institute of Marine Engineers

**IMCO** INTERNATIONAL RELATIONS Intergovernmental Maritime Consultative Organization

**IME** ONLINE in my experience (used in e-mails)

**IMechE** MECHANICAL ENGINEERING Institution of Mechanical Engineers

**IMF** ECONOMICS International Monetary Fund

**IMHO** ONLINE in my humble opinion (used in e-mails)

**IMinE** MINERAL EXTRACT Institution of Mining Engineers

**imit. 1.** imitation **2.** imitative (NOTE: The abbreviation **imit.** is sometimes used in dictionaries to indicate that a word is of onomatopoeic origin (i.e. it imitates the sound associated with the meaning of the word).)

**IMM 1.** SHIPPING International Mercantile Marine **2.** FINANCE International Monetary Market

**IMMA** FINANCE insured money market account

**immun. 1.** immunity **2.** immunization **3.** immunology

**IMO 1.** ONLINE in my opinion (used in e-mails) **2.** METEOROLOGY International Meteorological Organization **3.** MINERAL EXTRACT International Miners' Organization

**IMP 1.** imperial **2.** COMPUTING interface message processor **3.** BRIDGE International Match Point

**imp. 1.** GRAMMAR imperative **2.** imperfect **3.** imperial **4.** GRAMMAR impersonal **5.** COMMERCE import **6.** important **7.** COMMERCE imported **8.** COMMERCE importer **9.** PUBLISHING an authorization allowing a book or other work to be published. Full form **imprimatur**

**Imp. 1.** Emperor (NOTE: From the Latin *Imperator.*) **2.** Empress

**imperf. 1.** imperfect **2.** lacking a normal opening or perforations. Full form **imperforate**

**IMRO** FINANCE Investment Management Regulatory Organization

**IMRT** MEDICINE intensity modulated radiation therapy

**IMS 1.** HEALTH SERVICES Indian Medical Service **2.** INFORMATION SCIENCE information management systems **3.** MANAGEMENT Institute of Management Services

**in** ONLINE India (NOTE: The abbreviation **in** is seen at the end of Internet addresses, preceded by a dot.)

**In** CHEMICAL ELEMENTS indium

**IN** MAIL Indiana (NOTE: The abbreviation **IN** is part of the US sorting code on the last line of an Indiana address.)

**in.** MEASUREMENTS inch

**INAO** WINE a regulatory body in France that oversees wine production. Full form **Institut Nationale des Appellations d'Origine** (NOTE: From the French, 'National Institute of Origin Appelations'.)

**inc. 1.** included **2.** including **3.** inclusive **4.** income **5.** incomplete **6.** BUSINESS incorporated **7.** increase

**Inc.** BUSINESS Incorporated (NOTE: The abbreviation **Inc.** is used after the name of a US company or group of companies. The British equivalent is 'Ltd'.)

**incl. 1.** including **2.** inclusive

**incr. 1.** increase **2.** increased **3.** increasing **4.** increment

**IND** in God's name (NOTE: From the Latin *in nomine Dei*.)

**ind. 1.** independence **2.** independent **3.** index **4.** GRAMMAR indicative **5.** GRAMMAR indirect **6.** industrial **7.** industry

**Ind. 1.** Independent **2.** GEOGRAPHY India **3.** GEOGRAPHY Indian **4.** GEOGRAPHY Indies

**indef.** GRAMMAR indefinite

**indic. 1.** indicating **2.** GRAMMAR indicative **3.** indicator

**INDO** WINE a regulatory body in Spain that supervises the quality and origin of various food products such as wine and olive oil. Full form **Instituto Nacional de Denominaciones de Origen**

**indus. 1.** industrial **2.** industry

**INF** MILITARY intermediate-range nuclear forces

**infl. 1.** inflammable **2.** BOTANY inflorescence **3.** influence **4.** influenced

**info** ONLINE information (NOTE: The abbreviation **info** is seen in Internet addresses and means that the site is for general use.)

**INH** PHARMACOLOGY a drug used in the treatment of tuberculosis. Full form **isoniazid** (NOTE: The full name of the chemical compound is *isonicotinic acid hydrazide*, hence the abbreviation.)

**inj.** MEDICINE **1.** injection **2.** injury

**INLA** POLITICS Irish National Liberation Army

**INN** PHARMACEUTICAL INDUSTRY international nonproprietary name

**innit** /'ɪnɪt/ **1.** isn't it **2.** an all-purpose, question-forming word, corresponding not only to 'isn't it?' but to more or less all other similar phrases (*informal*) ○ *Arsenal are playing Spurs tonight, innit?*

**INPO** ONLINE in no particular order (*used in e-mails*)

**INRI** CHRISTIANITY Jesus of Nazareth, king of the Jews (NOTE: The abbreviation **INRI**, from the Latin *Iesus Nazarenus Rex Iudaeorum*, is seen in art as an inscription over the head of the crucified Jesus Christ.)

**ins. 1.** inscription **2.** inspector **3.** insulation **4.** insurance

**INSEAD** /'ɪnsiæd/ COMMERCE a leading European business school in Fontainebleau, France. Full form **Institut Européen d'Administration des Affaires** (NOTE: From the French, 'European Institute of Business Administration'.)

**INSET** /'ɪnset/ EDUCATION in-service education and training

The acronym **INSET** refers to extra training given to teachers during term time (on *INSET days*). It can also be short for 'in-service education of teachers' or simply 'in-service training'.

**insp. 1.** inspected **2.** inspector

**inst. 1.** instant (NOTE: The abbreviation **inst.** was formerly used in business correspondence, where 'instant' referred to the current month, as in *your letter of the 13th inst.*) **2.** instantaneous **3.** institute **4.** institution **5.** institutional

**Inst. 1.** Institute **2.** Institution

**instr. 1.** instruction **2.** instructor **3.** instrument **4.** instrumental

**int** ONLINE international organization (NOTE: The abbreviation **int** is seen at the end of Internet addresses, preceded by a dot.)

**int. 1.** MILITARY intelligence **2.** intercept **3.** FINANCE interest **4.** interim **5.** interior **6.** GRAMMAR interjection **7.** intermediate **8.** internal **9.** international **10.** interpreter **11.** MATHEMATICS intersection **12.** interval **13.** interview **14.** GRAMMAR intransitive

**Int.** International

**Intelsat** /'ɪntelsæt/ TELECOMMUNICATIONS an international organization that owns the communications satellites orbiting the Earth and whose members include the telecommunications agencies of most countries. Full form **International Telecommunication Satellite Organization** (NOTE: The abbreviation **Intelsat** is also used as a noun to denote a telecommunications satellite launched by this organization.)

**intens. 1.** GRAMMAR intensifier **2.** intensify **3.** intensive

**interj.** GRAMMAR interjection

**Interpol** /'ɪntəpɒl/ an association of national police forces that promotes cooperation and mutual assistance in apprehending international criminals and criminals who flee abroad to avoid justice. The headquarters of Interpol is in Paris. Full form **International Criminal Police Organization** (NOTE: The abbreviation **Interpol** is used as a noun in its own right, and the full form is rarely encountered in general usage.)

**interrog. 1.** interrogate **2.** interrogation **3.** GRAMMAR interrogative

**intl** international

**intro. 1.** introduction (NOTE: When **intro** is used informally as a noun in this sense (especially with reference to the opening bars of a piece of popular music), it is written without a full stop.) **2.** introductory

**introd. 1.** introduction **2.** introductory

**INTUC** /'ɪntʌk/ HUMAN RESOURCES Indian National Trade Union Congress

**inv. 1.** invariable **2.** invented **3.** invention **4.** inventor **5.** COMMERCE invoice

**io** ONLINE British Indian Ocean Territory (NOTE: The abbreviation **io** is seen at the end of Internet addresses, preceded by a dot.)

**I/O** COMPUTING input/output

**IOC** SPORTS International Olympic Committee

**IOD** BUSINESS Institute of Directors

**IOL** OPHTHALMOLOGY an artificial lens implanted in the eye to replace the natural lens after the surgical removal of a cataract. Full form **intraocular lens**

**IOM** GEOGRAPHY Isle of Man

**IOP** COMPUTING input/output processor

**IORQ** COMPUTING input/output request

**IOSCO** FINANCE International Organization of Securities Commissions

**IOU** FINANCE a written acknowledgment of a debt between the writer and somebody else
○ *If you lend him any money, make sure he gives you an IOU.*
The abbreviation **IOU**, representing the sound of the phrase 'I owe you', is used as a noun in its own right. Dating from the 18th century, it is an early example of the style of phonetic shorthand now much used in Internet communications.

**IOUS** MEDICINE intraoperative ultrasound

**IOW 1.** ONLINE in other words (*used in e-mails*) **2.** GEOGRAPHY Isle of Wight

**IP 1.** COMPUTING image processing **2.** COMPUTING information provider **3.** ONLINE the standard that controls the routing and structure of transmitted data. Full form **Internet protocol**

**I/P** COMPUTING input

**IPA 1.** MARKETING Institute of Practitioners in Advertising **2.** PHONETICS a system of letters and marks used internationally to represent speech sounds, e.g. in dictionaries. Full form **International Phonetic Alphabet**

**IPCC** ENVIRONMENT Intergovernmental Panel on Climate Change

**IPE** FINANCE International Petroleum Exchange

**IPL** COMPUTING **1.** initial program load **2.** initial program loader

**IPM 1.** AGRICULTURE integrated pest management **2.** HUMAN RESOURCES Institute of Personnel Management (NOTE: In the United Kingdom, the **IPM** has now been replaced by the **CIPD** (Chartered Institute of Personnel and Development).)

**IPO** STOCK EXCHANGE a first-time sale of company securities on a stock exchange to public investors. Full form **initial public offering**

**IPPV** MEDICINE a method of simulating normal breathing patterns in patients with chronic respiratory failure, either manually or using a mechanical ventilator. Full form **intermittent positive pressure ventilation**

**IPR 1.** WINE a mark indicating area of origin for lower-quality wines in Portugal. Full form **Indicação de Proveniencia Regulamentada** (NOTE: From the Portuguese, 'regulated mark of area of origin'.) **2.** LAW legal rights regarding the protection of original creative work, e.g. by means of a patent, trademark, or copyright. Full form **intellectual property rights**

**ips** MEASUREMENTS inches per second

**IPSE** COMPUTING integrated project support environment

**iq** ONLINE Iraq (NOTE: The abbreviation **iq** is seen at the end of Internet addresses, preceded by a dot.)

**IQ** PSYCHOLOGY a measure of a person's intelligence, obtained through a series of aptitude tests concentrating on different aspects of intellectual functioning. Full form **intelligence quotient**

    The abbreviation **IQ** is used as a noun in its own right (as in *a child with a high IQ*). IQ tests do not measure general knowledge, so the same test can theoretically be used for people of all ages and backgrounds. An IQ score of 100 represents 'average' intelligence.

**ir** ONLINE Iran (NOTE: The abbreviation **ir** is seen at the end of Internet addresses, preceded by a dot.)

**Ir** CHEMICAL ELEMENTS iridium

**IR 1.** COMPUTING a computer address register that is added to a reference address to provide a location to be accessed. Full form **index register 2.** COMPUTING information retrieval **3.** PHYSICS infrared (radiation) **4.** FINANCE Inland Revenue **5.** COMPUTING instruction register

**Ir. 1.** GEOGRAPHY Ireland **2.** LANGUAGE Irish

**IRA 1.** /ˈaɪrə/ PENSIONS in the United States, a pension plan that permits working people to invest money for retirement and pay no tax on the amount invested either at the time of investment or after retirement. Full form **Individual Retirement Account 2.** POLITICS an organization of Irish nationalists originally set up to strive for an independent Ireland by force of arms and still dedicated to achieving the unity of the island of Ireland. Full form **Irish Republican Army**

**IRBM** ARMS intermediate-range ballistic missile

**IRC** ONLINE an Internet facility that enables two or more people to participate in real-time online discussions. Full form **Internet relay chat**

**IRCA** HUMAN RESOURCES Industrial Relations Court of Australia

**IRD** *NZ* FINANCE Inland Revenue Department

**IRDS** MEDICINE infant respiratory distress syndrome

**IRL** ONLINE in real life (*used in e-mails, text messages and Internet chat rooms*)

**IRO 1.** FINANCE Inland Revenue Office **2.** INTERNATIONAL RELATIONS a former agency of the United Nations. Full form **International Refugee Organization 3.** INTERNATIONAL RELATIONS International Relief Organization

**IRQ** COMPUTING interrupt request

**IRR** BUSINESS internal rate of return

**IRS** FINANCE the US equivalent of the Inland Revenue. Full form **Internal Revenue Service**

**IRSG** ONLINE Internet research steering group

**IRTF** ONLINE Internet research task force

**is** ONLINE Iceland (NOTE: The abbreviation **is** is seen at the end of Internet addresses, preceded by a dot, and comes from the Icelandic name for the country 'Íslandi'.)

**IS 1.** SOCIAL WELFARE income support **2.** COMPUTING information services

**is.** GEOGRAPHY **1.** island **2.** isle

**Is. 1.** BIBLE Isaiah **2.** GEOGRAPHY Island **3.** GEOGRAPHY Isle

**ISA 1.** /ˈaɪsə/ FINANCE a savings account with tax-free interest, introduced in 1999. A person can invest up to £7,000 in each tax year. Full form **individual savings account** (NOTE: The abbreviation **ISA** is used as a noun in its own right.) **2.** COMPUTING a standard used for the 16-bit expansion bus in an IBM PC or compatible. Full form **Industry Standard Architecture 3.** AEROSPACE a hypothetical standard distribution of air pressure and temperature at various heights, internationally agreed as standard for aviation purposes. Full form **International Standard Atmosphere**

**Isa.** BIBLE Isaiah

**ISAM** COMPUTING indexed sequential access method

**ISBN** PUBLISHING International Standard Book Number

**ISC 1.** MEDICINE intermittent self-catheterization **2.** FINANCE Insurance and Superannuation Commission

**ISD** TELECOMMUNICATIONS international subscriber dialling

**ISDA** FINANCE International Swaps and Derivatives Association

**ISDN** ONLINE a digital telephone network that can transmit both voice and data messages. Full form **Integrated Services Digital Network**

**ISE** STOCK EXCHANGE International Stock Exchange

**ISIC** COMMERCE International Standard Industrial Classification

**IS-IS** COMPUTING intermediate system to intermediate system

**isl.** GEOGRAPHY **1.** island **2.** isle

**ISMA** STOCK EXCHANGE International Securities Market Association

**isn't** /ˈɪz(ə)nt/ is not

**ISO 1.** MILITARY Imperial Service Order **2.** COMMERCE International Organization for Standardization

Popularly thought to be short for 'International Standards Organization' in English-speaking countries, the abbreviation **ISO** was chosen by the International Organization for Standardization as a multilingual name, from Greek *isos*.

**ISP** ONLINE Internet service provider

**ISR** COMPUTING information storage and retrieval

**ISS 1.** ONLINE I said so (*used in e-mails, text messages and Internet chat rooms*) **2.** MEDICINE injury scoring system **3.** AEROSPACE International Space Station

**ISSN** PUBLISHING International Standard Serial Number

**Isth.** GEOGRAPHY isthmus

**ISWIM** ONLINE if (you) see what I mean (*used in e-mails*)

**it** ONLINE Italy (NOTE: The abbreviation **it** is seen at the end of Internet addresses, preceded by a dot.)

**IT 1.** FINANCE income tax **2.** COMPUTING information technology

**ITA 1.** TV formerly, an organisation regulating the ITV and Channel 4 television channels, a duty now undertaken by Ofcom. Full form **Independent Television Authority 2.** EDUCATION an alphabet of 44 symbols, each representing a single sound in English, devised in the early 1960s for the purpose of teaching children to read. Full form **Initial Teaching Alphabet**

**ital.** PUBLISHING **1.** italic **2.** italics

**Ital. 1.** LANGUAGE Italian **2.** GEOGRAPHY Italy

**ITC** TV Independent Television Commission

**ITCZ** GEOGRAPHY intertropical convergence zone

**it'd** /ˈɪt(ə)d/ **1.** it had **2.** it would

**it'll** /ˈɪt(ə)l/ it will

**ITM** ONLINE in the money (*used in e-mails*)

**ITRW** ONLINE in the real world (*used in e-mails, text messages and Internet chat rooms*)

**it's** /ɪts/ **1.** it has **2.** it is

**ITS** COMPUTING a special character transmitted to indicate to a device that the host computer is ready to receive messages. Full form **invitation to send**

**ITU 1.** HEALTH SERVICES intensive therapy unit **2.** TELECOMMUNICATIONS International Telecommunication Union

**ITV** TV Independent Television

**IU** MEASUREMENTS, PHARMACEUTICAL INDUSTRY the amount of a hormone or vitamin required to produce a specific response. Full form **international unit**

**IUCD** MEDICINE a plastic or metal device that is inserted into the cavity of the womb in order to prevent pregnancy. Full form **intrauterine contraceptive device**

**IUCN** ECOLOGY International Union for the Conservation of Nature (NOTE: The **IUCN** is now called the World Conservation Union.)

**IUD** MEDICINE intrauterine device. ◊ **IUCD**

**IUS** MEDICINE a plastic or metal device that functions like an IUCD, with an additional release of hormones to further ensure against pregnancy. Full form **intrauterine system**

**IV** MEDICINE **1.** intravenous **2.** intravenously

**I've** /aɪv/ I have

**IVF** MEDICINE the fertilization of an ovum by sperm outside the body, a technique developed in the 1970s as a means of assisted conception. Full form **in vitro fertilization**

The Latin phrase *in vitro* literally means 'in glass' and refers to the test tube or other artificial environment in which such fertilization takes place, hence the informal name *test-tube baby* for children conceived in this way.

**IVP** MEDICINE a procedure to determine whether the kidneys are functioning properly, by injecting a contrast dye into the bloodstream and monitoring its progress through the urinary system. Full form **intravenous pyelogram**

**IVR** TELECOMMUNICATIONS a term for computer-controlled pre-recorded telephone systems in which the caller can control the transaction through speech or dialled instructions. Full form **interactive voice response**

**IVU** MEDICINE intravenous urography. Same as **IVP**

**IWC** ECOLOGY International Whaling Commission

**IWIK** ONLINE I wish I knew (*used in e-mails, text messages and Internet chat rooms*)

**IWUTK** ONLINE I want you to know (*used in e-mails*)

**IWW** INDUSTRY Industrial Workers of the World

**IYKWIM** ONLINE if you know what I mean (*used in e-mails*)

**IYSS** ONLINE if you say so (*used in e-mails, text messages and Internet chat rooms*)

# J

**j 1.** ELECTRICITY electric current density **2.** MATHEMATICS the imaginary number &#8730;-1

**J 1.** CARD GAMES jack **2.** PRESS Journal **3.** MEASUREMENTS, PHYSICS joule **4.** LAW Judge **5.** LAW Justice

**Jam. 1.** GEOGRAPHY Jamaica **2.** BIBLE James

**Jan.** CALENDAR January

**JANET** /ˈdʒænɪt/ COMPUTING an Internet-linked computer network used by academics and researchers. Full form **Joint Academic Network**

**Jas.** James

**JATO** /ˈdʒeɪtəʊ/ AVIAT an auxiliary jet or rocket designed to aid the combined thrust of aircraft jet engines during takeoff. Full form **jet-assisted takeoff**

**jav.** ATHLETICS javelin

**Jav.** LANGUAGE Javanese

**JC 1.** CHRISTIANITY Jesus Christ **2.** ANCIENT HIST Julius Caesar **3.** LAW jurisconsult **4.** LAW Justice Clerk

**JCL** COMPUTING a powerful computer language for writing a script used to control the execution of programs in batch processing systems. Full form **job control language**

**JCR** EDUCATION in some colleges and universities, a room provided for general use by students, as distinct from the senior common room (SCR), reserved for staff. Full form **junior common room**

**JCS** MILITARY Joint Chiefs of Staff

**JD 1.** PRESS Diploma in Journalism **2.** COMPUTING in computer programming, a date expressed as the number of days since 1 January of the current year. Full form **Julian date 3.** *US* LAW Juris Doctor (NOTE: The UK equivalent is LLD.) **4.** CRIME juvenile delinquent

**JDBC** COMPUTING Java database connectivity

**je** ONLINE Jersey (NOTE: The abbreviation **je** is seen at the end of Internet addresses, preceded by a dot.)

**JEPI** E-COMMERCE joint electronic payment initiative

**Jer. 1.** BIBLE Jeremiah **2.** GEOGRAPHY Jersey **3.** GEOGRAPHY Jerusalem

**JET** /dʒet/ **1.** INDUST an international research project into the possibility of generating power from nuclear fusion, based in Culham, UK. Full form **Joint European Torus 2.** TRANSPORT Joint European Transport

**JFF** ONLINE just for fun (*used in e-mails*)

**JFK** 35th president of the United States (1961–63) ○ *We landed at JFK six hours later.* Full form **John Fitzgerald Kennedy** (NOTE: The abbreviation **JFK** is also used to denote the US international airport named after President Kennedy.)

**JHVH** JUDAISM an alternative transliteration of the Tetragrammaton, the four letters representing the Hebrew name of God in the Bible, usually transliterated as YHWH. The name Jehovah is an expansion of JHVH.

**JIC** ONLINE just in case (*used in e-mails*)

**JICRAR** /ˈdʒɪkrɑː/ RADIO Joint Industry Committee for Radio Audience Research

**JICTAR** /ˈdʒɪktɑː/ TV Joint Industry Committee for Television Advertising Research

**JIT** MANUFACTURING a manufacturing and stock-control system in which goods are produced and delivered as they are required. Full form **just-in-time**

**JJ 1.** BIBLE Judges **2.** LAW Justices

**Jl 1.** BIBLE Joel **2.** PUBLISHING Journal

**Jl.** CALENDAR July

**jm** ONLINE Jamaica (NOTE: The abbreviation **jm** is seen at the end of Internet addresses, preceded by a dot.)

**Jn** BIBLE John

**Jn.** CALENDAR June

**jnd** PSYCHOLOGY the amount by which something must be changed for that difference to be perceptible. Full form **just noticeable difference**

**jnr** junior

**Jnr** Junior

**jo** ONLINE Jordan (NOTE: The abbreviation **jo** is seen at the end of Internet addresses, preceded by a dot.)

**Jon.** BIBLE Jonah

**Josh.** BIBLE Joshua

**jour. 1.** journal **2.** PRESS journalist **3.** journeyman

**jp** ONLINE Japan (NOTE: The abbreviation **jp** is seen at the end of Internet addresses, preceded by a dot.)

**JP** LAW a person appointed to judge minor criminal cases, perform marriages, administer oaths, and refer cases to higher courts. Full form **justice of the peace** (NOTE: The abbreviation **JP** is used as a noun in its own right.)

**JPEG** /'dʒeɪ peg/ COMPUTING a format for encoding high-resolution graphic images as computer files for storage and transmission. Full form **Joint Photographic Experts Group** (NOTE: The abbreviation **JPEG** is also used as a noun to denote a file containing an image in this format.)

**Jpn** GEOGRAPHY Japan

**Jpn.** LANGUAGE Japanese

**JPO** E-COMMERCE Japanese payment option

**jr** junior

**Jr** Junior

**Jr.** BIBLE Jeremiah

**JSA** SOCIAL WELFARE Jobseeker's Allowance

**JSD** LAW Doctor of Juristic Science (NOTE: From the Latin *Juris Scientiae Doctor.*)

**JSYK** ONLINE just so you know (*used in e-mails*)

**JTLYK** ONLINE just to let you know (*used in e-mails*)

**Jud.** BIBLE **1.** Judges **2.** Judith

**Judg.** BIBLE Judges

**Jul.** CALENDAR July

**jun.** junior

**Jun.** CALENDAR June

**junr** junior

**JV** COMMERCE joint venture

**Jy** MEASUREMENTS, ASTRONOMY jansky

# K

**k 1.** MEASUREMENTS kilo- **2.** HANDICRAFT knit (NOTE: The abbreviation **k** is used in knitting patterns as an instruction to make a knit stitch as opposed to a purl stitch (p).) **3.** MEASUREMENTS knot

**K 1.** PHYSICS kaon **2.** MEASUREMENTS, PHYSICS kelvin **3.** MEASUREMENTS, COMPUTING kilobyte **4.** MEASUREMENTS kilometre **5.** PHYSICS kinetic energy **6.** CARD GAMES, CHESS king **7.** MILITARY Knight **8.** MUSIC Köchel (NOTE: The abbreviation **K**, followed by a number, is used in Köchel's catalogue of Mozart's works.) **9.** MONEY kopek **10.** MONEY krona **11.** MONEY krone **12.** MONEY kwacha **13.** MONEY kyat **14.** CHEMICAL ELEMENTS potassium (NOTE: From Modern Latin 'kalium'.) **15.** thousand

> The abbreviation **K**, from the prefix *kilo-*, is often used for large sums of money but is also found in other contexts (as in *a dissertation of 80K words*). In informal speech it means 'thousand pounds (or dollars)', as in *She must be earning at least 200K*.

**KAM** COMMERCE key account management

**Kb** MEASUREMENTS, COMPUTING kilobit

**KB 1.** MEASUREMENTS, COMPUTING kilobyte **2.** LAW King's Bench **3.** CHESS king's bishop **4.** MILITARY Knight Bachelor

**KBE** MILITARY Knight Commander of the Order of the British Empire

**Kbit** /'keɪbɪt/ COMPUTING kilobit

**KBP** CHESS king's bishop's pawn

**Kbps** COMPUTING kilobits per second

**Kbyte** /'keɪbaɪt/ COMPUTING kilobyte

**kc** MEASUREMENTS, PHYSICS kilocycle

**KC 1.** Kennel Club **2.** LAW a senior barrister (when the reigning monarch is male). Full form **King's Counsel 3.** CHRISTIANITY a member of a benevolent and fraternal organization of Roman Catholic men, founded in the United States in 1882. Full form **Knight of Columbus**

**kcal** /'keɪkæl/ MEASUREMENTS, PHYSICS kilocalorie

**KCB** MILITARY Knight Commander of the Order of the Bath

**KCMG** MILITARY Knight Commander of the Order of St Michael and St George

**KCVO** MILITARY Knight Commander of the Royal Victorian Order

**KD** BUSINESS knockdown (NOTE: The abbreviation **kd** is used to refer to furniture or other structures that can be assembled and disassembled easily by the customer.)

**ke** ONLINE Kenya (NOTE: The abbreviation **ke** is seen at the end of Internet addresses, preceded by a dot.)

**keV** MEASUREMENTS, PHYSICS kilo-electron volt

**kg 1.** MEASUREMENTS kilogram **2.** ONLINE Kyrgyzstan (NOTE: The abbreviation **kg** is seen at the end of Internet addresses, preceded by a dot.)

**KG** MILITARY Knight of the (Order of the) Garter

**KGB** POLICE the secret police of the former Soviet Union. Full form **Komitet Gosudarstvennoi Bezopasnosti** (NOTE: From the Russian, 'Committee of State Security'.)

**kgf** MEASUREMENTS, PHYSICS kilogram-force

**kh** ONLINE Cambodia (NOTE: The abbreviation **kh**, from 'Khmer', is seen at the end of Internet addresses, preceded by a dot.)

**KHYF** ONLINE know how you feel (*used in e-mails and text messages*)

**kHz** MEASUREMENTS, PHYSICS kilohertz

**ki** ONLINE Kiribati (NOTE: The abbreviation **ki** is seen at the end of Internet addresses, preceded by a dot.)

**KIA** ONLINE know-it-all (*used in e-mails*)

**Kild.** GEOGRAPHY Kildare

**kinda** /'kaɪndə/ kind of

**KIPS** COMPUTING kilo (= thousand) instructions per second

**KISS** /kɪs/ keep it short and simple

The acronym **KISS** is used in various contexts to encourage conciseness and intelligibility, e.g. in training manuals and sales presentations. Its more familiar interpretation, 'keep it simple, stupid', has a wider range of usage.

**kJ** MEASUREMENTS, PHYSICS kilojoule

**KKK** POLITICS Ku Klux Klan

**KKt** CHESS king's knight

**KKtP** CHESS king's knight's pawn

**KL** GEOGRAPHY Kuala Lumpur

**km 1.** MEASUREMENTS kilometre **2.** ONLINE Comoros (NOTE: The abbreviation **km** is seen at the end of Internet addresses, preceded by a dot.)

**km/h** MEASUREMENTS kilometres per hour

**kn 1.** MEASUREMENTS knot **2.** MONEY krona **3.** MONEY krone **4.** ONLINE St Kitts and Nevis (NOTE: The abbreviation **kn** is seen at the end of Internet addresses, preceded by a dot.)

**KN** CHESS king's knight

**KNP** CHESS king's knight's pawn

**Knt** CHESS knight

**KO** BOXING knockout ○ *The defending champion was KO'd in the first round.* (NOTE: The abbreviation **KO** is used informally as a noun in its own right. It is also used as a verb, meaning 'knock out'.)

**Kor. 1.** GEOGRAPHY Korea **2.** LANGUAGE Korean

**kp** ONLINE North Korea (NOTE: The abbreviation **kp** reflects the official name of the country, the Democratic People's Republic of Korea. It is seen at the end of Internet addresses, preceded by a dot.)

**KP 1.** CHESS king's pawn **2.** Knight of (the Order of) St Patrick

**kpc** MEASUREMENTS, ASTRONOMY kiloparsec

**kph** MEASUREMENTS kilometres per hour

**kr** ONLINE South Korea (NOTE: The abbreviation **kr** reflects the official name of the country, the Republic of Korea. It is seen at the end of Internet addresses, preceded by a dot.)

**Kr 1.** MONEY krona **2.** CHEMICAL ELEMENTS krypton

**KR** CHESS king's rook

**kr.** MONEY **1.** krona **2.** króna **3.** krone

**KRL** COMPUTING knowledge representation language

**KRP** CHESS king's rook's pawn

**KS** MAIL Kansas (NOTE: The abbreviation **KS** is part of the US sorting code on the last line of a Kansas address.)

**KSAM** /'keɪ sæm/ COMPUTING keyed sequential access method

**KSJ** RELIGION Knight of (the Order of) St John

**kt 1.** MEASUREMENTS, PHYSICS kiloton **2.** MEASUREMENTS knot

**Kt** CHESS knight

**KT 1.** Knight of the (Order of the) Thistle **2.** HISTORY, CHRISTIANITY Knight Templar

**kV** MEASUREMENTS, ELECTRICITY kilovolt

**kw** ONLINE Kuwait (NOTE: The abbreviation **kw** is seen at the end of Internet addresses, preceded by a dot.)

**kW** MEASUREMENTS, ELECTRICITY kilowatt

**KW** COMPUTING kiloword

**kWh** MEASUREMENTS kilowatt-hour

**KWIC** /kwɪk/ COMPUTING a library indexing system that uses keywords from the title of text of a book as an indexed entry followed by the text it relates to. Full form **key word in context**

**KWIM** ONLINE know what I mean (*used in e-mails and text messages*)

**KWOC** /kwɒk/ COMPUTING a library indexing system that indexes books or documents under any relevant keywords. Full form **key word out of context**

**ky** ONLINE Cayman Islands (NOTE: The abbreviation **ky**, from 'Kayman Islands', as the country is called by its own people, is seen at the end of Internet addresses, preceded by a dot.)

**KY** MAIL Kentucky (NOTE: The abbreviation **KY** is part of the US sorting code on the last line of a Kentucky address.)

**KYFC** ONLINE keep your fingers crossed (*used in e-mails and text messages*)

**kz** ONLINE Kazakhstan (NOTE: The abbreviation **kz** is seen at the end of Internet addresses, preceded by a dot.)

# L

**l 1.** GEOGRAPHY latitude **2.** law **3.** left **4.** length **5.** AVIAT lift **6.** line (NOTE: The abbreviation l, followed by a number, is often used in references to a particular line of printed text.) **7.** MONEY lira **8.** MEASUREMENTS litre **9.** ELECTRICITY live

**L 1.** PHYSICS angular momentum **2.** PHYSICS inductance **3.** MAPS Lake **4.** large **5.** PHYSICS latent heat **6.** LANGUAGE Latin **7.** SPORTS League **8.** AUTOMOTIVE learner **9.** POLITICS Liberal **10.** Licentiate **11.** MEASUREMENTS litre **12.** PHYSICS luminance **13.** ASTRONOMY luminosity

> An *L-plate*, a small square sign bearing a red **L** on a white background, must be attached to any vehicle driven by an *L-driver* (i.e. somebody who has not yet passed the driving test).

**L8R** ONLINE later (*used in e-mails and text messages*)

**la** ONLINE Laos (NOTE: The abbreviation **la** is seen at the end of Internet addresses, preceded by a dot.)

**La** CHEMICAL ELEMENTS lanthanum

**LA 1.** POLITICS legislative assembly **2.** LIBRARIES Library Association **3.** COMMERCE local agent **4.** GEOGRAPHY Los Angeles ○ *His sister lives in LA.* (NOTE: The abbreviation **LA** is frequently used in speech and writing in place of the full name of the city.) **5.** MAIL Louisiana (NOTE: The abbreviation **LA** is part of the US sorting code on the last line of a Louisiana address.)

**Lab. 1.** POLITICS Labour **2.** GEOGRAPHY Labrador

**LAC** MILITARY Leading Aircraftman

**LACW** MILITARY Leading Aircraftwoman

**LAFTA** /ˈlæftdə/ COMMERCE Latin American Free Trade Association

**LAI** BUSINESS a measure in vineyard management of the density of leaf cover on the vines and therefore the optimum spacing. Full form **leaf area index**

**LAMDA** /ˈlæmbdə/ PERFORMING ARTS London Academy of Music and Dramatic Art

**LAN** /læn/ COMPUTING a network of personal computers and peripheral devices linked by cable and able to share resources. Full form **local area network**

**Lancs.** GEOGRAPHY Lancashire

**laser** /ˈleɪzə/ ◊ see note at **Aids**

**lat.** GEOGRAPHY latitude

**Lat. 1.** LANGUAGE Latin **2.** GEOGRAPHY Latvia **3.** LANGUAGE Latvian

**LAUTRO** /ˈlaʊtrəʊ/ FINANCE Life Assurance and Unit Trust Regulatory Organization

**lb 1.** ONLINE Lebanon (NOTE: The abbreviation **lb** is seen at the end of Internet addresses, preceded by a dot.) **2.** CRICKET a run scored after the ball hits some part of the batsman's body other than the hand, without touching the bat. Full form **leg bye 3.** MEASUREMENTS pound (weight)

**LBD** CLOTHING little black dress

**LBJ** 36th president of the United States (1963–69). Full form **Lyndon Baines Johnson**

**LBO** COMMERCE a takeover strategy in which a controlling proportion of a company's shares is bought using borrowed money, the collateral for which is assets belonging to the purchased company. Full form **leveraged buyout**

**LBV** WINE late bottled vintage (NOTE: The abbreviation **LBV** refers to port that is six years old.)

**lbw** CRICKET leg before wicket (NOTE: The abbreviation **lbw** refers to the dismissal of a batsman hit on the leg by a ball that would otherwise have hit the wicket.)

**lc 1.** THEATRE left centre (of the stage) **2.** BANKING a letter from a bank, usually for presentation to another branch or bank, authorizing it to issue credit or money to the person named. Full form **letter of credit 3.** loco citato (NOTE: The abbreviation **lc** is used in textual references to a passage that has already been cited.) **4.** PRINTING lower case **5.** ONLINE St Lucia (NOTE: The abbreviation **lc** is seen at the end of Internet addresses, preceded by a dot.)

**LC 1.** MILITARY Lance Corporal **2.** NAVY landing craft **3.** ECOLOGY lethal concentration (NOTE: $LC50$ or $LC_{50}$ is the concentration of a harmful substance that kills 50% of organisms in experimental conditions.) **4.** LIBRARIES Library of Congress

**L/C** BANKING a letter from a bank, usually for presentation to another branch or bank, authorizing it to issue credit or money to the person named. Full form **letter of credit**

**LCD 1.** COMPUTING liquid-crystal display **2.** MATHEMATICS lowest common denominator

**LCE** STOCK EXCHANGE London Commodity Exchange

**LCH** BANKING London Clearing House

**LCM 1.** NAVY landing craft, mechanized **2.** FINANCE an accounting policy valuing assets at either market value or historical cost, whichever is the lower. Full form **lower of cost or market 3.** MATHEMATICS lowest common multiple

**LCP** COMPUTING rules defining the transmission of data over a channel. Full form **link control procedure**

**L/Cpl** MILITARY Lance Corporal

**ld 1.** PRINTING lead **2.** load

**Ld 1.** COMMERCE limited (company) (NOTE: The abbreviation **Ld** is a less frequent variant of *Ltd*.) **2.** Lord

**LD 1.** EDUCATION learning disability (or difficulty) **2.** EDUCATION learning-disabled **3.** PHARMACEUTICAL INDUSTRY lethal dose (NOTE: In toxological testing, $LD50$ or $LD_{50}$ is the dose that kills 50% of a group of test animals.)

**LDC** ECONOMICS **1.** a country with weak human resources and a low GDP by global standards. Full form **least-developed country 2.** a country defined by the UN as being at the lowest end of the global scale of development, based on criteria such as life expectancy, calorie intake and per capita GDP. Full form **less-developed country**

**ldg 1.** landing **2.** loading

**Ldg** MILITARY Leading

**LDL** BIOCHEMISTRY a complex of lipids and proteins that carries cholesterol to cells and tissue. Full form **low-density lipoprotein**

**LDR** ONLINE long-distance relationship (*used in e-mails and text messages*)

**LDS 1.** RELIGION Latter-Day Saints **2.** DENTISTRY Licentiate in Dental Surgery **3.** CHRISTIANITY praise be to God forever

**LDT** COMMERCE licensed deposit-taker

**LEA** EDUCATION Local Education Authority

**lea. 1.** MEASUREMENTS league **2.** leather

**lect.** EDUCATION **1.** lecture **2.** lecturer

**LED** ELECTRONICS a semiconductor that emits light when a current passes through it. LEDs of various colours are used as indicator lights on electronic equipment. Full form **light-emitting diode**

**leg. 1.** LAW legal **2.** INTERNATIONAL RELATIONS legate **3.** MUSIC legato **4.** POLITICS legislation **5.** POLITICS legislative **6.** POLITICS legislature

**legis.** POLITICS **1.** legislation **2.** legislative **3.** legislature

**Leics.** GEOGRAPHY Leicestershire

**LEM** /lem/ AEROSPACE lunar excursion module

**lemme** /ˈlemi/ let me

**let's** /lets/ let us

**LEV** AUTOMOTIVE low emission vehicle

**Lev.** BIBLE Leviticus

**lexicog. 1.** lexicographic **2.** lexicography

**LF** COMPUTING a control on a computer or printer that moves the cursor or printhead down by one line. Full form **line feed**

**LFS** BUSINESS labour force survey

**LGBT** lesbian, gay, bisexual, or transgender

**LGV 1.** VEHICLES large goods vehicle **2.** MEDICINE a sexually transmitted disease caused by a bacterial infection, in which there is swelling of the genital lymph nodes and, especially in men, a genital ulcer. Full form **lymphogranuloma venereum**

**lh** left hand

**LH 1.** left hand **2.** BIOCHEMISTRY a pituitary hormone that causes the ovary to produce one or more eggs, to secrete progesterone, and to form the corpus luteum, and that causes the testes to secrete male sex hormones. Full form **luteinizing hormone**

**l/h** COMMERCIAL LAW leasehold

**lhd** AUTOMOTIVE left-hand drive

**LH-RH** BIOCHEMISTRY a hormone released by the hypothalamus that triggers the secretion of luteinizing hormone. Full form **luteinizing hormone-releasing hormone**

**li** ONLINE Liechtenstein (NOTE: The abbreviation **li** is seen at the end of Internet addresses, preceded by a dot.)

**Li** CHEMICAL ELEMENTS lithium

**lib. 1.** librarian **2.** library

**Lib.** POLITICS Liberal

**Lib Dem** /ˌlɪb ˈdem/ POLITICS Liberal Democrat

**LIBID** BANKING London Interbank Bid Rate

**LIBOR** /ˈlaɪbɔː/ BANKING London Interbank Offered Rate

**Lieut.** MILITARY Lieutenant

**LIFFE** /ˈlɪfi/ FINANCE London International Financial Futures and Options Exchange

**LIFO** /ˈlaɪfəʊ/ last in, first out

The acronym **LIFO** is used in various contexts. It is probably most widely known as an informal reference to the system of selecting personnel for redundancy on the basis of their length of service. It also denotes a method of accounting in which it is assumed that the most recently purchased items in an inventory are the first to be sold, and a queue system in computing that reads the last item stored first.

**LILO** /ˈlaɪləʊ/ COMPUTING a data storage method in which data stored last is retrieved last. Full form **last in, last out**

**LIMEAN** BANKING London Interbank Mean Rate

**lin. 1.** lineal **2.** linear

**Lincs.** GEOGRAPHY Lincolnshire

**liq. 1.** liquid **2.** liquor

**LISP** /lɪsp/ COMPUTING a high-level computer programming language, used in artificial intelligence, that converts data into lists. Full form **list processing**

**lit. 1.** MEASUREMENTS litre **2.** literal **3.** literally **4.** literary **5.** literature

**LitB** EDUCATION Bachelor of Letters (or Literature) (NOTE: From the Latin *Litterarum Baccalaureus*.)

**LitD** EDUCATION Doctor of Letters (or Literature) (NOTE: From the Latin *Litterarum Doctor*.)

**lith.** PRINTING **1.** lithograph **2.** lithography

**Lith. 1.** GEOGRAPHY Lithuania **2.** LANGUAGE Lithuanian

**litho.** PRINTING **1.** lithograph **2.** lithography

**lithog.** PRINTING **1.** lithograph **2.** lithography

**LittB** EDUCATION Bachelor of Letters (or Literature) (NOTE: From the Latin *Litterarum Baccalaureus.*)

**LittD** EDUCATION Doctor of Letters (or Literature) (NOTE: From the Latin *Litterarum Doctor.*)

**LJ** LAW Lord Justice

**lk** ONLINE Sri Lanka (NOTE: The abbreviation **lk** is seen at the end of Internet addresses, preceded by a dot.)

**ll** lines

**'ll** /əl/ **1.** shall **2.** will

**LL 1.** LANGUAGE late Latin **2.** LAW Lord Lieutenant

**LLB** EDUCATION Bachelor of Laws (NOTE: From the Latin *Legum Baccalaureus.*)

**LLC** COMPUTING logical link control

**LLD** EDUCATION Doctor of Laws (NOTE: From the Latin *Legum Doctor.*)

**LLL** COMPUTING low-level language

**LLM** EDUCATION Master of Laws (NOTE: From the Latin *Legum Magister.*)

**lm** PHYSICS lumen

**LMC 1.** HEALTH SERVICES local medical committee **2.** ONLINE lost my connection (*used in Internet chat rooms*)

**LMDS** TELECOMMUNICATIONS Local Multipoint Distribution Service

**LME** FINANCE London Metal Exchange

**LMK** ONLINE let me know (*used in e-mails*)

**LMKOWOTO** ONLINE let me know one way or the other (*used in e-mails*)

**ln** MATHEMATICS natural logarithm

**LNG** INDUST liquefied natural gas

**loadsa** /ˈləʊdzə/ loads of

**loc. cit.** loco citato (NOTE: The abbreviation **loc. cit.**, from the Latin, 'in the place cited', is used in textual references to a passage that has already been cited.)

**LOGO** /ˈləʊgəʊ/ COMPUTING a high-level programming language used mainly for educational purposes, with graphical commands that are easy to use

**LOL** ONLINE laughing out loud (*used in e-mails and Internet chat rooms*)

**LOMBARD** /ˈlɒmbɑːd/ SOCIAL SCIENCES ◊ see note at **dinky**

**long.** GEOGRAPHY longitude

**LOS** line of sight

**lotta** /ˈlɒtə/ lot of

**LP 1.** MUSIC long-playing (record) (NOTE: The abbreviation **LP** is used as a noun in its own right.) **2.** PUBLIC ADMINISTRATION Lord Provost **3.** low pressure

**LPG** INDUST liquefied petroleum gas

**LPM** MEASUREMENTS, COMPUTING a measure of printing speed. Full form **lines per minute**

**LPN** HEALTH SERVICES licensed practical nurse

**LPS 1.** MICROBIOLOGY a complex of lipid and polysaccharide that forms the outer layer of some bacteria. Full form **lipopolysaccharide 2.** POLITICS Lord Privy Seal

**LQ** COMPUTING of a high quality comparable to conventional printing. Full form **letter quality**

**lr** ONLINE Liberia (NOTE: The abbreviation **lr** is seen at the end of Internet addresses, preceded by a dot.)

**Lr** CHEMICAL ELEMENTS lawrencium

**LR 1.** BUILDINGS living room (*used in property advertisements*) **2.** INSURANCE Lloyd's Register (of Shipping)

**LRCP** MEDICINE Licentiate of the Royal College of Physicians

**LRP** INDUST lead replacement petrol

**LRU** COMPUTING least recently used (algorithm)

**LRV** RAIL light rail vehicle

**ls** ONLINE Lesotho (NOTE: The abbreviation **ls** is seen at the end of Internet addresses, preceded by a dot.)

**LSA** HEALTH SERVICES Local Supervising Authority

**LSB** COMPUTING least significant bit

**LSD 1.** COMPUTING least significant digit **2.** DRUGS lysergic acid diethylamide (NOTE: The abbreviation **LSD** is used as a noun in its own right.) **3.** MONEY pounds, shillings, pence (NOTE: The abbreviation **LSD** refers to the old-style system of UK currency that was replaced by the decimal system in 1971. The pound sign (£) is a stylized form of the letter 'L'.)

**LSE 1.** EDUCATION London School of Economics **2.** STOCK EXCHANGE London Stock Exchange

**LSI** ELECTRONICS the process of integrating a large number of circuits, often several thousand, on a silicon chip. Full form **large-scale integration**

**LSO** MUSIC London Symphony Orchestra

**LSZ** *NZ* ROADS limited speed zone

**lt** ONLINE Lithuania (NOTE: The abbreviation **lt** is seen at the end of Internet addresses, preceded by a dot.)

**LTA** TENNIS Lawn Tennis Association

**LTC** COMPUTING a time signal that is integrated into an audio tape recording as a track running lengthways along the tape. Full form **longitudinal time code**

**Lt Cdr** MILITARY Lieutenant Commander

**Lt Col.** MILITARY Lieutenant Colonel

**Ltd** COMMERCE limited (company) (NOTE: The abbreviation **Ltd** after a company name indicates that the shareholders' liability for any debts or losses is restricted.)

**Lt Gen.** MILITARY Lieutenant General

**LTOM** STOCK EXCHANGE London Traded Options Market

**LTR** ONLINE long-term relationship (NOTE: The abbreviation **LTR** is used in e-mails, text messages, and personal advertisements.)

**LTV** BUSINESS the amount of a mortgage or other loan relative to the value of the property bought with it, including resale value and penalties on the loan. Full form **loan to value**

**lu** ONLINE Luxembourg (NOTE: The abbreviation **lu** is seen at the end of Internet addresses, preceded by a dot.)

**Lu** CHEMICAL ELEMENTS lutetium

**LU** COMPUTING logical unit

**LUT** COMPUTING look-up table

**lv** ONLINE Latvia (NOTE: The abbreviation **lv** is seen at the end of Internet addresses, preceded by a dot.)

**LV** COMPUTING a recording and playback system similar to modern CDs, using a laser to scan information stored on the pitted surface of a disc, but in analogue rather than digital format. Full form **LaserVision** (NOTE: The system essentially died out in the early 1980s and is now used only rarely by industry and schools as an information library system.)

**LV-ROM** /ˌel viː ˈrɒm/ COMPUTING a 12-inch diameter optical disc, developed by Philips, that can store both analog video and digital data

**LW 1.** RADIO long wave **2.** OCEANOGRAPHY low water

**LWM** low water mark

**LWR** INDUST light-water reactor

**lx** PHYSICS lux

**ly** ONLINE Libya (NOTE: The abbreviation **ly** is seen at the end of Internet addresses, preceded by a dot.)

**LY 1.** ECOLOGY an aggressive disease of coconut palms, characterised by the dropping of unripe fruit and the yellowing of fronds until the top of the tree drops away, leaving a bare trunk. Full form **lethal yellowing 2.** ONLINE love you (*used in e-mails and text messages*)

# M

**m 1.** PRINTING em dash **2.** PHYSICS magnetic moment **3.** CRICKET maiden (over) **4.** male **5.** married **6.** GRAMMAR masculine **7.** PHYSICS mass **8.** medium **9.** MEASUREMENTS metre **10.** MEASUREMENTS mile **11.** MEASUREMENTS milli- **12.** million **13.** MEASUREMENTS, TIME minute **14.** CALENDAR month **15.** PHYSICS mutual inductance

**M 1.** PRINTING em dash **2.** Majesty **3.** male **4.** GEOGRAPHY Manitoba **5.** CHEMISTRY mass **6.** EDUCATION Master (NOTE: The abbreviation **M** is used in degree titles, as in *MSc*.) **7.** medieval **8.** CLOTHING medium (NOTE: The abbreviation **M** is used as a size of clothing.) **9.** MEASUREMENTS mega- **10.** Member **11.** middle **12.** LOGIC a term that appears in both premises of a syllogism but not in the conclusion. Full form **middle term 13.** million **14.** CHEMISTRY molar **15.** CALENDAR Monday **16.** the French equivalent of Mr. Full form **Monsieur 17.** ROADS motorway **18.** GEOGRAPHY mountain

**M8** ONLINE mate (*used in e-mails and text messages*)

**mA** MEASUREMENTS, ELECTRICITY milliampere

**MA 1.** MAIL Massachusetts (NOTE: The abbreviation **MA** is part of the US sorting code on the last line of a Massachusetts address.) **2.** EDUCATION Master of Arts **3.** SOCIAL WELFARE maternity allowance **4.** PSYCHOLOGY mental age **5.** MILITARY Military Academy

**MAAG** HEALTH SERVICES medical audit advisory group

**MAB** ENVIRONMENT Man and the Biosphere (programme)

**MAC 1.** ENVIRONMENT maximum allowable concentration **2.** COMPUTING media access control **3.** /mæk/ TV a system for transmitting pictures to colour televisions using satellites. Full form **multiplexed analogue component**

**Mac.** BIBLE Maccabees

**Macc.** BIBLE Maccabees

**MAD** /mæd/ **1.** PSYCHIATRY major affective disorder **2.** MILITARY the enormous reciprocal damage that the superpowers and their allies would inflict on each other in the event of a nuclear war. Full form **mutual assured destruction**

**MAFF** /mæf/ GOVERNMENT a former government department whose responsibilities have now been transferred to the Department of the Environment, Food, and Rural Affairs (DEFRA). Full form **Ministry of Agriculture, Fisheries, and Food**

**mag. 1.** magazine (NOTE: When *mag* is used informally as a noun in this sense (with reference to a periodical publication), it is written without a full stop.) **2.** CHEMISTRY magnesium **3.** PHYSICS magnet **4.** magnetic (NOTE: When *mag* is used informally as an adjective in this sense (as in *mag tape*), it is written without a full stop.) **5.** PHYSICS magnetism **6.** magnitude **7.** magnum

**maj.** MUSIC major

**Maj.** MILITARY Major

**Maj. Gen.** MILITARY Major General

**Mal. 1.** BIBLE Malachi **2.** LANGUAGE Malay **3.** GEOGRAPHY Malayan **4.** GEOGRAPHY Malaysia **5.** GEOGRAPHY Malaysian

**MAN** /mæn/ COMPUTING a network extending over a limited geographical area, usually a city. Full form **metropolitan area network**

**man.** manual

**Man. 1.** PAPER Manila (paper) **2.** GEOGRAPHY Manitoba

**M & A** BUSINESS mergers and acquisitions

**manuf. 1.** manufacture **2.** manufactured **3.** manufacturer **4.** manufacturing

**MAO** BIOCHEMISTRY an enzyme that breaks down monoamine neurotransmitters (e.g. adrenaline and serotonin). Full form **monoamine oxidase**

**MAOI** PHARMACOLOGY an antidepressant drug that blocks the action of monoamine oxidase in the brain. Full form **monoamine oxidase inhibitor**

**MAR** COMPUTING memory address register

**mar. 1.** maritime **2.** married

**Mar.** March

**MArch** ARCHITECTURE Master of Architecture

**March.** Marchioness

**marg. 1.** margin **2.** marginal

**Marq. 1.** Marquess **2.** Marquis

**masc.** GRAMMAR masculine

**MASH** /mæʃ/ MILITARY mobile army surgical hospital

The acronym **MASH** was popularized in the wider world during the 1970s and 1980s by the film and long-running television series *M\*A\*S\*H*, a black comedy set in a US mobile army surgical hospital during the Korean War.

**masint** /ˈmæsɪnt/ MILITARY intelligence data acquired, typically by electronic means, about possible attacks using weapons of mass destruction. Full form **materials intelligence**

**mat.** THEATRE matinée

**math. 1.** mathematical **2.** mathematically **3.** mathematician **4.** mathematics

**MATV** TV master antenna television

**MAU** COMPUTING multistation access unit

**max.** maximum

**may've** /ˈmeɪ(ə)v/ may have

**mb** MEASUREMENTS, PHYSICS millibar

**Mb** MEASUREMENTS, COMPUTING megabit

**MB 1.** MEDICINE Bachelor of Medicine (NOTE: From the Latin *Medicinae Baccalaureus*.) **2.** MILITARY Medal of Bravery **3.** MEASUREMENTS, COMPUTING megabyte **4.** ONLINE another name for the bulletin board system (BBS). Full form **message board**

**MBA** BUSINESS Master of Business Administration

**MBE** MILITARY Member of the Order of the British Empire

**MBI** COMMERCE the acquisition of a subsidiary company by outside directors. Full form **management buyin**

**MBO 1.** COMMERCE the takeover of a company by its own employees, usually senior management. Full form **management buyout 2.** MANAGEMENT management by objectives

**MBps** MEASUREMENTS, COMPUTING **1.** megabits per second **2.** megabytes per second

**MBR** COMPUTING memory buffer register

**MBWA** MANAGEMENT management by walking around

**Mbyte** /ˈembaɪt/ MEASUREMENTS, COMPUTING megabyte

**mc 1.** MEASUREMENTS, PHYSICS millicurie **2.** ONLINE Monaco (NOTE: The abbreviation **mc** is seen at the end of Internet addresses, preceded by a dot.)

**MC 1.** master of ceremonies (NOTE: The abbreviation **MC** is used informally as a noun in its own right, sometimes written *emcee*. The latter form is also used as a verb, meaning 'to act as master of ceremonies'.) **2.** MILITARY Medical Corps **3.** ASTROLOGY the point on the apparent annual path of the Sun in the celestial sphere where the meridian is crossed, or the sign of the zodiac that contains it. Full form **Midheaven 4.** MILITARY Military Cross

**MCA 1.** COMPUTING media control architecture **2.** E-COMMERCE merchant certificate authority

**MCC** CRICKET Marylebone Cricket Club

**MCG** CRICKET Melbourne Cricket Ground

**MCh** SURGERY Master of Surgery (NOTE: From the Latin *Magister Chirurgiae*.)

**MCom** COMMERCE Master of Commerce

**MCP 1.** male chauvinist pig **2.** COMPUTING master control program

**MCPP** AGRICULTURE a pesticide used for weed control. Full form **mecoprop**

**MCT** BUSINESS mainstream corporation tax

**MCU** MEDICINE a procedure to determine urinary tract health and function, by passing a contrast dye through the system which can then be x-rayed. Full form **micturating cysto-urethrogram**

**MCUG** MEDICINE micturating cysto-urethrogram

**md** ONLINE Moldova (NOTE: The abbreviation **md** is seen at the end of Internet addresses, preceded by a dot.)

**Md** CHEMICAL ELEMENTS mendelevium

**MD 1.** MEDICINE Doctor of Medicine (NOTE: From the Latin *Medicinae Doctor.*) **2.** ONLINE mailed (*used in e-mails and text messages*) **3.** MANAGEMENT managing director **4.** MAIL Maryland (NOTE: The abbreviation **MD** is part of the US sorting code on the last line of a Maryland address.) **5.** BANKING memorandum of deposit **6.** HOUSEHOLD minidisc **7.** MEDICINE muscular dystrophy **8.** MUSIC musical director

**m/d** COMMERCE months after date

**MDA** COMPUTING monochrome display adapter

**MDF** INDUSTRY a type of hardboard suitable for indoor construction use. Full form **medium density fibreboard** (NOTE: The abbreviation **MDF** is used as a noun in its own right.)

**MDiv** RELIGION Master of Divinity

**MDMA** DRUGS the technical name for the drug ecstasy. Full form **methylenedioxymethamphetamine**

**MDR** COMPUTING memory data register

**MDS** DENTISTRY Master of Dental Surgery

**mdse** COMMERCE merchandise

**Me** CHEMISTRY methyl

**ME 1.** MAIL Maine (NOTE: The abbreviation **ME** is part of the US sorting code on the last line of a Maine address.) **2.** MECHANICAL ENGINEERING mechanical engineer **3.** CHRISTIANITY Methodist Episcopal **4.** LANGUAGE Middle English **5.** MINERAL EXTRACT mining engineer **6.** Most Excellent **7.** MEDICINE an illness without a known cause that is characterized by long-term exhaustion, muscle weakness, depression, and sleep disturbances. Also known as chronic fatigue syndrome (CFS) or postviral syndrome (PVS), it may occur as a reaction to a viral infection. Full form **myalgic encephalomyelitis** (NOTE: The abbreviation **ME** is used as a noun in its own right.)

**meas. 1.** measure **2.** measurement

**MEC** BUSINESS the discount that, if applied to the returns from a particular investment or asset, would make its present value equal to its original supply price. Full form **marginal efficiency of capital**

**mech. 1.** mechanical **2.** mechanics **3.** mechanism

**MEcon** ECONOMICS Master of Economics

**MEd** EDUCATION Master of Education

**med. 1.** medical **2.** medicine **3.** medieval **4.** medium

**Medit.** Mediterranean

**mem. 1.** member **2.** LITERATURE memoir **3.** COMMERCE memorandum **4.** memorial

**MEMS** ELECTRICAL ENGINEERING micro-electromechanical system

**Mencap** /'menkæp/ EDUCATION a UK charity for people with learning disabilities
The name **Mencap** is a contraction of *mental handicap* or *mentally handicapped*. The charity, now officially called the Royal Mencap Society, was formerly known as the Royal Society for Mentally Handicapped Children and Adults.

**MEng** ENGINEERING Master of Engineering

**MEP 1.** ENGINEERING Master of Engineering Physics **2.** POLITICS Member of the European Parliament

**mer.** GEOGRAPHY meridian

**MES** BUSINESS minimum efficient scale

**Met** /met/ **1.** METEOROLOGY Meteorological (Office) **2.** MUSIC Metropolitan Opera House (in New York) **3.** POLICE Metropolitan Police

**met. 1.** metallurgy **2.** LANGUAGE metaphor **3.** PHILOSOPHY metaphysics **4.** meteorological **5.** meteorology **6.** metropolitan

**metal. 1.** metallurgical **2.** metallurgy

**metall. 1.** metallurgical **2.** metallurgy

**meteor.** meteorology

**meteorol.** meteorology

**Meth.** CHRISTIANITY Methodist

**MeV** MEASUREMENTS, PHYSICS million electron volts

**Mex.** GEOGRAPHY **1.** Mexican **2.** Mexico

**MEY** AGRICULTURE maximum economic yield

**mf** MUSIC mezzo forte (NOTE: The abbreviation **mf**, usually italicized, is used on sheet music at a passage that is to be played or sung moderately loudly.)

**mF** MEASUREMENTS, PHYSICS millifarad

**MF 1.** RADIO medium frequency **2.** LANGUAGE Middle French

**M/F** male or female (NOTE: The abbreviation **M/F** is used in advertisements for accommodation, jobs and personal connections.)

**MFA** ARTS Master of Fine Arts

**mfd** manufactured

**mfg** manufacturing

**MFM** RADIO modified frequency modulation

**MFN** COMMERCE a nation accorded the most favourable trading terms by another nation. Full form **most favoured nation**

**mfr** MANUFACTURING manufacturer

**mfr.** MANUFACTURING manufacture

**MFS** COMPUTING Macintosh filing system

**mg 1.** ONLINE Madagascar (NOTE: The abbreviation **mg** is seen at the end of Internet addresses, preceded by a dot.) **2.** MEASUREMENTS milligram

**Mg** CHEMICAL ELEMENTS magnesium

**MG 1.** ARMS machine gun **2.** MILITARY Major General

**MGB** POLICE the secret police of the former Soviet Union from 1946 to 1954. Full form **Ministerstvo Gosudarstvennoi Bezopasnosti** (NOTE: From the Russian, 'Ministry of State Security'.)

**mgmt** management

**mgr** manager

**Mgr 1.** a title for certain dignitaries, e.g. bishops and princes, in France and other French-speaking countries. Full form **Monseigneur 2.** CHRISTIANITY a title for certain clerics of the Roman Catholic Church. Full form **Monsignor**

**mgt** management

**mh** ONLINE Marshall Islands (NOTE: The abbreviation **mh** is seen at the end of Internet addresses, preceded by a dot.)

**mH** MEASUREMENTS millihenry

**MH 1.** MAIL Marshall Islands **2.** PSYCHOLOGY mental health

**MHA** *Aus, Can* GOVERNMENT Member of the House of Assembly

**MHC** GENETICS a group of genes in mammals that serve to make cells separate and distinguishable from those of other organisms. Full form **major histocompatibility complex**

**MHD** PHYSICS magnetohydrodynamics

**MHG** LANGUAGE Middle High German

**MHL** EDUCATION Master of Hebrew Literature

**MHz** MEASUREMENTS, PHYSICS megahertz

**MI 1.** MAIL Michigan (NOTE: The abbreviation **MI** is part of the US sorting code on the last line of a Michigan address.) **2.** MILITARY Military Intelligence (NOTE: *MI5* is the British security and counterintelligence service, and *MI6* is the British secret intelligence and espionage service.) **3.** MEDICINE a condition in which the heart's mitral valve does not form a complete seal on closing, allowing blood to reflux into the left atrium. Full form **mitral incompetence 4.** MEDICINE the death of a segment of heart muscle, caused by a blood clot in the coronary artery interrupting blood supply. Full form **myocardial infarction**

**mi.** MEASUREMENTS mile

**MIA** MILITARY missing in action (NOTE: The abbreviation **MIA** is used in US English as a noun to denote a soldier reported missing during military action.)

**MIC** CHEMISTRY a toxic liquid used in the manufacture of herbicides. Full form **methyl isocyanate**

**Mic.** BIBLE Micah

**Mich.** CALENDAR Michaelmas

**mid.** middle

**Mid.** MILITARY Midshipman

**Middx** GEOGRAPHY Middlesex

**MIDI** /'mɪdi/ COMPUTING the interface between an electronic musical instrument and a computer, used in composing and editing music. Full form **musical instrument digital interface**

**MiG** /mɪg/ AIR FORCE a high-speed high-altitude fighter aircraft built in Russia (NOTE: The name of the aircraft is an acronym derived from the surnames of its designers, A. I. Mikoyan and M. I. Gurevich.)

**MIG 1.** BUSINESS formerly, a means-tested scheme to top up state pensions falling below a minimum amount. Full form **Minimum Income Guarantee** (NOTE: The **MIG** was replaced in 2003 by the Pensions Credit scheme.) **2.** FINANCE mortgage indemnity guarantee

**MIGA** FINANCE Multilateral Investment Guarantee Agency

**mightn't** /'maɪt(ə)nt/ might not

**might've** /'maɪt(ə)v/ might have

**mil** ONLINE military organization (NOTE: The abbreviation **mil** is seen at the end of Internet addresses, preceded by a dot.)

**mil. 1.** military **2.** militia

**milit.** military

**MIME** /maɪm/ ONLINE a set of Internet standards for handling multimedia and non-ASCII material. Full form **Multipurpose Internet Mail Extensions**

**min. 1.** mineralogical **2.** mineralogy **3.** MEASUREMENTS minim **4.** minimum **5.** MINERAL EXTRACT mining **6.** minister **7.** MUSIC minor **8.** MEASUREMENTS, TIME minute

**Min.** GOVERNMENT **1.** Minister **2.** Ministry

**MING** ONLINE mailing (*used in e-mails and text messages*)

**MIP 1.** INSURANCE marine insurance policy **2.** FINANCE monthly investment plan

**MIPS** /mɪps/ **1.** ONLINE meaningless information per second (NOTE: **Mips** in this sense is a humorous corruption of the original meaning 'million instructions per second', coined by computer hackers.) **2.** COMPUTING million instructions per second

**MIRAS** /ˈmaɪræs/ FINANCE a former tax relief system on mortgages, whereby tax was deducted from the amount before repayment instead of being paid and then reclaimed. Full form **mortgage interest relief at source**

**MIRV** /mɜːv/ MILITARY part of a ballistic missile containing more than one nuclear weapon, each capable of being independently steered and aimed at a different target. Full form **multiple independently targeted re-entry vehicle**

**MIS** COMPUTING **1.** management information service **2.** management information system

**misc. 1.** miscellaneous **2.** miscellany

**MI-SET** E-COMMERCE merchant-initiated secure electronic transactions

**Miss. 1.** Mission **2.** RELIGION Missionary

**MIT 1.** FINANCE an order to sell or purchase a commodity as soon as a particular price is reached. Full form **market if touched 2.** EDUCATION Massachusetts Institute of Technology

**MIU** HEALTH SERVICES minor injuries unit

**MJPEG** /ˈem peg/ COMPUTING a version of the JPEG image compression system that supports video. Full form **motion JPEG**

**mk 1.** ONLINE Macedonia (NOTE: The abbreviation **mk** is seen at the end of Internet addresses, preceded by a dot.) **2.** MONEY mark **3.** MONEY markka

**Mk 1.** BIBLE Mark **2.** AUTOMOTIVE mark (NOTE: The abbreviation **Mk**, followed by a number, is used to denote one of a series of car designs or models, as in *Ford Escort Mk I*.)

**MKDIR** COMPUTING a DOS command used to create a new directory on a disc. Full form **make directory**

**mks** MEASUREMENTS metre-kilogram-second (NOTE: The *mks units* form the basis of the metric system of measurement that has the metre, kilogram, and second as its basic units of length, mass, and time, respectively.)

**mksA** MEASUREMENTS metre-kilogram-second-ampere (NOTE: The **mksA** system was introduced in the 1930s in an effort to standardise international units of measurements. It now forms a subset of the SI system.)

**mkt** COMMERCE market

**mktg** marketing

**ml 1.** ONLINE Mali (NOTE: The abbreviation **ml** is seen at the end of Internet addresses, preceded by a dot.) **2.** MEASUREMENTS mile **3.** MEASUREMENTS millilitre

**mL** MEASUREMENTS millilambert

**ML** ONLINE more later (*used in e-mails and text messages*)

**M-L** WINE a process in wine fermentation in which malic acid is converted into lactic acid by bacteria, making the wine less fruity and crisp. Full form **malolactic (fermentation)**

**MLA 1.** EDUCATION Master of Landscape Architecture **2.** *Aus, Can* GOVERNMENT Member of the Legislative Assembly **3.** LANGUAGE Modern Language Association

**MLD** MEDICINE minimum lethal dose

**MLF** MILITARY multilateral (nuclear) force

**MLG** LANGUAGE Middle Low German

**MLitt** /ˈem ˈlɪt/ EDUCATION Master of Letters (NOTE: From the Latin *Magister Litterarum*.)

**Mlle** the French equivalent of Miss. Full form **Mademoiselle**

**Mlles** the plural of Mademoiselle (Mlle). Full form **Mesdemoiselles**

**MLR 1.** BANKING minimum lending rate **2.** MILITARY multiple-launch rockets

**MLSO** HEALTH SERVICES medical laboratory scientific officer

**mm 1.** MEASUREMENTS millimetre **2.** ONLINE Myanmar (NOTE: The abbreviation **mm** is seen at the end of Internet addresses, preceded by a dot.)

**MM 1.** the plural of Monsieur (M). Full form **Messieurs** (NOTE: *Messrs*, an alternative abbreviation of *Messieurs*, is used as the plural of the English title *Mr.*) **2.** MILITARY Military Medal

**MMC** BUSINESS Monopolies and Mergers Commission

**MMDA** FINANCE money market deposit account

**MMDS** RADIO multipoint microwave distribution system

**Mme** the French equivalent of Mrs. Full form **Madame**

**Mmes** the plural of Madame (Mme). Full form **Mesdames**

**mmf 1.** PHYSICS magnetomotive force **2.** ONLINE make money fast (*used in e-mails and text messages*)

**mmHg** MEASUREMENTS, PHYSICS a unit for measuring atmospheric pressure. Full form **millimetre of mercury**

**MMI** COMPUTING man-machine interface

**MMM** MILITARY Member of the Order of Military Merit

**mmol** MEASUREMENTS, CHEMISTRY millimole

**MMP** *NZ* POLITICS an electoral system in which half of the governmental seats are awarded by proportional representation, and half by majoritarian (first-past-the-post) election. Full form **Mixed Member Proportional**

**MMPI** PSYCHOLOGY Minnesota Multiphasic Personality Inventory

**MMR** IMMUNOLOGY measles, mumps, rubella (vaccine) (NOTE: *Rubella* is the technical name for German measles.)

**MMS** a system that enables sounds, images, or animations to be incorporated into text messages sent (usually) from mobile phones. Full form **multimedia messaging service**

**MMU** COMPUTING memory management unit

**MMus** MUSIC Master of Music

**mn** ONLINE Mongolia (NOTE: The abbreviation **mn** is seen at the end of Internet addresses, preceded by a dot.)

**Mn** CHEMICAL ELEMENTS manganese

**MN 1.** NAVIGATION magnetic north **2.** NAVY Merchant Navy **3.** MAIL Minnesota (NOTE: The abbreviation **MN** is part of the US sorting code on the last line of a Minnesota address.)

**MNA** GOVERNMENT Member of the National Assembly (of Quebec)

**MNC 1.** ONLINE Mother Nature calls (*used in e-mails, text messages and Internet chat rooms*) **2.** COMMERCE multinational company (or corporation)

**MND** MEDICINE motor neurone disease

**MNE** COMMERCE multinational enterprise

**mngr** manager

**Mo** CHEMICAL ELEMENTS molybdenum

**MO 1.** COMPUTING magneto-optical **2.** COMMERCE mail order **3.** MEDICINE medical officer **4.** MAIL Missouri (NOTE: The abbreviation **MO** is part of the US sorting code on the last line of a Missouri address.) **5.** modus operandi **6.** FINANCE money order

**mo.** TIME month

**m.o. 1.** COMMERCE mail order **2.** modus operandi **3.** FINANCE money order

**MoD** GOVERNMENT Ministry of Defence

**MOD** /mɒd/ BUSINESS the remainder after the division of one number by another. Full form **modulus**

**mod. 1.** moderate **2.** MUSIC moderato **3.** modern

**modif. 1.** modification **2.** GRAMMAR modifier

**MODS** MEDICINE multiple organ dysfunction syndrome

**MOF 1.** male or female (NOTE: The abbreviation **MOF** is used in e-mails, text messages, Internet chat rooms, and personal advertisements.) **2.** MEDICINE multi-organ failure

**MOH** HEALTH SERVICES Medical Officer of Health

**MOI** GOVERNMENT a government department set up during World War 2 to gather and disseminate information to help the war effort. In 1946 it was replaced by the non-Ministerial Central Office of Information. Full form **Ministry of Information**

**mol** CHEMISTRY mole

**mol.** CHEMISTRY **1.** molecular **2.** molecule

**mol. wt** CHEMISTRY molecular weight

**m.o.m.** COMMERCE middle of the month

**MOMI** /ˈməʊmi/ Museum of the Moving Image

**mon. 1.** CHRISTIANITY monastery **2.** FINANCE monetary

**Mon. 1.** CALENDAR Monday **2.** CHRISTIANITY a title for certain clerics of the Roman Catholic Church. Full form **Monsignor**

**MONEP** FINANCE Marché des Options Négociables de Paris (NOTE: From the French, 'Paris traded options market'.)

**MOO** /muː/ ONLINE a virtual online space in which several participants can meet at a given time to discuss a given topic. Full form **multi-user domain, object-oriented**

**MOP** FINANCE a person who has assets such as shares that are nominally worth a million pounds (or dollars) but that may never be realizable in cash. Full form **millionaire on paper**

**MOPP** /mɒp/ MILITARY the correct amount and type of protective clothing that should be worn in case of a chemical attack when carrying out a military mission, bearing in mind the precise threat and the type of mission. Full form **Mission Oriented Protective Posture**

**MOR** MUSIC middle-of-the-road (NOTE: The abbreviation **MOR** is used especially in radio programming.)

**mor.** INDUSTRY morocco (leather)

**Mor.** GEOGRAPHY **1.** Moroccan **2.** Morocco

**MORF** ONLINE male or female (NOTE: The abbreviation **MORF** is used in e-mails, text messages, Internet chat rooms, and personal advertisements.)

**MORI** /ˈmɔːri/ MARKETING Market and Opinion Research Institute

**morph.** BIOLOGY, LINGUISTICS **1.** morphological **2.** morphology

**morphol.** BIOLOGY, LINGUISTICS **1.** morphological **2.** morphology

**MOS** COMPUTING metal oxide semiconductor

**mos.** TIME months

**MOSFET** /ˈmɒsfet/ COMPUTING metal oxide semiconductor field effect transistor

**MOT** Ministry of Transport ○ *I have to get my car MOT'd next week.*

Although the Ministry of Transport no longer exists under this name (it is now the Department for Transport, or DfT), the abbreviation **MOT** is still used as a noun to denote the annual inspection of a vehicle to test its roadworthiness (a legal requirement in the United Kingdom) and the certificate awarded to vehicles that pass. It is also used as a verb, meaning 'to carry out an MOT test on a vehicle'.

**MOTAS** ONLINE member of the appropriate sex (*used in Internet bulletin boards*)

**MOTD** ONLINE message of the day (NOTE: The abbreviation **MOTAS** is used in e-mails, text messages, Internet chat rooms, and personal advertisements.)

**MOTOS** ONLINE member of the opposite sex (NOTE: The abbreviation **MOTOS** is used in e-mails, text messages, Internet chat rooms, and personal advertisements.)

**MOTSS** ONLINE member of the same sex (NOTE: The abbreviation **MOTSS** is used in e-mails, text messages, Internet chat rooms, and personal advertisements.)

**mouse** /maʊs/ MILITARY minimum orbital unmanned satellite of the Earth

**MOW** GOVERNMENT Ministry of Works

**MOX** /mɒks/ INDUST a reactor fuel made from plutonium that has been separated from spent nuclear fuel by chemical reprocessing and mixed with natural or depleted uranium

**Moz.** GEOGRAPHY Mozambique

**mp 1.** CHEMISTRY melting point **2.** MUSIC mezzo piano (NOTE: The abbreviation **mp** is seen at the end of Internet addresses, preceded by a dot.) **3.** ONLINE Northern Mariana Islands (NOTE: The abbreviation **mp**, usually italicized, is used on sheet music at a passage that is to be played or sung moderately softly.)

**MP 1.** GOVERNMENT Member of Parliament (NOTE: The abbreviation **MP** is used as a noun in its own right in this sense.) **2.** POLICE Metropolitan Police **3.** MILITARY military police **4.** POLICE mounted police

**MP3** ONLINE a computer file standard for downloading compressed music from the Internet, playable on a multimedia computer with appropriate software. Full form **Moving Picture Experts Group, Audio Layer 3**

**MPA** PUBLIC ADMINISTRATION Master of Public Administration

**MPC 1.** ECONOMICS marginal propensity to consume **2.** BUSINESS Monetary Policy Committee

**MPD** PSYCHIATRY multiple personality disorder

**MPEG** /ˈempeg/ COMPUTING a computer file standard for compressing, storing, and transmitting digital video and audio. Full form **Moving Picture Experts Group** (NOTE: The abbreviation **MPEG** is also used as a noun to denote a file containing digital video and audio in this format.)

**mpg** MEASUREMENTS, AUTOMOTIVE miles per gallon

**MPG** EDUCATION the basic salary scale for a teacher in Britain. Full form **main professional grade**

**mph** MEASUREMENTS miles per hour

**MPhil** /emˈfɪl/ EDUCATION Master of Philosophy

**MPM** ECONOMICS marginal propensity to import

**MPP** BUSINESS maternity pay period

**MPS 1.** ECONOMICS marginal propensity to save **2.** PHARMACOLOGY Member of the Pharmaceutical Society **3.** COMPUTING microprocessor system

**MPT** ECONOMICS marginal propensity to tax

**MPU** COMPUTING microprocessor unit

**MPV** AUTOMOBILES a large car that can carry more than five people, typically seven people in three rows of seats. Full form **multipurpose vehicle** (NOTE: The abbreviation **MPV** is used as a noun in its own right. The full form is rarely encountered, but such a vehicle is often called a *people carrier*.)

**mq** ONLINE Martinique (NOTE: The abbreviation **mq** is seen at the end of Internet addresses, preceded by a dot.)

**mr** ONLINE Mauritania (NOTE: The abbreviation **mr** is seen at the end of Internet addresses, preceded by a dot.)

**MR** LAW Master of the Rolls

**MRBM** ARMS medium-range ballistic missile

**MRC** MEDICINE Medical Research Council

**MRCA** AIR FORCE multirole combat aircraft

**MRCGP** MEDICINE Member of the Royal College of General Practitioners

**MRCP** MEDICINE Member of the Royal College of Physicians

**MRCS** SURGERY Member of the Royal College of Surgeons

**MRCVS** VETERINARY MEDICINE Member of the Royal College of Veterinary Surgeons

**MRE** MILITARY meal, ready to eat

**MRI** MEDICINE an imaging technique that uses electromagnetic radiation to obtain images of the body's soft tissues, e.g. the brain and spinal cord ○ *MRI scanning* Full form **magnetic resonance imaging**

**MRIA** Member of the Royal Irish Academy

**MRL** ENVIRONMENT maximum residue level

**mRNA** GENETICS a form of RNA (ribonucleic acid) that is transcribed from a strand of DNA and translated into a protein sequence at a cell ribosome. Full form **messenger RNA**

**MRP** COMMERCE manufacturer's recommended price

**MRS** BUSINESS the point at which a consumer is willing to give up one good for another and is equally satisfied with either. Full form **marginal rate of substitution**

**MRSA** MICROBIOLOGY a strain of a common pathogenic bacterium that has become resistant to treatment by the antibiotic methicillin and is therefore a hazard in places such as hospitals. Full form **methicillin-resistant *Staphylococcus aureus***

**MRSC** CHEMISTRY Member of the Royal Society of Chemistry

**ms 1.** MEASUREMENTS millisecond **2.** ONLINE Montserrat (NOTE: The abbreviation **ms** is seen at the end of Internet addresses, preceded by a dot.)

**MS 1.** PUBLISHING manuscript **2.** SURGERY Master of Surgery **3.** MAIL Mississippi (NOTE: The abbreviation **MS** is part of the US sorting code on the last line of a Mississippi address.) **4.** MEDICINE the narrowing of the heart's mitral valve (the one-way valve between the upper and lower chambers, on the left side) as the result of disease. Full form **mitral stenosis 5.** ONLINE more (of the) same (*used in e-mails and text messages*) **6.** BOAT motor ship **7.** MEDICINE multiple sclerosis **8.** sacred to the memory of (NOTE: The abbreviation **MS** is seen on gravestones.)

**m/s** MEASUREMENTS metres per second

**MSB 1.** COMPUTING most significant bit **2.** BANKING mutual savings bank

**MSc** SCIENCE Master of Science

**MS-DOS** /ˌem es ˈdɒs/ COMPUTING a trademark for a widely used computer operating system. Full form **Microsoft Disk Operating System**

**msec** MEASUREMENTS millisecond

**MSF** HUMAN RESOURCES Manufacturing, Science, Finance (Union)

**MSG** CHEMISTRY monosodium glutamate

**msg.** message

**Msgr 1.** a title for certain dignitaries, e.g. bishops and princes, in France and other French-speaking countries. Full form **Monseigneur 2.** CHRISTIANITY a title for certain clerics of the Roman Catholic Church. Full form **Monsignor**

**MSH** BIOCHEMISTRY melanocyte-stimulating hormone

**MSI** COMPUTING medium scale integration

**MSP** GOVERNMENT Member of the Scottish Parliament

**MSS** PUBLISHING manuscripts

**MST** TIME Mountain Standard Time

**MSU** MEDICINE midstream specimen of urine

**mSv** MEASUREMENTS, SCIENCE millisievert

**MSX** COMPUTING a hardware and software standard for home computers that can use interchangeable software. Full form **Microsoft Extended**

**MSY** AGRICULTURE maximum sustainable yield

**mt 1.** ONLINE Malta (NOTE: The abbreviation **mt** is seen at the end of Internet addresses, preceded by a dot.) **2.** GEOGRAPHY mount

**Mt 1.** BIBLE Matthew **2.** CHEMICAL ELEMENTS meitnerium **3.** GEOGRAPHY Mount **4.** GEOGRAPHY Mountain

**MT 1.** MEASUREMENTS megaton **2.** MEASUREMENTS metric ton **3.** MAIL Montana (NOTE: The abbreviation **MT** is part of the US sorting code on the last line of a Montana address.) **4.** TIME Mountain Time

**mt. 1.** MEASUREMENTS megaton **2.** GEOGRAPHY mountain

**MTA** COMPUTING mail transfer agent

**MTB** NAVY motor torpedo boat

**MTBE** CHEMISTRY a lead-free antiknock petrol additive. Full form **methyl tertiary-butyl ethyl**

**MTBF** COMPUTING mean time between failures

**MTCE** MEASUREMENTS million tonnes of coal equivalent

**MTech** /'emtek/ EDUCATION Master of Technology

**MTF** COMPUTING mean time to failure

**MTFS** BUSINESS Medium-Term Financial Strategy

**mtg** meeting

**mtg.** FINANCE mortgage

**MTM** MANAGEMENT methods-time measurement

**mtn** GEOGRAPHY mountain

**Mt Rev.** CHRISTIANITY Most Reverend

**mts** GEOGRAPHY **1.** mountains **2.** mounts

**MTTR** MANUFACTURING mean time to repair

**mu** ONLINE Mauritius (NOTE: The abbreviation **mu** is seen at the end of Internet addresses, preceded by a dot.)

**MU 1.** Mothers' Union **2.** ONLINE multiuser (online space) **3.** MUSIC Musicians' Union

**MUA** COMPUTING mail user agent

**MUD** /mʌd/ ONLINE a virtual online space in which several participants can contribute to a communal project such as a collaboratively written story or a game for several players. Full form **multiuser domain**

**mus. 1.** museum **2.** music **3.** musical **4.** musician

**MusB** MUSIC Bachelor of Music (NOTE: From the Latin *Musicae Baccalaureus*.)

**MusD** MUSIC Doctor of Music (NOTE: From the Latin *Musicae Doctor*.)

**MusM** MUSIC Master of Music (NOTE: From the Latin *Musicae Magister*.)

**mustn't** /'mʌs(ə)nt/ must not

**MUX** COMPUTING multiplexer

**mv 1.** ONLINE Maldives (NOTE: The abbreviation **mv** is seen at the end of Internet addresses, preceded by a dot.) **2.** MUSIC a musical direction indicating that a passage is to be sung or played with moderate volume from the voice or instrument. Full form **mezza voce**

**mV** MEASUREMENTS millivolt

**MV 1.** COMMERCE market value **2.** STATISTICS mean variation **3.** MEASUREMENTS megavolt **4.** SHIPPING merchant vessel **5.** BOAT motor vessel **6.** ARMS muzzle velocity

**MVA** COMMERCE **1.** market value added **2.** market value adjuster

**MVD** POLICE the Ministry for Internal Affairs of the former Soviet Union from 1946 to 1960, which acted as its secret police. Full form **Ministerstvo vnutrennikh dyel**

**MVO** MILITARY Member of the Royal Victorian Order

**MVP 1.** ECOLOGY minimum viable population **2.** *N Am* SPORTS most valuable player (award)

**MVS** VETERINARY MEDICINE Master of Veterinary Surgery

**MVSc** VETERINARY MEDICINE Master of Veterinary Science

**mw** ONLINE Malawi (NOTE: The abbreviation **mw** is seen at the end of Internet addresses, preceded by a dot.)

**mW** MEASUREMENTS, ELECTRICITY milliwatt

**MW 1.** WINE Master of Wine **2.** RADIO medium wave **3.** MEASUREMENTS, ELECTRICITY megawatt **4.** CHEMISTRY molecular weight

**MWCA** FINANCE Monetary Working Capital Adjustment

**mx** ONLINE Mexico (NOTE: The abbreviation **mx** is seen at the end of Internet addresses, preceded by a dot.)

**Mx** MEASUREMENTS, PHYSICS maxwell

**MX 1.** COMPUTING mail exchange (record) **2.** MOTOR SPORTS motocross

**mxd** mixed

**my 1.** ONLINE Malaysia (NOTE: The abbreviation **my** is seen at the end of Internet addresses, preceded by a dot.) **2.** MEASUREMENTS, TIME million years

**MY** BOAT motor yacht

**MYOB** ONLINE mind your own business (*used in e-mails and text messages*)

**myth. 1.** mythological **2.** mythology

**mythol. 1.** mythological **2.** mythology

**mz** ONLINE Mozambique (NOTE: The abbreviation **mz** is seen at the end of Internet addresses, preceded by a dot.)

# N

**n 1.** PHYSICS amount of substance **2.** PRINTING en dash **3.** MEASUREMENTS nano- **4.** COMMERCE net **5.** GRAMMAR neuter **6.** PHYSICS neutron **7.** GRAMMAR nominative **8.** TIME noon **9.** MUSIC note **10.** GRAMMAR noun **11.** number **12.** PHYSICS refractive index

**N 1.** PHYSICS Avogadro's number **2.** PRINTING en dash **3.** CHESS knight (NOTE: The abbreviation **N**, representing the initial sound (rather than the initial letter) of the word, is used to distinguish the knight from the king (K).) **4.** MONEY naira **5.** AUTOMOTIVE neutral **6.** GEOGRAPHY New (NOTE: The abbreviation **N** is used in placenames.) **7.** MEASUREMENTS, PHYSICS newton **8.** CHEMICAL ELEMENTS nitrogen **9.** LANGUAGE Norse **10.** north **11.** northern **12.** CALENDAR November

**na** ONLINE Namibia (NOTE: The abbreviation **na** is seen at the end of Internet addresses, preceded by a dot.)

**Na** CHEMICAL ELEMENTS sodium (NOTE: From the modern Latin *natrium*.)

**NA** GEOGRAPHY North America

**n/a 1.** not applicable **2.** not available

**NAACP** LAW National Association for the Advancement of Colored People

**NAAFI** /'næfi/ MILITARY an organization that provides canteens and shops for people who work in the armed forces. Full form **Navy, Army, and Air Force Institutes** (NOTE: The acronym **NAAFI** is used as a noun denoting a canteen or shop provided by this organization.)

**NAC** DOMESTIC National Advisory Council

**NACODS** /'neɪkɒdz/ HUMAN RESOURCES National Association of Colliery Overmen, Deputies, and Shotfirers

**NACRO** /'nækrəʊ/ CRIME National Association for the Care and Resettlement of Offenders

**NAD** BIOCHEMISTRY a coenzyme that plays a role in the electron transport chain, where it is vital in the production of energy. Full form **nicotinamide adenine dinucleotide**

**NADH** BIOCHEMISTRY the reduced form of NAD. Full form **NAD hydrogen**

**NADP** BIOCHEMISTRY a coenzyme involved in anabolism, consisting of NAD with an extra phosphate group. Full form **nicotinamide adenine dinucleotide phosphate**

**NADPH** BIOCHEMISTRY the reduced form of NADP. Full form **NADP hydrogen**

**NAFTA** /'næftə/ a free trade agreement signed between the United States and Canada in 1989, and extended to include Mexico in 1994. Full form **North American Free Trade Agreement**

**Nah.** BIBLE Nahum

**NAHT** EDUCATION National Association of Headteachers

**NAI** LAW nonaccidental injury

**NAIRU** /'neɪruː/ ECONOMICS nonaccelerating inflation rate of unemployment

**NAK** /næk/ COMPUTING an ASCII control code used to indicate to the sender that a transmitted message has not been properly received. Full form **negative acknowledgment**

**NALGO** /'nælgəʊ/ HUMAN RESOURCES a former trade union, now part of UNISON. Full form **National Association of Local Government Officers**

**N Am.** GEOGRAPHY **1.** North America **2.** North American

**NAND** /nænd/ COMPUTING a logic operator used in computing that produces an output signal only if at least one of its inputs has no signal, thus being the inverse of an AND operator. Full form **not and**

**NAO** FINANCE National Audit Office

**NAPO** /ˈnæpəʊ/ HUMAN RESOURCES National Association of Prison Officers

**NAS** NAVY naval air station

**NASA** /ˈnæsə/ AEROSPACE the US government agency responsible for nonmilitary programmes in the exploration and scientific study of space. Full form **National Aeronautics and Space Administration** (NOTE: The acronym **NASA** is used as a noun in its own right.)

**NASD** FINANCE National Association of Securities Dealers

**NASDAQ** /ˈnæzdæk/ FINANCE in the United States, an electronic communications system that links all over-the-counter securities dealers to form a single market

**NAS/UWT** HUMAN RESOURCES National Association of Schoolmasters/Union of Women Teachers

**nat. 1.** national **2.** native **3.** natural

**NATFHE** /ˈnætfiː/ HUMAN RESOURCES National Association of Teachers in Further and Higher Education

**natl** national

**NATO** /ˈneɪtəʊ/ INTERNATIONAL RELATIONS an international organization established in 1949 to promote mutual defence and collective security. Full form **North Atlantic Treaty Organization** (NOTE: The acronym **NATO** is used as a noun in its own right.)

**NATSOPA** /nætˈsəʊpə/ HUMAN RESOURCES National Society of Operative Printers, Graphical and Media Personnel (NOTE: The organization was formerly called the National Society of Printers and Assistants, hence the acronym.)

**naut.** nautical

**NAV** FINANCE net asset value

**nav. 1.** naval **2.** navigable **3.** navigation

**NAVSAT** /ˈnævsæt/ navigation satellite

**nb** CRICKET no ball

**Nb** CHEMICAL ELEMENTS niobium

**NB 1.** GEOGRAPHY New Brunswick **2.** used to draw attention to something particularly important, usually an addition to or qualification of a previous statement. Full form **nota bene** (NOTE: From the Latin, 'mark well'.)

**NBA 1.** BASKETBALL National Basketball Association **2.** BOXING National Boxing Association **3.** PUBLISHING a former agreement in the British book trade that prevented booksellers from selling books at prices lower than those fixed by the publishers. Full form **Net Book Agreement**

**NBC 1.** *US* BROADCASTING National Broadcasting Company **2.** MILITARY nuclear, biological, and chemical (weapons or warfare)

**NBCD** COMPUTING natural binary coded decimal

**NBD** ONLINE no big deal (*used in e-mails and text messages*)

**NbE** north by east

**NBER** ECONOMICS National Bureau of Economic Research

**NBFI** FINANCE nonbank financial institution

**NBG** no bloody good

**NBL** PUBLISHING National Book League

**NBTD** ONLINE nothing better to do (*used in e-mails and text messages*)

**NBV** ACCOUNTING net book value

**NbW** north by west

**nc** ONLINE New Caledonia (NOTE: The abbreviation **nc** is seen at the end of Internet addresses, preceded by a dot.)

**NC 1.** EDUCATION a UK qualification in a vocational subject that is roughly equivalent to a GCSE. Full form **National Certificate 2.** EDUCATION National Curriculum **3.** COMPUTING network computer **4.** COMMERCE no charge **5.** MAIL North Carolina (NOTE: The abbreviation **NC** is part of the US sorting code on the last line of a North Carolina address.) **6.** COMPUTING numerical control

**n/c** COMMERCE no charge

**NCB** BANKING national central bank

**NCC 1.** DOMESTIC National Consumer Council **2.** EDUCATION National Curriculum Council **3.** ENVIRONMENT Nature Conservancy Council

**NCO** MILITARY noncommissioned officer (NOTE: The abbreviation **NCO** is used as a noun in its own right.)

**NCSA** COMPUTING National Center for Supercomputing Applications

**NCT** MEDICINE National Childbirth Trust

**NCU** HUMAN RESOURCES National Communications Union

**NCUA** FINANCE National Credit Union Administration

**Nd** CHEMICAL ELEMENTS neodymium

**ND 1.** EDUCATION a UK vocational qualification that is roughly equivalent to two A levels. Full form **National Diploma 2.** no date (NOTE: The abbreviation **nd** is used when citing a source that has no date, after the author's name in parentheses.) **3.** MAIL North Dakota (NOTE: The abbreviation **ND** is part of the US sorting code on the last line of a North Dakota address.)

**NDA** BUSINESS **1.** nondisclosure agreement **2.** nondisparagement agreement

**NDE** PARANORMAL a sensation that people on the brink of death have described as leaving their own bodies and observing them as though they were bystanders. Full form **near-death experience**

**NDIP** FINANCE nondeposit investment product

**NDP** ECONOMICS net domestic product

**NDPB** GOVERNMENT a public body, often statutory, that is able to act independently of the government that creates and finances it. The Arts Council and industrial tribunals are examples of NDPBs. Full form **non-departmental public body** (NOTE: **NDBP** is the more formal term that has come to replace **quango**, which acquired negative associations because quangos were thought of as being unelectable and unaccountable.)

**NDT** TIME Newfoundland Daylight Time

**NDU** HEALTH SERVICES Nursing Development Unit

**ne** ONLINE Niger (NOTE: The abbreviation **ne** is seen at the end of Internet addresses, preceded by a dot.)

**Ne** CHEMICAL ELEMENTS neon

**NE 1.** MAIL Nebraska (NOTE: The abbreviation **NE** is part of the US sorting code on the last line of a Nebraska address.) **2.** GEOGRAPHY New England **3.** northeast **4.** northeastern

**NEA** *US* EDUCATION National Education Association

**NEB 1.** BUSINESS National Enterprise Board **2.** BIBLE New English Bible

**NEbE** northeast by east

**NEbN** northeast by north

**NEC 1.** BUSINESS National Executive Committee **2.** COMMERCE National Exhibition Centre (Birmingham)

**NEDC** /'nedi/ ECONOMICS National Economic Development Council (NOTE: The **NEDC** is informally called *Neddy*.)

**needn't** /ˈniːd(ə)nt/ need not

**NEF** ENVIRONMENT noise exposure forecast

**neg.** negative

**Neh.** BIBLE Nehemiah

**nem. con.** /ˌnem ˈkɒn/ LAW without opposition ○ *The motion was carried nem. con.* (NOTE: From the Latin *nemine contradicente* 'with no one contradicting'.)

**NEO** ASTRONOMY near-earth object

**NEPAD** ECONOMICS an organization established in 2001 by Africa's political leaders to implement an integrated social and economic development programme for the whole continent. Full form **New Partnership for Africa's Development**

**NEQ** COMPUTING nonequivalence

**NERC** /nɜːk/ ENVIRONMENT Natural Environment Research Council

**net** ONLINE networking organization (NOTE: The abbreviation **net** is seen at the end of Internet addresses, preceded by a dot.)

**NetBIOS** /ˈnet ˌbaɪɒs/ COMPUTING a commonly used standard set of commands, originally developed by IBM, that allow application programs to carry out basic operations such as file sharing and transferring data between nodes over a network. Full form **Network Basic Input Output System**

**Neth.** GEOGRAPHY Netherlands

**neurol.** MEDICINE **1.** neurological **2.** neurology

**neut.** GRAMMAR neuter

**NEW** MILITARY nonexplosive warfare

**New Eng.** GEOGRAPHY New England

**Newf.** GEOGRAPHY Newfoundland

**nf** ONLINE Norfolk Island (NOTE: The abbreviation **nf** is seen at the end of Internet addresses, preceded by a dot.)

**NF 1.** POLITICS National Front **2.** MEDICINE an inherited disorder causing visual and hearing defects, other nervous disorders, and sometimes major deformities. Full form **neurofibromatosis 3.** GEOGRAPHY Newfoundland **4.** BANKING no funds **5.** LANGUAGE Norman French

**Nfd** GEOGRAPHY Newfoundland

**NFER** EDUCATION National Foundation for Educational Research

**NFL** AMERICAN FOOTBALL National Football League

**Nfld** GEOGRAPHY Newfoundland

**NFS 1.** EMERGENCIES National Fire Service **2.** COMPUTING network file service **3.** COMPUTING network file system **4.** not for sale

**NFT 1.** CINEMA National Film Theatre **2.** TIME Newfoundland Time

**NFU** AGRICULTURE National Farmers' Union

**NFWI** National Federation of Women's Institutes

**ng 1.** ONLINE Nigeria (NOTE: The abbreviation **ng** is seen at the end of Internet addresses, preceded by a dot.) **2.** no good

**NGO** nongovernmental organization

**NH** MAIL New Hampshire (NOTE: The abbreviation **NH** is part of the US sorting code on the last line of a New Hampshire address.)

**NHI** HEALTH SERVICES National Health Insurance

**NHS** HEALTH SERVICES National Health Service

**ni** ONLINE Nicaragua (NOTE: The abbreviation **ni** is seen at the end of Internet addresses, preceded by a dot.)

**Ni** CHEMICAL ELEMENTS nickel

**NI 1.** FINANCE National Insurance **2.** *NZ* GEOGRAPHY North Island **3.** GEOGRAPHY Northern Ireland

**NIC 1.** FINANCE National Insurance contribution(s) **2.** COMPUTING network interface card **3.** BUSINESS newly industrialized country

**Nic.** GEOGRAPHY Nicaragua

**NiCad** /'naɪkæd/ ELECTRICITY nickel-cadmium (battery)

**NICAM** /'naɪkæm/ near-instantaneous companded audio multiplex

**NICE** /naɪs/ MEDICINE National Institute for Clinical Excellence

**NIDA** /'naɪdə/ PERFORMING ARTS Australia's premier drama school. Full form **National Institute of the Dramatic Arts**

**NIEO** ECONOMICS New International Economic Order

**NIESR** ECONOMICS National Institute of Economic and Social Research

**NIF** BUSINESS a facility by which a company obtains a short-term loan from a bank and can use this to issue small Eurocurrency notes to replace ones which have expired. Full form **note issuance facility**

**Nig.** GEOGRAPHY **1.** Nigeria **2.** Nigerian

**NIH 1.** *US* HEALTH SERVICES National Institutes of Health **2.** ECOLOGY a stubborn refusal to make use of an existing solution to a problem, simply because it originated outside the company. Full form **not invented here**

**NIHE** EDUCATION National Institute for Higher Education

**NII** INDUST Nuclear Installations Inspectorate

**NIMBY** /'nɪmbi/ ENVIRONMENT a person who objects to something unattractive or potentially dangerous being located near his or her home. Full form **not in my back yard**

> The acronym **NIMBY** is usually derogatory, implying that the person would have no objection to the offending installation if a different location were proposed (regardless of the potential risk or inconvenience to others). It is also used to describe the attitude of such people.

**NiMH** ELECTRICITY nickel metal hydride (battery)

**NIRC** HUMAN RESOURCES National Industrial Relations Court

**N Ire.** Northern Ireland

**NIREX** /'naɪreks/ INDUST Nuclear Industry Radioactive Waste Executive

**NJ** MAIL New Jersey (NOTE: The abbreviation **NJ** is part of the US sorting code on the last line of a New Jersey address.)

**nl 1.** ONLINE Netherlands (NOTE: The abbreviation **nl** is seen at the end of Internet addresses, preceded by a dot.) **2.** PRINTING new line

**NL** LANGUAGE New Latin

**NLF** POLITICS National Liberation Front

**NLP 1.** COMPUTING natural language processing **2.** PSYCHOLOGY neurolinguistic programming

**NLQ** COMPUTING of a high quality comparable to typewritten text. Full form **near letter quality**

**nm 1.** MEASUREMENTS nanometre **2.** MEASUREMENTS, NAUTICAL nautical mile **3.** MEASUREMENTS nuclear magneton

**NM 1.** MEASUREMENTS nautical mile **2.** MAIL New Mexico (NOTE: The abbreviation **NM** is part of the US sorting code on the last line of a New Mexico address.)

**NMC** HEALTH SERVICES Nursing and Midwifery Council

**NMI** COMPUTING a high-priority interrupt signal that cannot be blocked and overrides all other commands. Full form **nonmaskable interrupt**

**nmol** MEASUREMENTS, CHEMISTRY nanomole

**NMR** PHYSICS the energy pulse released by an atomic nucleus exposed to high-frequency radiation in a magnetic field, which is used to provide data about the atom that can be transformed into an image by computer techniques. Full form **nuclear magnetic resonance** (NOTE: **NMR** is used in medicine in the diagnostic technique of magnetic resonance imaging (MRI).)

**NNE** north-northeast

**NNI** ENVIRONMENT a model used to assess average noise pollution by aircraft in an area. Full form **noise and number index**

**NNP** ECONOMICS net national product

**NNR** ECOLOGY National Nature Reserve

**NNTP** COMPUTING network news transfer protocol

**NNW** north-northwest

**no** ONLINE Norway (NOTE: The abbreviation **no** is seen at the end of Internet addresses, preceded by a dot.)

**No** CHEMICAL ELEMENTS nobelium

**no. 1.** north **2.** northern **3.** number

**No.** number (NOTE: From the Latin *numero*, ablative of *numerus*.)

**n.o.** CRICKET not out

**NOHSC** HEALTH National Occupational Health and Safety Commission

**Nol** ISLAM Nation of Islam

**nol. pros.** LAW an entry made in a court record when a plaintiff or a prosecutor decides not to proceed further with a case or action. Full form **nolle prosequi** (NOTE: From the Latin, 'be unwilling to pursue'.)

**nom.** GRAMMAR nominative

**NOP** National Opinion Polls

**Nopo** /ˈnəʊpəʊ/ RAIL a train that is controlled automatically and needs no driver. Full form **no person operated train**

**NOR** /nɔː/ LOGIC a logic operator with two arguments that returns true if and only if both arguments are false. Full form **not or**

**Nor. 1.** HISTORY Norman **2.** North **3.** GEOGRAPHY Norway **4.** LANGUAGE Norwegian

**Norf.** GEOGRAPHY Norfolk

**norm.** MATHEMATICS normal

**Norm.** HISTORY Norman

**Northants.** GEOGRAPHY Northamptonshire

**Norw. 1.** GEOGRAPHY Norway **2.** LANGUAGE Norwegian

**NOS** COMPUTING network operating system

**nos.** numbers

**Nos.** numbers

**n.o.s.** not otherwise specified

**Notts.** GEOGRAPHY Nottinghamshire

**Nov.** CALENDAR November

**NOW** /naʊ/ National Organization for Women

**NOx** ENVIRONMENT nitrogen oxides

**NOYB** ONLINE none of your business (*used in e-mails and text messages*)

**np 1.** ONLINE Nepal (NOTE: The abbreviation **np** is seen at the end of Internet addresses, preceded by a dot.) **2.** PRINTING new paragraph

**Np 1.** MEASUREMENTS, ELECTRICITY neper **2.** CHEMICAL ELEMENTS neptunium

**NP 1.** POLITICS National Party **2.** MEDICINE neuropsychiatry **3.** PRINTING new paragraph **4.** LAW notary public **5.** GRAMMAR noun phrase

**NPA** PRESS Newspaper Publishers' Association

**NPD** MARKETING new product development

**NPK** AGRICULTURE nitrogen, phosphorus, and potassium (in fertilizers) (NOTE: The abbreviation **NPK** is made up of the chemical symbols of the three elements.)

**NPL** 1. PHYSICS National Physical Laboratory 2. ENVIRONMENT noise pollution level

**NPN** CHEMISTRY nonprotein nitrogen

**NPP** ECOLOGY net primary productivity

**NPV** FINANCE 1. no par value 2. net present value

**NPWS** *Aus* ECOLOGY National Parks and Wildlife Service

**NQA** ONLINE no questions asked (*used in e-mails and text messages*)

**nr** 1. ONLINE Nauru (NOTE: The abbreviation **nr** is seen at the end of Internet addresses, preceded by a dot.) 2. near

**NRA** 1. ARMS National Rifle Association 2. ENVIRONMENT National Rivers Authority

**NRC** INDUST Nuclear Regulatory Commission

**NRDC** BUSINESS National Research and Development Corporation

**NRDS** MEDICINE neonatal respiratory distress syndrome

**NREM** PHYSIOLOGY used to describe a stage of sleep in which rapid eye movement (REM) does not occur ○ *NREM sleep* Full form **nonrapid eye movement**

**NRI** an Indian citizen who has migrated to another country. Full form **nonresident Indian**

**NRMA** AUTOMOTIVE the largest motoring organization in Australia, providing roadside assistance, travel information, and other motor-related services to its members, as well as insurance and travel services to the general public. Full form **National Roads and Motorists Association**

**NRN** ONLINE no reply necessary (*used in e-mails and text messages*)

**NRPB** HEALTH SERVICES National Radiological Protection Board

**NRV** FINANCE net realizable value

**NRWT** FINANCE tax payable by a non-resident of a country on any income which has been made in that country, such as royalties or share dividends. Full form **nonresident withholding tax**

**NRZ** COMPUTING transmission of binary data which does not return to a zero volts signal in between each bit of data. Full form **nonreturn to zero**

**ns** MEASUREMENTS, TIME nanosecond

**NS** 1. CALENDAR New Style (NOTE: The abbreviation **NS** is seen after a date reckoned according to the Gregorian calendar, especially one falling before or around the time of the changeover from the Julian calendar.) 2. BANKING not sufficient (funds) 3. GEOGRAPHY Nova Scotia 4. SHIPPING nuclear ship

**n.s.** 1. nearside 2. new series 3. not specified

**n/s** BANKING not sufficient (funds)

**N/S** 1. nonsmoker 2. nonsmoking

**NSA** 1. *US* National Security Agency 2. ACCOUNTING National Society of Accountants 3. ENVIRONMENT nitrate-sensitive area

**NSAID** PHARMACOLOGY any of a group of drugs taken orally or applied externally for the relief of pain or inflammation. Aspirin and ibuprofen are NSAIDs. Full form **nonsteroid(al) anti-inflammatory drug**

**NS & I** FINANCE National Savings and Investments

**NSB** BANKING National Savings Bank

**NSC** 1. National Safety Council 2. FINANCE National Savings Certificate 3. *US* National Security Council

**nsec** MEASUREMENTS, TIME nanosecond

**NSF** BANKING not sufficient funds

**NSG** EDUCATION nonstatutory guidelines

**NSPCA** *US* VETERINARY MEDICINE National Society for the Prevention of Cruelty to Animals

**NSPCC** SOCIAL WELFARE National Society for the Prevention of Cruelty to Children

**NSU** MEDICINE nonspecific urethritis

**NSW** GEOGRAPHY New South Wales

**NT 1.** National Trust **2.** BIBLE New Testament **3.** CARD GAMES no trump **4.** TIME Nome Time **5.** *Aus* GEOGRAPHY Northern Territory **6.** *Can* GEOGRAPHY Northwest Territories

**NTA** FINANCE net tangible assets

**NTB** BUSINESS a restriction on import and export over a country's borders that is not tariff-related, e.g. the lack of a market for the product in that country. Full form **nontariff barrier**

**Nth** north

**NTIM** ONLINE not that it matters (*used in e-mails and text messages*)

**NTL** ONLINE (*used in e-mails and text messages*) **1.** nevertheless **2.** nonetheless

**NTP 1.** COMPUTING network time protocol **2.** MEASUREMENTS, PHYSICS normal temperature and pressure

**NTSC** *US* TV a standard that defines the minimum definition quality for colour broadcasts in the US. Full form **National Television Systems Committee**

**NTW 1.** ONLINE not to worry (*used in e-mails and text messages*) **2.** no time-wasters (NOTE: In the meaning 'no time-wasters', the abbreviation **NTW** is used in personal ads and online dating.)

**nt wt** MEASUREMENTS net weight

**nu** ONLINE Niue (NOTE: The abbreviation **nu** is seen at the end of Internet addresses, preceded by a dot.)

**NUAAW** HUMAN RESOURCES National Union of Agricultural and Allied Workers

**NUCPS** HUMAN RESOURCES National Union of Civil and Public Servants

**NUDETS** MILITARY nuclear detection system

**NUJ** HUMAN RESOURCES National Union of Journalists

**NUM** HUMAN RESOURCES National Union of Mineworkers

**num. 1.** number **2.** numeral

**Num.** BIBLE Numbers

**NUPE** /'njuːpiː/ HUMAN RESOURCES a former trade union, now part of UNISON. Full form **National Union of Public Employees**

**NURMTW** HUMAN RESOURCES National Union of Rail, Maritime, and Transport Workers

**NUS 1.** HUMAN RESOURCES National Union of Seamen **2.** EDUCATION National Union of Students

**NUT** HUMAN RESOURCES National Union of Teachers

**NV 1.** MAIL Nevada (NOTE: The abbreviation **NV** is part of the US sorting code on the last line of a Nevada address.) **2.** WINE nonvintage **3.** FINANCE used to describe a share that does not give the holder the right to vote at company meetings. Full form **nonvoting**

**N/V** BANKING no value

**NVC** ECOLOGY a system for studying and classifying all plant matter in the UK. Full form **national vegetation classification**

**nvCJD** MEDICINE a form of Creutzfeldt-Jakob disease (CJD) that has a much shorter incubation period than previously recognized types but is clinically identical. Full form **new variant CJD**

**NVQ** EDUCATION a UK qualification, awarded at a variety of levels in a technical or vocational subject, certifying the holder's proficiency in a range of work-related activities. Full form **National Vocational Qualification** (NOTE: The abbreviation **NVQ** is used as a noun in its own right.)

**NVZ** ENVIRONMENT nitrate-vulnerable zone

**NW 1.** northwest **2.** northwestern

**NWbN** northwest by north

**NWbW** northwest by west

**Nwfld** GEOGRAPHY Newfoundland

**NWT** *Can* GEOGRAPHY Northwest Territories

**n.wt** MEASUREMENTS net weight

**NY** MAIL New York (State) (NOTE: The abbreviation **NY** is part of the US sorting code on the last line of an address in the state of New York.)

**NYC** GEOGRAPHY New York City

**NYCE** FINANCE New York Cotton Exchange

**NYFE** FINANCE New York Futures Exchange

**NYLON** /ˈnaɪlɒn/ relating to a transatlantic lifestyle divided between New York and London, as lived by successful business executives (NOTE: The abbreviation **NY-LON** is a combination of the abbreviations for *Nw York* and *London*.)

**NYMEX** /ˈnaɪmeks/ FINANCE New York Mercantile Exchange

**NYO** MUSIC National Youth Orchestra

**NYP** PUBLISHING not yet published

**NYSE** STOCK EXCHANGE New York Stock Exchange

**nz** ONLINE New Zealand (NOTE: The abbreviation **nz** is seen at the end of Internet addresses, preceded by a dot.)

**NZ** New Zealand

**NZBC** New Zealand Broadcasting Corporation

**N Zeal.** New Zealand

**NZMA** MEDICINE New Zealand Medical Association

**NZRFU** RUGBY New Zealand Rugby Football Union

**NZSE** STOCK EXCHANGE New Zealand Stock Exchange

**O 1.** GEOGRAPHY ocean **2.** PRINTING octavo **3.** old **4.** MATHEMATICS order **5.** BASEBALL out **6.** CRICKET over(s) **7.** PHARMACOLOGY pint

**o'** /ə/ of

**O 1.** GEOGRAPHY ocean **2.** PRINTING octavo **3.** CALENDAR October **4.** old **5.** MATHEMATICS order **6.** BASEBALL out **7.** ONLINE over (*used in e-mails, text messages and Internet chat rooms*) **8.** CRICKET over(s) **9.** CHEMICAL ELEMENTS oxygen

**OA 1.** COMPUTING office automation **2.** MEDICINE osteoarthritis

**o/a** on or about

**OAC** COMMERCE on approved credit

**OAM** MILITARY Medal of the Order of Australia

**O & M** BUSINESS a process of examining how an office works, and suggesting how it can be made more efficient. Full form **organization and method**

**OAP** SOCIAL SCIENCES a person who is entitled to draw a state pension on reaching a specific age, usually after retirement. Full form **old-age pensioner** (NOTE: The abbreviation **OAP** is used as a noun in its own right.)

**OAS** POLITICS Organization of American States

**OAUS** ONLINE on an unrelated subject (*used in e-mails and text messages*)

**OB 1.** MEDICINE obstetric **2.** MEDICINE obstetrician **3.** MEDICINE obstetrics **4.** BROADCASTING outside broadcast

**ob. 1.** he or she died (NOTE: From the Latin *obiit*.) **2.** MUSIC oboe **3.** MEDICINE obstetric **4.** MEDICINE obstetrician **5.** MEDICINE obstetrics

**Ob.** BIBLE Obadiah

**Obad.** BIBLE Obadiah

**obb.** MUSIC obbligato

**OBC** *S Asia* SOCIOLOGY Other Backward Classes

**OBE** MILITARY Officer of the (Order of the) British Empire

**OBI** E-COMMERCE open buying on the Internet

**obj. 1.** GRAMMAR object **2.** objection **3.** GRAMMAR objective

**obl.** PRINTING oblique

**o.b.o.** COMMERCE or best offer (NOTE: The abbreviation **o.b.o.** is used in classified advertisements following a guide price.)

**obs. 1.** obscure **2.** observation **3.** ASTRONOMY observatory **4.** obsolete **5.** MEDICINE obstetrics

**Obs.** ASTRONOMY Observatory

**OBSF** FINANCE off-balance-sheet financing

**obstet.** MEDICINE **1.** obstetric **2.** obstetrics

**OBTW** ONLINE oh, by the way (*used in e-mails and text messages*)

**OC 1.** MILITARY Officer Commanding **2.** PHARMACOLOGY oral contraceptive **3.** BIOCHEMISTRY organic carbon **4.** STAMPS original cover

**Oc.** GEOGRAPHY Ocean

**o.c.** in the work or works cited (NOTE: The abbreviation **o.c.**, from the Latin *opus citatum* or *opere citato*, is a less frequent variant of *op. cit.*)

**o/c** FINANCE overcharge

**OCAM** ECONOMICS African and Malagasy Common Organization (NOTE: From the French *Organisation commune africaine et malgache*.)

**occ. 1.** GEOGRAPHY occident **2.** occupation

**OCCAM** /ˈɒkəm/ COMPUTING a computer programming language used in large multiprocessor or multi-user systems

**occas. 1.** occasional **2.** occasionally

**OCD** PSYCHIATRY obsessive-compulsive disorder

**OCE** COMPUTING open collaboration environment

**OCF** FINANCE operating cash flow

**OCR 1.** FINANCE official cash rate **2.** COMPUTING optical character reader **3.** COMPUTING optical character recognition

**OCS** *US* MILITARY Officer Candidate School

**oct.** PRINTING octavo

**Oct.** CALENDAR October

**OD 1.** OPHTHALMOLOGY Doctor of Optometry **2.** MILITARY Officer of the Day **3.** MILITARY greyish-green cloth used for military uniforms, or a uniform made of this cloth. Full form **olive drab 4.** MAPS the sea-level standard adopted by the Ordnance Survey for mapmaking purposes. Full form **ordnance datum 5.** MEDICINE overdose (NOTE: The abbreviation **OD** is used informally as a noun or verb, both in the literal sense of overdosing on a drug and in the figurative sense of overindulgence in anything.) **6.** BANKING overdraft **7.** BANKING overdrawn

**o.d. 1.** BANKING on demand **2.** MEASUREMENTS outside diameter **3.** OPHTHALMOLOGY right eye

**O/D** BANKING **1.** overdraft **2.** overdrawn

**ODA** HEALTH SERVICES operating department assistant

**ODP** ENVIRONMENT ozone-depleting potential

**Oe** MEASUREMENTS, PHYSICS oersted

**OE** LANGUAGE Old English

**OECD** COMMERCE Organization for Economic Cooperation and Development

**OEIC** /ɔɪk/ FINANCE a limited company managing a portfolio of investments for investors with holdings in the form of units representing a fraction of the value of the investments that are issued and bought back by the managers. Full form **open-ended investment company**

**OEM** COMPUTING original equipment manufacturer

**OEO** *US* ECONOMICS Office of Economic Opportunity

**Ofcom** /ˈɒfkɒm/ TV, RADIO an organisation formed in late 2003, regulating independent television and radio communications in the UK. Full form **Office of Communications**

**OFEX** /ˈɒfeks/ STOCK EXCHANGE private trading facilities for buying and selling shares in companies that are not quoted on the London Stock Exchange. Full form **off exchange**

**off. 1.** office **2.** officer **3.** official

**OFFER** /ˈɒfə/ UTILITIES a regulatory body set up to supervise the electricity industry in the United Kingdom after privatization and deregulation. Full form **Office of Electricity Regulation**

**OFGAS** /ˈɒfgæs/ UTILITIES a regulatory body set up to supervise the gas industry in the United Kingdom after privatization and deregulation. Full form **Office of Gas Supply**

**OFM** CHRISTIANITY Order of Minor Friars (NOTE: The abbreviation **OFM**, from the Latin *Ordo Fratrum Minorum*, is used by Franciscan friars.)

**OFSTED** /ˈɒfsted/ EDUCATION the government department that monitors educational standards in schools and colleges in England and Wales. Full form **Office for Standards in Education**

**OFT** COMMERCE Office of Fair Trading

**OFTEL** /'ɒftel/ TELECOMMUNICATIONS a regulatory body set up to supervise the telecommunications industry in the United Kingdom after privatization and deregulation. Full form **Office of Telecommunications**

**OFWAT** /'ɒfwɒt/ UTILITIES a regulatory body set up to supervise water services in the United Kingdom after privatization and deregulation. Full form **Office of Water Services**

**OG 1.** MILITARY Officer of the Guard **2.** STAMPS original gum

**o.g. 1.** STAMPS original gum **2.** SPORTS own goal

**OGD** MEDICINE oesophagogastroduodenoscopy

**O grade** EDUCATION a former lower-level examination for the Scottish Certificate of Education, now replaced by Standard grade. Full form **Ordinary grade**

**OH 1.** HEALTH SERVICES occupational health **2.** MAIL Ohio (NOTE: The abbreviation **OH** is part of the US sorting code on the last line of an Ohio address.)

**OHG** LANGUAGE Old High German

**OHMS** On Her (or His) Majesty's Service

**OHP** overhead projector

**OHV 1.** VEHICLES off-highway vehicle **2.** MECHANICAL ENGINEERING overhead valve

**OI** BUSINESS operating income

**OIC** ONLINE oh, I see (*used in e-mails and text messages*)

**OINK** /ɔɪŋk/ SOCIAL SCIENCES ◊ see note at **dinky**

**OIRO** COMMERCE offers in the region of

> The abbreviation **OIRO** is used in classified advertisements, followed by a guide price. It is one of several standard abbreviations used by estate agents: others include *ch* ('central heating'), *dbl bed* ('double bedroom'), *d/g* ('double-glazing'), *f/h* ('freehold'), *l/h* ('leasehold'), *p/b* ('purpose-built') and *OSP* ('off-street parking').

**OJ** BEVERAGES orange juice

**OJT** HUMAN RESOURCES on-the-job training

**OK 1.** all right (NOTE: The abbreviation **OK** is part of the US sorting code on the last line of an Oklahoma address.) **2.** MAIL Oklahoma

> The abbreviation **OK** (often 'spelt out' as *okay*) is of uncertain origin. It may be short for *orl korrect*, a facetious misspelling of 'all correct', or *Old Kinderhook*, a nickname of Martin Van Buren, 8th president of the United States (1837–41), who was born in Kinderhook, New York State. The abbreviation is used as an adjective (*Is that OK with you?*), an adverb (*if everything goes OK*), a noun (*until they give us the OK*), a verb (*I'll OK it with my boss*), and an interjection indicating agreement or approval.

**OLE** COMPUTING object linking and embedding

**O level** EDUCATION a former examination primarily for 16-year-olds in England and Wales that was replaced (along with the Certificate of Secondary Education) by the General Certificate of Secondary Education (GCSE). It was the lower of two levels of the General Certificate of Education (GCE), the other being Advanced level (A level). Full form **Ordinary level** (NOTE: The abbreviation **O level** is used as a noun to denote both the level (*studying Latin at O level*) and the qualification (*candidates with five or more O levels*).)

**OLS** BUSINESS ordinary least squares

**om** ONLINE Oman (NOTE: The abbreviation **om** is seen at the end of Internet addresses, preceded by a dot.)

**OM** MILITARY Order of Merit

**OMB** BUSINESS Office of Management and Budget

**OMLX** FINANCE London Securities and Derivatives Exchange

**OMOV** /'əʊmɒv/ POLITICS one member one vote

**OMR** COMPUTING **1.** optical mark reader **2.** optical mark recognition

**ON 1.** LANGUAGE Old Norse **2.** GEOGRAPHY Ontario

**ONI** NAVY Office of Naval Intelligence

**o.n.o.** COMMERCE or near(est) offer (NOTE: The abbreviation **o.n.o.** is used in classified advertisements following a guide price.)

**ONS** STATISTICS Office for National Statistics

**Ont.** GEOGRAPHY Ontario

**o.o.** COMMERCE on order

**OOD** NAVY officer of the deck

**OOG** COMPUTING graphics images present in a computer as actual instructions to draw objects and not as bit maps. Full form **object-oriented graphics**

**OOP** COMPUTING a form of computer programming based on objects arranged in a branching hierarchy. Full form **object-oriented programming**

**OOTB** ONLINE (*used in e-mails and text messages*) **1.** out of the blue **2.** out of the box

**OP 1.** MILITARY observation post **2.** CHRISTIANITY Order of Preachers (NOTE: The abbreviation **OP** is used by Dominican friars.) **3.** CHEMISTRY organophosphate **4.** PUBLISHING out of print **5.** MEDICINE outpatient

**op. 1.** MUSIC opera **2.** operation (NOTE: When *op* is used informally as a noun in this sense (especially with reference to a surgical operation), it is written without a full stop.) **3.** opposite **4.** OPTICS optical **5.** a creative piece of work, especially in music or literature. Full form **opus**

**Op.** MUSIC Opus (NOTE: The abbreviation **Op.**, followed by a number, is used to identify one of series of works by the same composer arranged to show the order in which they were written or catalogued.)

**O/P** COMPUTING output

**OPA** BUSINESS offre publique d'achat (NOTE: From the French, 'public offer to buy'.)

**OPAP** WINE Appellation of Origin of Superior Quality

**op art** /ˈɒp ɑːt/ ART a 20th-century school of abstract art using geometric patterns and colour to create the illusion of movement. Full form **optical art**

**OPB** PENSIONS Occupational Pensions Board

**op. cit.** in the work or works quoted (NOTE: The abbreviation **op.cit.**, from the Latin *opus citatum* or *opere citato*, is used in textual references to a source already mentioned.)

**OPE** WINE Controlled Appellation of Origin

**OPEC** /ˈəʊpek/ INDUSTRY an organization of oil-producing countries that share the same policies regarding the sale of petroleum. Full form **Organization of Petroleum Exporting Countries** (NOTE: The acronym **OPEC** is used as a noun in its own right.)

**ophthal.** MEDICINE **1.** ophthalmologist **2.** ophthalmology

**ophthalmol.** MEDICINE **1.** ophthalmologist **2.** ophthalmology

**OPM** FINANCE other people's money

**OPP** oriented polypropylene (NOTE: *OPP film* is a plastic film used for packaging.)

**opp.** opposite

**op shop** /ˈɒp ʃɒp/ ANZ COMMERCE a charity shop selling second-hand goods donated by members of the public. Full form **opportunity shop**

**OPT** MANUFACTURING optimized production technology

**opt. 1.** GRAMMAR optative **2.** optical **3.** OPHTHALMOLOGY optician **4.** optics **5.** optimum **6.** optional

**OR 1.** /ɔː/ LAW own recognizance **2.** FINANCE an official appointed to manage a bankrupt's property prior to the appointment of a trustee. Full form **Official Receiver 3.** MEDICINE the US name for an operating theatre. Full form **operating room 4.** BUSINESS analysis of the problems that exist in complex systems such as those used to run a business or a military campaign, designed to give a scientific basis for decision-making. Full form **operations (or operational) research 5.** MAIL Oregon (NOTE: The abbreviation **OR** is part of the US sorting code on the last line of an Oregon address.) **6.** MILITARY other ranks **7.** INSURANCE owner's risk

**ORB** COMPUTING object request broker

**orch.** MUSIC **1.** orchestra **2.** orchestrated by

**ord. 1.** order **2.** ordinal **3.** ordinance **4.** ordinary **5.** MILITARY ordnance

**ordn.** MILITARY ordnance

**org** /ɔːg/ ONLINE noncommercial organization (NOTE: The abbreviation **org** is seen at the end of Internet addresses, preceded by a dot.)

**org. 1.** organic **2.** organization **3.** organized

**orig. 1.** origin **2.** original **3.** originally

**ornith.** BIRDS **1.** ornithological **2.** ornithology

**OROM** /ˈəʊ rɒm/ COMPUTING optical read-only memory

**ORT** MEDICINE oral rehydration therapy

**orth.** MEDICINE **1.** orthopaedic **2.** orthopaedics

**ORV** VEHICLES off-road vehicle

**Os** CHEMICAL ELEMENTS osmium

**OS 1.** OPHTHALMOLOGY left eye (NOTE: From the Latin *oculus sinister.*) **2.** LAW old series **3.** CALENDAR Old Style (NOTE: The abbreviation **OS** is seen after a date reckoned according to the Julian calendar, especially one falling before or around the time of the changeover to the Gregorian calendar.) **4.** COMPUTING operating system **5.** MILITARY Ordinary Seaman **6.** MAPS Ordnance Survey **7.** COMMERCE out of stock **8.** CLOTHING outsize **9.** BANKING outstanding

**o.s. 1.** LAW old series **2.** COMMERCE out of stock **3.** BANKING outstanding

**O/S** COMMERCE out of stock

**OSA 1.** MEDICINE cessation or restriction of breathing during sleep that results in loud snoring. Full form **obstructive sleep apnoea 2.** CHRISTIANITY Order of Saint Augustine

**OSB** CHRISTIANITY Order of Saint Benedict

**OSCE** POLITICS Organization for Security and Cooperation in Europe

**OSD** CHRISTIANITY Order of Saint Dominic

**OSF 1.** COMPUTING Open Software Foundation **2.** CHRISTIANITY Order of Saint Francis

**OSI** COMPUTING open systems interconnection

**OSPF** COMPUTING open shortest path first

**OSU** CHRISTIANITY Order of Saint Ursula

**OT 1.** HEALTH SERVICES occupational therapist **2.** HEALTH SERVICES occupational therapy **3.** BIBLE Old Testament **4.** HUMAN RESOURCES overtime

**OTC 1.** MILITARY Officers' Training Corps **2.** STOCK EXCHANGE, PHARMACOLOGY over-the-counter

**OTE** HUMAN RESOURCES on-target earnings (NOTE: The abbreviation **OTE** is used in advertisements for jobs that pay commission.)

**OTEC** /ˈəʊtek/ METEOROLOGY Ocean Thermal Energy Conversion

**OTL** ONLINE out to lunch (*used in e-mails and text messages*)

**OTO** BUSINESS one time only

**OTOH** ONLINE on the other hand (*used in e-mails and text messages*)

**otol.** MEDICINE otology

**OTP** E-COMMERCE open trading protocol

**OTS 1.** MILITARY Officers' Training School **2.** MARKETING opportunities to see

**OTT** ridiculously or outrageously exaggerated or excessive ○? Full form **over the top** (NOTE: The abbreviation **OTT** is used as an adjective in its own right.)

**OU** EDUCATION Open University

**OV** COMPUTING overflow

**OWTTE** ONLINE or words to that effect (*used in e-mails and text messages*)

**Oxon. 1.** EDUCATION of (the University of) Oxford (NOTE: The abbreviation **Oxon.**, from the Latin *Oxoniensis*, is used after titles of academic awards.) **2.** GEOGRAPHY Oxfordshire

**oz 1.** ONLINE Australia (NOTE: The abbreviation **oz** is seen at the end of Internet addresses, preceded by a dot.) **2.** MEASUREMENTS ounce

# P

**p 1.** PUBLISHING page **2.** part **3.** GRAMMAR participle **4.** GRAMMAR past **5.** MONEY pence **6.** MONEY penny **7.** per **8.** MUSIC piano (NOTE: The abbreviation **p**, usually italicized, is used on sheet music at a passage that is to be played or sung softly.) **9.** MEASUREMENTS pico- **10.** MEASUREMENTS pint **11.** pipe **12.** population **13.** HANDICRAFT purl (NOTE: The abbreviation **p** is used in knitting patterns as an instruction to make a purl stitch as opposed to a knit stitch (k).)

**P 1.** PHYSICS parity **2.** AUTOMOTIVE park (NOTE: The abbreviation **P** is used on the gear selector of a motor vehicle with automatic transmission.) **3.** CHRISTIANITY Pastor **4.** MONEY pataca **5.** CHESS pawn **6.** MONEY the former unit of currency in Spain and Andorra, replaced by the euro in 2002. Symbol for **peseta 7.** MONEY peso **8.** MEASUREMENTS peta- **9.** CHEMICAL ELEMENTS phosphorus **10.** SPORTS played **11.** PHYSICS power **12.** President **13.** PHYSICS pressure **14.** CHRISTIANITY Priest **15.** Prince **16.** MONEY pula

**P2P** ONLINE **1.** used to describe payments or linkups made between two individuals via the Internet. Full form **peer-to-peer 2.** used to describe software enabling commercial or private users of the Internet to communicate or share resources without the use of intermediaries such as servers. Full form **person-to-person**

**pa** ONLINE Panama (NOTE: The abbreviation **pa** is seen at the end of Internet addresses, preceded by a dot.)

**Pa 1.** PHYSICS pascal **2.** CHEMICAL ELEMENTS protactinium

**PA 1.** INSURANCE insurance for goods being shipped against partial damage or loss, usually that caused by the shipping process itself. Full form **particular average 2.** MAIL Pennsylvania (NOTE: The abbreviation **PA** is part of the US sorting code on the last line of a Pennsylvania address.) **3.** BANKING personal account **4.** personal appearance **5.** BUSINESS personal assistant (NOTE: The abbreviation **PA** is used as a noun in its own right in this sense.) **6.** US HEALTH SERVICES physician's assistant **7.** MILITARY Post Adjutant **8.** LAW power of attorney **9.** COMMUNICATION press agent **10.** PRESS Press Association **11.** US LAW prosecuting attorney **12.** an electronic amplification system used to increase the sound level of speech or music in a large or open space such as a stadium or auditorium ○ *An announcement was made over the PA.* Full form **public-address (system)** (NOTE: The abbreviation **PA** is used as a noun in its own right in this sense.)

**p.a.** FINANCE per annum

**P/A** LAW power of attorney

**PABA** /ˈpæbə/ BIOCHEMISTRY a form of aminobenzoic acid, part of the B vitamin complex, that is used in sunscreen lotions. Full form **para-aminobenzoic acid**

**PABX** TELECOMMUNICATIONS private automatic branch exchange

**PACE** LAW Police and Criminal Evidence Act

**PACT** MEDICINE prescribing analyses and cost

**PAD** COMPUTING packet assembler/disassembler

**PAH** CHEMISTRY a toxic pollutant caused by industrial processes such as burning waste, thought to be carcinogenic in humans. Full form **polycyclic aromatic hydrocarbon**

**PAL** /pæl/ TV the system used for broadcasting television programmes in the United Kingdom and many other European countries. Full form **phase alternation line**

**PAN 1.** POLITICS the main political party in opposition in Mexico. Full form **Partido Acción Nacional** (NOTE: From the Spanish, 'National Action Party'.) **2.** CHEMISTRY a toxic, irritating compound which can cause widespread damage to vegetation at very low concentrations. Full form **peroxyacetyl nitrate** **3.** E-COMMERCE primary account number

**p & h** *Aus, US* MAIL postage and handling

**P & L** ACCOUNTING profit and loss

**p & p** MAIL postage and packing

**PANSE** MANAGEMENT an Internet-based Mp3 streaming audio program open to all users for the development of experimental audiovisual art. Full form **Public Access Network Sound Engine**

**PAR** FINANCE a requirement that a bank most hold a percentage of the value of its total liabilities in specified high-security investments. Full form **prime assets ratio**

**par. 1.** paragraph **2.** parallel **3.** parenthesis **4.** parish

**Par.** GEOGRAPHY Paraguay

**Parl.** GOVERNMENT **1.** Parliament **2.** parliamentary

**PASCAL** /'pæskæl/ COMPUTING a high-level general-purpose programming language designed to encourage structured programming. Full form **Programme Appliqué à la Sélection et la Compilation Automatique de la Littérature** (NOTE: The **PASCAL** language, from the French, 'program applied to the selection and compilation of literature', is partly named in honour of the 17th-century French mathematician Blaise Pascal.)

**pat. 1.** patent **2.** patented

**patd** patented

**Pat. Off.** GOVERNMENT Patent Office

**pat. pend.** patent pending

**PAU** INTERNATIONAL RELATIONS Pan American Union

**PAX** TELECOMMUNICATIONS private automatic exchange

**PAYE** FINANCE a system in which income tax is deducted from salary or wages as they are earned and paid directly to the government by the employer. Full form **pay-as-you-earn**

**PAYG** FINANCE the Australian equivalent of PAYE (pay-as-you-earn). Full form **pay-as-you-go**

**Pb** CHEMICAL ELEMENTS lead (NOTE: From the Latin *plumbum*.)

**PB 1.** SPORTS personal best **2.** COMPUTING petabyte **3.** AUTOMOTIVE power brakes **4.** CHRISTIANITY prayer book

**p/b** CONSTRUCTION purpose-built

**PBB** CHEMISTRY an organic compound generally used as a fire retardant. Full form **polybrominated biphenyl** (NOTE: A quantity of **PBBs** entered the food chain accidentally in Michigan in1973, causing organ damage and weakened appetite and disease resistance in livestock and humans.)

**PBR** BUSINESS payment by results

**PBX** TELECOMMUNICATIONS private branch exchange

**PC 1.** POLITICS Parish Council **2.** POLITICS Parish Councillor **3.** MILITARY Past Commander **4.** COMPUTING personal computer (NOTE: The abbreviation **PC** is used as a noun in its own right in this sense.) **5.** POLICE Police Constable **6.** politically correct (NOTE: The abbreviation **PC** is used as an adjective in its own right in this sense.) **7.** MILITARY Post Commander **8.** Prince Consort **9.** ELECTRONICS printed circuit **10.** POLITICS Privy Council **11.** POLITICS Privy Councillor **12.** COMPUTING program counter **13.** *Can* POLITICS Progressive Conservative

**p.c. 1.** PHARMACOLOGY after meals (NOTE: The abbreviation **p.c.**, from the Latin *post cibum* 'after food', is used in prescriptions.) **2.** per cent **3.** BUSINESS petty cash **4.** FINANCE price current

**P/C 1.** BUSINESS petty cash **2.** photocopy

**PCB 1.** BUSINESS petty cash book **2.** CHEMISTRY a compound derived from biphenyl and containing chlorine that is a hazardous pollutant. Full form **polychlorinated biphenyl** **3.** ELECTRONICS printed circuit board

**PCC** MEDICINE Professional Conduct Committee

**PC-DOS** /ˌpiː siː ˈdɒs/ COMPUTING Personal Computer Disk Operating System

**PCG** HEALTH SERVICES primary care group

**PCI** COMPUTING a specification for extending the internal circuitry that transmits data from one part of a computer to another by inserting circuit boards. Full form **peripheral component interconnect**

**PCL** COMPUTING printer control language

**pcm** per calendar month

**PCM** TELECOMMUNICATIONS a way of transmitting information using a series of electrical pulses, the duration, amplitude or frequency of the pulses being modified to carry the information. Full form **pulse code modulation**

**PCMCIA** COMPUTING **1.** a specification for extending the internal circuitry that transmits data from one part of a computer to another, used to add memory or connect credit-card-sized peripheral devices. Full form **personal computer memory card interface adapter 2.** an international organization that has developed a standard for adding memory to personal computers using credit-card-sized devices. Full form **Personal Computer Memory Card International Association**

**PCOD** MEDICINE polycystic ovary disease

**PCOS** MEDICINE polycystic ovary (or ovarian) syndrome

**PCP 1.** DRUGS a drug used as an anaesthetic in veterinary medicine and illegally as a hallucinogen (with the slang name 'angel dust'). Full form **phencyclidine** (NOTE: The full name of the drug is made up of the elements pheno-, cyclo-, and piperidine, hence the abbreviation.) **2.** MEDICINE a form of pneumonia that mainly affects people with weakened immune systems. Full form *Pneumocystis carinii* **pneumonia 3.** POLITICS a Canadian federal and provincial political party. Full form **Progressive Conservative Party**

**PCR** BIOTECHNOLOGY a technique used to replicate a fragment of DNA and produce a large amount of that sequence. Full form **polymerase chain reaction**

**PCS** COMPUTING personal communications services

**PCT** HEALTH SERVICES primary care trust

**PC/TV** COMPUTING a personal computer that can receive, decode and display standard television images

**PCU** COMPUTING peripheral control unit

**PCV** TRANSPORT passenger-carrying vehicle

**pd** paid

**Pd** CHEMICAL ELEMENTS palladium

**PD 1.** BUSINESS activities associated with the efficient moving of goods from the supplier to the consumer. Full form **physical distribution 2.** *US* POLICE police department **3.** MAIL postal district **4.** COMPUTING the condition of not being protected by patent or copyright and therefore freely available for use. Full form **public domain**

**p.d. 1.** per diem (NOTE: From the Latin, 'per day'.) **2.** PHYSICS potential difference

**P-D** STOCK EXCHANGE price-dividend (ratio)

**PDA 1.** COMPUTING a small hand-held computer with a built-in notebook, diary, and fax capability, usually operated using a stylus rather than a keyboard. Full form **personal digital assistant 2.** ONLINE public display of affection (*used in e-mails and text messages*)

**PDF** COMPUTING a format for a computer file that enables a document to be processed and printed on any computer using any printer or word-processing software. Full form **portable document format**

**PDL** COMPUTING **1.** page description language **2.** program design language

**PDN** COMPUTING public data network

**pdq** pretty damn quick (NOTE: The abbreviation **pdq** is used in informal language in place of 'at once' or 'immediately'.)

**PDR** STOCK EXCHANGE price-dividend ratio

**PDSA** VETERINARY MEDICINE People's Dispensary for Sick Animals

**PDT** TIME Pacific Daylight Time

**pe** ONLINE Peru (NOTE: The abbreviation **pe** is seen at the end of Internet addresses, preceded by a dot.)

**PE 1.** EDUCATION gymnastics, athletics, team sports, and other forms of physical exercise taught to children at school ○ *PE teacher* Full form **physical education** (NOTE: The abbreviation **PE** is used as a noun in its own right.) **2.** PHYSICS potential energy **3.** CALENDAR Present Era (NOTE: The abbreviation **PE** is sometimes used after a date as a non-Christian alternative for AD.) **4.** GEOGRAPHY Prince Edward Island **5.** STATISTICS probable error **6.** CHRISTIANITY Protestant Episcopal

**p.e.** PRINTING printer's error

**P/E** FINANCE price/earnings (NOTE: The abbreviation **P/E** is seen in phrases such as *P/E ratio* and *P/E multiple*.)

**PEEP** MEDICINE the insertion of a valve into the respiratory system to ensure that the lungs do not completely empty on expiration, to improve the absorption of oxygen into the blood. Full form **positive end-expiratory pressure**

**PEFR** MEDICINE a measure of expiration function used to diagnose whether there are any airway or lung obstructions or disease. Full form **peak expiratory flow rate**

**PEI** GEOGRAPHY Prince Edward Island

**pel** COMPUTING picture element (NOTE: The abbreviation **pel** has been almost entirely superseded by the variation 'pixel'.)

**PEN** /pen/ LITERATURE International Association of Poets, Playwrights, Editors, Essayists, and Novelists

**Pen.** GEOGRAPHY Peninsula

**PEP** /pep/ FINANCE a tax-free investment plan that allows small investors to own shares in UK companies. Full form **Personal Equity Plan**

**PER** STOCK EXCHANGE price-earnings ratio

**perf. 1.** GRAMMAR perfect **2.** STAMPS perforated **3.** performance

**PERLA** MEDICINE a measure of the eye's reaction to stimulus, used in assessing the conscious state of the person examined. Full form **pupils equal, react to light and accommodation**

**per pro** /pə ˈprəʊ/ BUSINESS a fuller form of the abbreviation *pp.* Full form **per procurationem**

**PERT** /pɜːt/ MANAGEMENT a method of charting and scheduling a complex set of interrelated activities that identifies the most time-critical events in the process. Full form **programme evaluation and review technique**

**PESA** MEDICINE a technique used in assisted conception, in which sperm for intracytoplasmic sperm injection (ICSI) are removed directly from the epididimis. Full form **percutaneous epididymal sperm aspiration**

**PESC** BUSINESS Public Expenditure Survey Committee

**PET** /pet/ **1.** CHEMISTRY a fully-recyclable plastic resin used in making food and drinks containers. Full form **polyethylene terephthalate 2.** MEDICINE a method of medical imaging capable of displaying the metabolic activity of organs in the body, and useful in diagnosing cancer, locating brain tumours, and investigating other brain disorders ○ *PET scan* Full form **positron emission tomography**

**Pet.** BIBLE Peter

**petrol.** GEOLOGY petrology

**pf** ONLINE French Polynesia (NOTE: The abbreviation **pf** is seen at the end of Internet addresses, preceded by a dot.)

**pF** MEASUREMENTS, ELECTRICITY picofarad

**pf. 1.** preferred **2.** GRAMMAR perfect **3.** MONEY a coin formerly used in Germany, worth one hundredth of a Deutschmark (replaced by the euro in 2002). Full form **pfennig**

**PFBC** INDUSTRY an advanced type of FBC that automatically feeds the coal into the combustion system and uses the steam produced to drive gas turbines. Full form **pressurized fluidized-bed combustion**

**PFC** CHEMISTRY a potent greenhouse gas produced by industrial processes such as the manufacture of aluminium. Full form **perfluorocarbon**

**PFD 1.** NAUTICAL the US term for a life jacket. Full form **personal flotation device 2.** *US* STOCK EXCHANGE preferred (NOTE: *Preferred stock* is the US term for *preference shares*, i.e. shares whose holders are the first to receive dividends from available profit.)

**PFI** FINANCE Private Finance Initiative

**pg** ONLINE Papua New Guinea (NOTE: The abbreviation **pg** is seen at the end of Internet addresses, preceded by a dot.)

**PG 1.** CINEMA a rating indicating that a film may be inappropriate for children and that parents should exercise caution. Full form **parental guidance 2.** paying guest **3.** EDUCATION postgraduate

**Pg.** LANGUAGE Portuguese

**PGA** GOLF Professional Golfers' Association

**PGCA** E-COMMERCE payment gateway certificate authority

**PGCE** EDUCATION a teaching qualification taken by somebody who has already graduated from a university or college with a first degree. Full form **Postgraduate Certificate of Education**

**PgDn** COMPUTING page down (key)

**PGEA** MEDICINE formerly, an allowance given to general practitioners attending educational courses, intended to cover expenses involved in this. Full form **postgraduate education allowance**

**PGP** E-COMMERCE a program used to encrypt data for security purposes when transmitting over public networks such as the Internet. PGP uses public key encryption, a system that provides privacy for and authentication of both the sender and the receiver of the message. Full form **Pretty Good Privacy**

**PgUp** COMPUTING page up (key)

**PGx** PHARMACOLOGY pharmacogenetics

**ph** ONLINE Philippines (NOTE: The abbreviation **ph** is seen at the end of Internet addresses, preceded by a dot.)

**pH** CHEMISTRY a measure of acidity or alkalinity in which the pH of pure water is 7, with lower numbers indicating acidity and higher numbers indicating alkalinity. Full form **potential of hydrogen**

**Ph** CHEMISTRY phenyl group

**PH** PUBLIC ADMINISTRATION public health

**pharm. 1.** pharmaceutical **2.** pharmacist **3.** pharmacy

**Pharm.** Pharmacopoeia

**PhB** EDUCATION Bachelor of Philosophy (NOTE: From the Latin *Philosophiae Baccalaureus*.)

**PhD** EDUCATION Doctor of Philosophy (NOTE: From the Latin *Philosophiae Doctor*.)

**PHI** /faɪ/ INSURANCE permanent health insurance

**PHIGS** /fɪgz/ COMPUTING programmers' hierarchical interactive graphics standard

**phil. 1.** philological **2.** philology **3.** philosopher **4.** philosophical **5.** philosophy

**Phil. 1.** MUSIC Philharmonic **2.** BIBLE Philippians **3.** GEOGRAPHY Philippines

**Phil. I.** GEOGRAPHY Philippine Islands

**PHS** *US* HEALTH SERVICES Public Health Service

**PI 1.** performance indicator **2.** CRIME private investigator

**PIA 1.** COMPUTING peripheral interface adapter **2.** FINANCE Personal Investment Authority

**PIB** FINANCE permanent interest-bearing share

**PIBOR** /ˈpaɪbɔː/ BANKING Paris Interbank Offered Rate

**PIBS** FINANCE permanent interest-bearing shares

**PIC 1.** COMPUTING picture **2.** CHEMISTRY product of incomplete combustion

**Pick** /pɪk/ COMPUTING a multi-user, multitasking operating system that runs on mainframe, mini or personal computers

**PICS** /pɪks/ COMPUTING platform for Internet content selection

**PID 1.** MEDICINE pelvic inflammatory disease **2.** COMPUTING personal identification device **3.** MEDICINE prolapsed intervertebral disc

**PIDS** MEDICINE immunodeficiency arising from a congenital fault in the cells rather than caused by a virus. Full form **primary immune deficiency syndrome**

**PIH** MEDICINE pregnancy-induced hypertension

**PILOT** /ˈpaɪlət/ COMPUTING programmed inquiry, learning, or teaching

**PIM** /pɪm/ COMPUTING a piece of software that organizes random notes, contacts, and appointments for fast access. Full form **personal information manager**

**PIN** /pɪn/ FINANCE a multidigit number that is used to gain access to an account at a cashpoint machine and in various other situations. Full form **personal identification number** (NOTE: The acronym **PIN** is used as a noun in its own right. A PIN is sometimes called a *PIN number*, although the word *number* is technically redundant.)

**PIO** COMPUTING parallel input/output

**PIP** MEDICINE proximal interphalangeal (joint) (NOTE: The *PIP joint* is the finger joint nearest the knuckle, in the middle of the finger.)

**PIPO** COMPUTING parallel input/parallel output

**pippie** SOCIAL SCIENCES ◊ see note at **dinky**

**PISO** COMPUTING parallel input/serial output

**PIW** HUMAN RESOURCES period of incapacity for work

**pk 1.** pack **2.** ONLINE Pakistan (NOTE: The abbreviation **pk** is seen at the end of Internet addresses, preceded by a dot.) **3.** park **4.** peak **5.** MEASUREMENTS peck

**PK** PARAPSYCHOLOGY psychokinesis

**PKD** MEDICINE polycystic kidney disease

**PKI** E-COMMERCE a method of encrypting data using one key to encrypt and another to decrypt, using digital certificates issued by certificate authorities. Full form **public key infrastructure**

**pkt** packet

**PKU** MEDICINE a condition, resulting from a genetic mutation, in which the body lacks the enzyme to metabolize phenylalanine. If untreated, it results in developmental deficiency, seizures, and tumours. Full form **phenylketonuria**

**Pky** *Aus, US* ROADS a wide stretch of public highway with grassy areas on both sides, often divided by a grassy central reservation. Full form **parkway**

**pl 1.** GRAMMAR plural **2.** ONLINE Poland (NOTE: The abbreviation **pl** is seen at the end of Internet addresses, preceded by a dot.)

**PL** LAW public law

**Pl.** ROADS Place (NOTE: The abbreviation **Pl.** is used in addresses.)

**PLA 1.** SHIPPING Port of London Authority **2.** COMPUTING programmable logic array

**PLAN** /plæn/ COMPUTING a low-level programming language. Full form **Packet Language for Active Networks**

**plc** COMMERCE a company whose shares can be bought and sold on the stock market and whose shareholders are subject to restricted liability for any debts or losses. Full form **public limited company** (NOTE: The lower-case form **plc** is probably the most frequent, but some companies prefer PLC or Plc.)

**PLC** MARKETING product life cycle

**PLD** COMPUTING programmable logic device

**PLO** POLITICS Palestine Liberation Organization

**PLP** POLITICS Parliamentary Labour Party

**PLR** LIBRARIES a system whereby authors receive a small fee every time their books are borrowed from public libraries in the United Kingdom. Full form **Public Lending Right**

**PLS** ONLINE please (*used in e-mails and text messages*)

**PLSS** MEDICINE portable life-support system

**PLZ** ONLINE please (*used in e-mails and text messages*)

**pm 1.** TELECOMMUNICATIONS phase modulation **2.** MEDICINE postmortem **3.** premium **4.** ONLINE St-Pierre and Miquelon (NOTE: The abbreviation **pm** is seen at the end of Internet addresses, preceded by a dot.)

**Pm** CHEMICAL ELEMENTS promethium

**PM 1.** MEDICINE solid or liquid particles dispersed in the air. Full form **particulate matter 2.** a former holder of the position of master of a fraternity. Full form **Past Master 3.** MAIL postmaster **4.** MEDICINE postmortem **5.** GOVERNMENT Prime Minister **6.** ONLINE private message (*used in e-mails and text messages*) **7.** MILITARY Provost Marshal

**p.m.** TIME in the period between noon and midnight. Full form **post meridiem** (NOTE: The abbreviation **p.m.**, from the Latin, 'after noon', is used after a specific time in the 12-hour clock. It is sometimes written PM or pm.)

**PMA** MEDICINE progressive muscular atrophy

**PME** COMMERCE petites et moyennes entreprises (NOTE: From the French, 'small and medium-sized businesses'.)

**PMG 1.** GOVERNMENT Paymaster General **2.** MAIL Postmaster General **3.** MILITARY Provost Marshal General

**pmol** CHEMISTRY picomole

**PMR** MEDICINE polymyalgia rheumatica

**PMS** MEDICINE premenstrual syndrome

**PMT** MEDICINE premenstrual tension

**PMTS** MANAGEMENT predetermined motion-time system

**pn** ONLINE Pitcairn Island (NOTE: The abbreviation **pn** is seen at the end of Internet addresses, preceded by a dot.)

**PN** FINANCE promissory note

**PNdB** MEASUREMENTS, ACOUSTICS perceived noise decibel

**PNL** ACOUSTICS perceived noise level

**PNS** ANATOMY peripheral nervous system

**Po** CHEMICAL ELEMENTS polonium

**PO 1.** MILITARY Petty Officer **2.** MILITARY Pilot Officer **3.** MAIL post office **4.** FINANCE postal order **5.** BUSINESS purchase order

**p.o.** PHARMACOLOGY by mouth (NOTE: The abbreviation **p.o.**, from the Latin *per os*, is used in prescriptions.)

**POA** HUMAN RESOURCES Prison Officers' Association

**PO Box** /ˌpiː 'əʊ ˌbɒks/ MAIL Post Office Box (NOTE: The abbreviation **PO Box**, followed by a number, is used in addresses, identifying a private numbered box in a post office where letters are held until collected by the addressee.)

**POD** MAIL pay on delivery

**POE 1.** MILITARY port of embarkation **2.** SHIPPING port of entry

**poet. 1.** poetic **2.** poetical **3.** poetry

**POETS day** /ˈpəʊəts deɪ/ an informal name for Friday, referring to shorter hours worked (officially or unofficially) on that day. Full form **push (or piss) off early, tomorrow's Saturday**

**POEU** HUMAN RESOURCES Post Office Engineers Union

**POL 1.** MILITARY petroleum, oil, and lubricants **2.** COMPUTING problem-oriented language

**pol. 1.** political **2.** politics

**POM 1.** ONLINE phase of (the) moon (NOTE: The abbreviation **POM** is used in Internet chatting as a humorous random parameter on which something is supposed to depend, meaning that it is unreliable.) **2.** PHARMACOLOGY prescription-only medicine

**POP 1.** ENVIRONMENT persistent organic pollutant **2.** COMPUTING a location where a user can connect to a network, e.g. a place where subscribers can dial in to an Internet service provider. Full form **point of presence 3.** COMMERCE point of purchase **4.** MAIL Post Office Preferred (NOTE: The abbreviation **POP** refers to the size of envelopes and packages.) **5.** PHARMACOLOGY an oral contraceptive that contains progestogen but not oestrogen, also known as a *minipill*. Full form **progestogen-only pill 6.** COMMERCE proof of purchase

**pop. 1.** popular **2.** population

**POPA** MARKETING point-of-purchase advertising

**POS 1.** ONLINE parents over shoulder (*used in e-mails, text messages and Internet chat rooms*) **2.** COMMERCE point of sale

**POSSLQ** /ˈpɒs(ə)lkjuː/ an informal name for either member of an unmarried cohabiting couple. Full form **person of the opposite sex sharing living quarters**

**POST 1.** COMMERCE point-of-sale terminal **2.** COMPUTING power-on self-test

**Postcomm** /ˈpəʊstkɒm/ MAIL the independent regulatory body for postal services in the United Kingdom. Full form **Postal Services Commission**

**post-obit** LAW coming into effect after somebody's death. Full form **post-obitum** (NOTE: A *post-obit bond*, from the Latin, 'after death', is a bond that pays after the death of somebody from whom the issuer of the bond expects to inherit.)

**POTUS** /ˈpəʊtəs/ US GOVERNMENT President of the United States (NOTE: The acronym **POTUS** is used by White House staff in memos and internal documents to refer to the president.)

**POV** ONLINE point of view (*used in e-mails and text messages*)

**POW** MILITARY prisoner of war (NOTE: The abbreviation **POW** is used as a noun in its own right.)

**pp 1.** pages **2.** GRAMMAR past participle **3.** BUSINESS per procurationem (NOTE: The abbreviation **pp**, usually italicized, is used on sheet music at a passage that is to be played or sung very softly.) **4.** MUSIC pianissimo **5.** PRINTING privately printed

The abbreviation **pp** is used when signing documents on behalf of somebody else. If Anne Smith is signing on behalf of Mary Jones, she should write 'Mary Jones pp Anne Smith', although in practice the names are often reversed.

**PP 1.** MAIL parcel post **2.** CHRISTIANITY parish priest **3.** GOVERNMENT past president **4.** MAIL postpaid **5.** MAIL prepaid **6.** GRAMMAR prepositional phrase

**p.p.** PHARMACOLOGY after a meal (NOTE: The abbreviation **p.p.**, from the Latin *post prandium*, is used in prescriptions.)

**ppb** MEASUREMENTS parts per billion

**PPBS** BUSINESS Planning Programming Budgeting System

**PPD** MEDICINE an antigen that is injected into the arm and the reaction assessed to determine whether a patient has ever had tuberculosis. Full form **purified protein derivative**

**PPH** MEDICINE postpartum haemorrhage

**pphm** MEASUREMENTS parts per hundred million

**ppm** MEASUREMENTS parts per million

**PPP 1.** PENSIONS personal pension plan **2.** ONLINE petty pet peeve (*used in e-mails and text messages*) **3.** ONLINE a protocol for dial-up access to the Internet using a modem. Full form **point-to-point protocol 4.** ENVIRONMENT polluter-pays principle **5.** BUSINESS public-private partnership **6.** FINANCE purchasing-power parity

**pptm** MEASUREMENTS parts per thousand million

**PPU** COMPUTING peripheral processing unit

**PPV 1.** TV pay-per-view **2.** MEDICINE any method of simulating normal breathing patterns in patients with chronic respiratory failure, either manually or using a mechanical ventilator. Full form **positive pressure ventilation**

**pr 1.** pair **2.** ONLINE Puerto Rico (NOTE: The abbreviation **pr** is seen at the end of Internet addresses, preceded by a dot.)

**Pr** CHEMICAL ELEMENTS praseodymium

**PR 1.** POLITICS an electoral system in which each party's share of the seats in government is the same as its share of all the votes cast. Full form **proportional representation 2.** BUSINESS public relations (NOTE: The abbreviation **PR** is used as a noun in its own right.) **3.** GEOGRAPHY Puerto Rico

**pr.** GRAMMAR pronoun

**PRB** ARTS Pre-Raphaelite Brotherhood (NOTE: The abbreviation **PRB** is used after the name of a painter belonging to this group: *WH Hunt PRB*.)

**PRC** GEOGRAPHY People's Republic of China

**pref. 1.** PUBLISHING preface **2.** prefatory **3.** preference **4.** preferred **5.** GRAMMAR prefix

**PREP** MEDICINE post-registration education and practice

**prep. 1.** preparation (NOTE: When *prep* is used informally as a noun in this sense (especially with reference to homework or private study at a boarding school), it is written without a full stop.) **2.** preparatory (NOTE: When *prep* is used informally in the phrase *prep school* (short for *preparatory school*), it is written without a full stop.) **3.** GRAMMAR preposition

**pres. 1.** GRAMMAR present **2.** POLITICS presidential

**Pres.** GOVERNMENT President

**p.r.n.** PHARMACOLOGY as required (NOTE: The abbreviation **p.r.n.**, from the Latin *pro re nata*, is used in prescriptions.)

**pro** ONLINE professional practice (NOTE: The abbreviation **pro** is seen at the end of Internet addresses, preceded by a dot.)

**PRO 1.** Public Record Office **2.** BUSINESS public relations officer

**Prof.** EDUCATION Professor

**PROFS** /prɒfs/ COMPUTING Professional Office System

**prog. 1.** program **2.** programme **3.** progress **4.** progressive

**Prog.** POLITICS Progressive

**Prolog** /ˈprəʊlɒg/ COMPUTING a high-level programming language based on logical rather than mathematical relationships. Full form **programming logic**

**PROM** /prɒm/ COMPUTING programmable read-only memory

**prom.** GEOGRAPHY promontory

**pron.** **1.** GRAMMAR pronominal **2.** GRAMMAR pronoun **3.** PHONETICS pronounced **4.** PHONETICS pronunciation

**prop.** **1.** GRAMMAR proper **2.** properly **3.** property (NOTE: When *prop* is used informally as a noun in this sense (especially with reference to an object used during the performance of a play or film), it is written without a full stop.) **4.** proposition **5.** COMMERCE proprietor

**propr.** COMMERCE proprietor

**pros.** LITERATURE prosody

**Pros. Atty** *US* LAW prosecuting attorney

**Prot.** **1.** Protectorate **2.** CHRISTIANITY Protestant

**prov.** **1.** GEOGRAPHY province **2.** provincial **3.** provisional

**Prov.** **1.** LANGUAGE Provençal **2.** BIBLE Proverbs **3.** Provost

**prox.** BUSINESS occurring during the next month. Full form **proximo**

**PRP** FINANCE **1.** performance-related pay **2.** profit-related pay

**prs** pairs

**PRT** FINANCE petroleum revenue tax

**pS** MEASUREMENTS, TIME picosecond

**PS** **1.** BOAT passenger steamer **2.** GOVERNMENT Permanent Secretary **3.** GRAMMAR phrase structure **4.** POLICE Police Sergeant **5.** postscript (NOTE: The abbreviation **PS** precedes extra information or a short message added after the signature on a letter.) **6.** private secretary **7.** THEATRE prompt side

**Ps.** BIBLE Psalms

**PSA** **1.** BIOCHEMISTRY an enzyme produced by prostate cells. Elevated levels of PSA in the blood are associated with prostate cancer. ○ *PSA test* Full form **prostate specific antigen 2.** *Aus, NZ* GOVERNMENT Public Service Association

**Psa.** BIBLE Psalms

**PSBR** ECONOMICS the amount that the government needs to borrow in any fiscal year in order to be able to meet its budgeted costs. Full form **public-sector borrowing requirement**

**PSDR** ECONOMICS public-sector debt repayment

**PSE** EDUCATION the study of social (especially health-related) issues as a school subject. Full form **personal and social education**

**pseud.** pseudonym

**psf** MEASUREMENTS pounds per square foot

**PSFD** ECONOMICS public-sector financial deficit

**Psge** ROADS Passage (NOTE: The abbreviation **Psge** is used in addresses.)

**PSHE** EDUCATION the study of social (especially health-related) issues as a school subject. Full form **personal, social, and health education**

**psi** MEASUREMENTS pounds per square inch

**psia** MEASUREMENTS pounds per square inch, absolute

**psid** MEASUREMENTS pounds per square inch, differential

**psig** MEASUREMENTS pounds per square inch, gauge

**PSL** ECONOMICS private sector liquidity

**PSN** COMPUTING packet switched network

**PSNCR** ECONOMICS public-sector net cash requirement

**PSNI** Police Service of Northern Ireland

**PSS** COMPUTING **1.** packet switching service **2.** packet switching system

**PST** **1.** TIME Pacific Standard Time **2.** *Can* FINANCE provincial sales tax

**PSTN** TELECOMMUNICATIONS public switched telephone network

**PSU** ELECTRICITY power supply unit

**PSV** TRANSPORT public service vehicle

**PSW** COMPUTING processor status word

**psych. 1.** psychological **2.** psychology

**psychoanal.** psychoanalysis

**psychol. 1.** psychological **2.** psychologist **3.** psychology

**pt 1.** part **2.** MEDICINE patient **3.** FINANCE payment **4.** MEASUREMENTS pint **5.** point **6.** port **7.** ONLINE Portugal (NOTE: The abbreviation **pt** is seen at the end of Internet addresses, preceded by a dot.)

**Pt 1.** CHEMICAL ELEMENTS platinum **2.** GEOGRAPHY Point (NOTE: The abbreviation **Pt** is used in placenames.) **3.** GEOGRAPHY Port (NOTE: The abbreviation **Pt** is used in placenames.)

**PT 1.** TIME Pacific Time **2.** the US name for physiotherapy. Full form **physical therapy 3.** SPORTS physical training (NOTE: The abbreviation **PT** is used as a noun in its own right.) **4.** TELECOMMUNICATIONS postal telegraph

**pt.** GRAMMAR preterite

**p.t. 1.** HUMAN RESOURCES part-time **2.** GRAMMAR past tense **3.** at the present time but not permanently. Full form **pro tem(pore)**

**pta** MONEY the former unit of currency in Spain and Andorra, replaced by the euro in 2002. Symbol for **peseta**

**PTA 1.** EDUCATION Parent-Teacher Association **2.** TRANSPORT Passenger Transport Authority

**PTB** ONLINE powers that be (*used in e-mails and text messages*)

**PTC** CHEMISTRY a crystalline compound that tastes extremely bitter to people who possess a particular dominant gene, used in testing for that gene. Full form **phenylthiocarbamide**

**Pte 1.** BUSINESS private limited company **2.** MILITARY Private

**PTE** TRANSPORT Passenger Transport Executive

**PTFE** CHEMISTRY a durable substance widely used to coat metal surfaces, especially in the manufacture of nonstick cooking utensils. Full form **polytetrafluoroethylene**

**ptg** printing

**PTH** BIOCHEMISTRY a hormone secreted by the parathyroid glands that controls calcium and phosphorus balance in the body. Full form **parathyroid hormone**

**PTN** TELECOMMUNICATIONS public telephone network

**PTO 1.** *US* Patent and Trademark Office **2.** please turn over (NOTE: The abbreviation **PTO** is written at the bottom of a page to indicate that the text continues overleaf.)

**PTR** COMPUTING paper tape reader

**pts 1.** parts **2.** FINANCE payments **3.** points **4.** ports

**PTSD** PSYCHOLOGY post-traumatic stress disorder

**PTV** TV pay television

**Pty** BUSINESS a company that is privately owned and run. Full form **proprietary company** (NOTE: The abbreviation *Pty Ltd* is used to indicate a private limited company.)

**Pu** CHEMICAL ELEMENTS plutonium

**pub** public house

> The word *pub*, written without a full stop, is short for 'public house', denoting a building where alcoholic (and other) drinks can be bought and consumed. Shortenings such as this are not generally classed as abbreviations. Many have entered the language as nouns in their own right, replacing full forms that now sound old-fashioned (e.g. *bra* 'brassiere', *bus* 'omnibus', *cello* 'violoncello', *fax* 'facsimile', *mac* 'mackintosh', *piano* 'pianoforte', *pram* 'perambulator', *zoo* 'zoological garden'). Sometimes the full form remains in use in formal contexts, but the short form is found in standard speech and writing (e.g. *amp* 'ampere', *disco* 'discotheque', *exam* 'examination', *flu* 'influenza', *fridge* 'refrigerator', *gym* 'gymnasium', *lab* 'laboratory',

*memo* 'memorandum', *phone* 'telephone', *photo* 'photograph', *plane* 'aeroplane', *quad* 'quadruplet', *vet* 'veterinary surgeon'). In other cases, the shortening is restricted to informal usage (e.g. *ad* 'advertisement', *deli* 'delicatessen', *demo* 'demonstration', *hippo* 'hippopotamus', *info* 'information', *limo* 'limousine', *marg* 'margarine', *panto* 'pantomime', *rhino* 'rhinoceros', *specs* 'spectacles', *telly* 'television'). Note that the spelling of the short form is sometimes adjusted to match the sound (e.g. *fax*, *fridge*, *pram*, *telly*). Where the first part of the word is dropped (as in *bus*, *flu*, *phone*, and *plane*), some people mark the omission with an apostrophe, but this is not necessary.

**pub. 1.** public **2.** publication **3.** published **4.** publisher **5.** publishing

**publ. 1.** publication **2.** published **3.** publisher

**PUC** *S Asia* EDUCATION preuniversity college

**putts** WINE a measure of the richness of Hungarian wines, defined by the number of puttonyos (basketfuls of sweet intense grapes) that went into its making. Full form **puttonyos**

**PV 1.** ELECTRICITY photovoltaic **2.** BUSINESS present value

**PVA** CHEMISTRY a colourless resin used in adhesives and paints. Full form **polyvinyl acetate**

**PVC** INDUSTRY a hard-wearing synthetic resin made by polymerizing vinyl chloride and used in clothing, flooring, and piping. Full form **polyvinyl chloride**

**PVS** MEDICINE **1.** a medical condition in which a patient has severe brain damage and as a result is unable to stay alive without the aid of a life-support system, showing no response to stimuli. Full form **persistent vegetative state 2.** an illness without a known cause that is characterized by long-term exhaustion, muscle weakness, depression, and sleep disturbances. Also known as myalgic encephalomyelitis (ME) or chronic fatigue syndrome (CFS), it may occur as a reaction to a viral infection. Full form **postviral syndrome**

**Pvt.** MILITARY Private

**pw** ONLINE Palau (NOTE: The abbreviation **pw** is seen at the end of Internet addresses, preceded by a dot.)

**PW 1.** GEOGRAPHY Palau **2.** POLICE Policewoman

**p.w.** per week

**PWA** MEDICINE person with Aids

**PWC** NAUT the US name for a jet-propelled vehicle for one or two people that is used for travelling on water. The Jet-Ski by Kawasaki is the best known example of a personal watercraft. Full form **personal watercraft**

**PWR** INDUST pressurized-water reactor

**pwt** MEASUREMENTS pennyweight

**PX 1.** WINE a white-wine grape grown in the Jeréz region of Spain. Full form **Pedro Ximénez 2.** MILITARY a store in a US military base selling goods to military personnel and their families, as well as to some authorized civilians. Full form **Post Exchange**

**py** ONLINE Paraguay (NOTE: The abbreviation **py** is seen at the end of Internet addresses, preceded by a dot.)

**PYB** FINANCE preceding year basis

**PYO** AGRICULTURE used to describe fruit, vegetables, or flowers that can be picked directly from the fields by customers and bought for less than the normal shop price. Full form **pick your own**

# Q

**q 1.** MEASUREMENTS quart **2.** quarter **3.** quarterly **4.** PAPER quarto **5.** query **6.** question **7.** MEASUREMENTS quintal **8.** MEASUREMENTS, PAPER quire

**Q 1.** PHYSICS heat **2.** MILITARY quartermaster **3.** PAPER quarto **4.** GEOGRAPHY Quebec **5.** CARD GAMES, CHESS queen **6.** MONEY quetzal

**qa** ONLINE Qatar (NOTE: The abbreviation **qa** is seen at the end of Internet addresses, preceded by a dot.)

**QAM** COMPUTING a data encoding method used by high-speed modems. Full form **quadrature amplitude modulation**

**Q & A** question and answer

**QB 1.** LAW Queen's Bench **2.** CHESS queen's bishop

**QBE** COMPUTING a simple method of retrieving information from a database by entering an example of the data which is then matched with it. Full form **query by example**

**QBP** CHESS queen's bishop's pawn

**QC 1.** BUSINESS a group of employees from different levels of a company who meet regularly to discuss ways of improving quality and to resolve any problems related to production. Full form **quality circle 2.** GEOGRAPHY Quebec **3.** a senior barrister (when the reigning monarch is female). Full form **Queen's Counsel**

**QCD** QUANTUM PHYSICS quantum chromodynamics

**q.e.** which is (NOTE: From the Latin *quod est*.)

**QED 1.** QUANTUM PHYSICS quantum electrodynamics **2.** quod erat demonstrandum (NOTE: The abbreviation **QED** is used to indicate that a particular fact is proof of the theory that has just been advanced (or of the statement that has just been made).)

**QEF** quod erat faciendum (NOTE: From the Latin, 'which was to be done'.)

**QF** ARMS quick-firing

**QFD** BUSINESS a strategy to ensure that the customer's wants and needs are being directly addressed by the product being manufactured, e.g. by using an HOQ. Full form **quality function deployment**

**q.i.d.** PHARMACOLOGY four times a day (NOTE: The abbreviation **q.i.d.**, from the Latin *quater in die*, is used in prescriptions.)

**QISAM** COMPUTING queued indexed sequential access method

**QKt** CHESS queen's knight

**QKtP** CHESS queen's knight's pawn

**ql** MEASUREMENTS quintal

**QL** COMPUTING query language

**q.l.** PHARMACOLOGY as much as you like (NOTE: The abbreviation **q.l.**, from the Latin *quantum libet*, is used in prescriptions.)

**Qld** GEOGRAPHY Queensland

**qlty** quality

**QM** MILITARY quartermaster

**q.m.** PHARMACOLOGY every morning (NOTE: The abbreviation **q.m.**, from the Latin *quaque mane*, is used in prescriptions.)

**QMC** MILITARY quartermaster corps

**QMG** MILITARY Quartermaster General

**QMS** MILITARY Quartermaster Sergeant

**qn** question

**QN** CHESS queen's knight

**q.n.** PHARMACOLOGY every night (NOTE: The abbreviation **q.n.**, from the Latin *quaque nocte*, is used in prescriptions.)

**QNP** CHESS queen's knight's pawn

**QOS** COMPUTING quality of service

**QP** CHESS queen's pawn

**qq.** questions

**qqv** which see (NOTE: The abbreviation **qqv**, from the Latin *quae vide*, is used after a cross reference to more than one item within the same book or article.)

**QR** CHESS queen's rook

**qr.** **1.** quarter **2.** quarterly **3.** MEASUREMENTS, PAPER quire

**QRP** CHESS queen's rook's pawn

**QS** LAW quarter sessions

**q.s.** **1.** PHARMACOLOGY as much as is sufficient (NOTE: The abbreviation **q.s.**, from the Latin *quantum sufficit*, is used in prescriptions.) **2.** *N Am* MEASUREMENTS a tract of land measuring one quarter of a square mile. Full form **quarter section**

**QSAM** COMPUTING queued sequential access method

**QSO** **1.** RADIO conversation (*used in amateur radio*) **2.** ASTRONOMY a compact object in space, usually with a large red shift indicating extreme remoteness, that emits huge amounts of energy, sometimes equal to the energy output of an entire galaxy. Full form **quasi-stellar object**

**qt** **1.** quantity **2.** MEASUREMENTS quart

**q.t.** quiet (NOTE: The informal abbreviation **q.t.** is used in the phrase *on the q.t.*, meaning 'quietly and secretly'.)

**qto** PAPER quarto

**qty** quantity

**qu.** **1.** queen **2.** query **3.** question

**quad.** MATHEMATICS **1.** quadrangle (NOTE: When *quad* is used informally as a noun in this sense (with reference to a rectangular yard), it is written without a full stop.) **2.** quadrant **3.** quadrilateral

**quango** /ˈkwæŋgəʊ/ ◊ see note at **Aids, NDPB**

**quant.** quantitative

**quar.** **1.** quarter **2.** quarterly

**qubit** /ˈkjuːbɪt/ COMPUTING an elementary particle such as an electron or photon that can store data and perform computational tasks within a quantum computer's processor and memory. Full form **quantum bit**

**Que.** GEOGRAPHY Quebec

**ques.** question

**quot.** quotation

**qv** which see (NOTE: The abbreviation **qv**, from the Latin *quod vide*, is used after a cross reference to an item within the same book or article.)

**QWERTY** /ˈkwɜːti/ COMPUTING used to describe a typewriter or computer keyboard in which the top row of alphabetic characters begins with the letters Q, W, E, R, T, Y. This is the standard layout in English-speaking countries (and in many other countries that use the Roman alphabet).

The enduring popularity of the **QWERTY** keyboard is a fine example of product 'lock-in', i.e. that the first product onto the market becomes so entrenched that later, more efficient versions fail to catch on. The illogical arrangement of keys on the **QWERTY** keyboard is assumed to have been an attempt to stop early keyboards from jamming, either by keeping frequent combinations of keys far apart or by slowing down typing in general. Although later arrangements such as the Dvorak keyboard were proven to increase typing speed, the **QWERTY** layout is now so widespread that there is little point in learning to type on any other style of keyboard.

**QWL** BUSINESS quality of working life

**qy** query

# R

**r 1.** MATHEMATICS radius **2.** TRANSPORT railway **3.** MONEY rouble **4.** rare **5.** PRINTING recto **6.** right **7.** GEOGRAPHY river **8.** road **9.** MEASUREMENTS rod **10.** SPORTS run(s) **11.** MONEY rupee

**R 1.** PHYSICS gas constant **2.** JUDAISM rabbi **3.** CHEMISTRY radical **4.** MATHEMATICS radius **5.** RAIL railway **6.** MONEY rand **7.** GEOGRAPHY range **8.** MEASUREMENTS, PHYSICS Réaumur scale **9.** CHRISTIANITY rector **10.** Regina (NOTE: The abbreviation **R** is used after the name of a queen.) **11.** POLITICS Republican **12.** ELECTRICAL ENGINEERING resistance **13.** CHRISTIANITY response (NOTE: The abbreviation **R** is used to indicate a phrase sung or spoken by the choir or congregation in reply to the officiant during a church service.) **14.** CINEMA a rating indicating that a film may only be watched by people over the age of 18 (in Australia) or over the age of 17 unless accompanied by an adult (in the United States). Full form **restricted 15.** Rex (NOTE: The abbreviation **R** is used after the name of a king.) **16.** right **17.** GEOGRAPHY river **18.** road **19.** MEASUREMENTS, PHYSICS roentgen **20.** CHESS rook **21.** MONEY rouble **22.** royal **23.** MONEY rupee

**Ra** CHEMICAL ELEMENTS radium

**RA 1.** MILITARY Rear Admiral **2.** ASTRONOMY right ascension **3.** ARTS Royal Academician **4.** ARMY Royal Artillery

**RAA** ARTS Royal Academy of Arts

**RAAF** AIR FORCE Royal Australian Air Force

**RAC 1.** ARMY Royal Armoured Corps **2.** AUTOMOTIVE Royal Automobile Club

**rad** MATHEMATICS radian

**rad. 1.** radiator **2.** MATHEMATICS radical **3.** radio **4.** MATHEMATICS radius **5.** MATHEMATICS radix

**RADA** /ˈrɑːdə/ THEATRE Royal Academy of Dramatic Art

**radar** /ˈreɪdɑː/ ◊ see note at **Aids**

**RADM** MILITARY Rear Admiral

**RAEC** ARMY Royal Army Educational Corps

**RAF** AIR FORCE Royal Air Force

**RAFDS** HEALTH SERVICES Royal Australian Flying Doctor Service

**RAFVR** AIR FORCE Royal Air Force Volunteer Reserve

**RAID** /reɪd/ COMPUTING a fast disk drive system in which many hard drives are linked together to save data simultaneously. Full form **redundant array of independent (or inexpensive) disks**

**rall.** MUSIC rallentando

**RAM** /ræm/ **1.** COMPUTING random-access memory (NOTE: The acronym **RAM** is used as a noun in its own right.) **2.** PHYSICS relative atomic mass **3.** ENGINEERING rocket-assisted motor **4.** MUSIC Royal Academy of Music

**RAMC** ARMY Royal Army Medical Corps

**RAMDAC** /ˈræmdæk/ COMPUTING an electronic component on a video graphics adapter that converts the digital colour signals into electrical signals that are sent to the monitor. Full form **random-access memory digital-to-analogue converter**

**RAN 1.** MILITARY request for authority to negotiate **2.** NAVY Royal Australian Navy

**R & B** MUSIC a style of popular music with elements of blues and jazz, adapted from a style originally developed by African American musicians. Full form **rhythm and blues**

**R & D** BUSINESS research and development

**R & R** rest and recreation (or relaxation or recuperation) (NOTE: Of military origin, the abbreviation **R & R** has now entered general usage.)

**RAOC** ARMY Royal Army Ordnance Corps

**RAR** FINANCE risk-adjusted return (on capital)

**RAS 1.** AGRICULTURE Royal Agricultural Society **2.** ASTRONOMY Royal Astronomical Society

**RATO** /ˈreɪtəʊ/ AVIAT rocket-assisted takeoff

**RAVC** ARMY Royal Army Veterinary Corps

**Rb** CHEMICAL ELEMENTS rubidium

**RBA** BANKING Reserve Bank of Australia

**RBC** MEDICINE red blood cell ○ *RBC count*

**RBE** BIOLOGY relative biological effectiveness

**RBNZ** BANKING Reserve Bank of New Zealand

**RBTL** ONLINE read between the lines (*used in e-mails and text messages*)

**rc** CONSTRUCTION reinforced concrete

**RC 1.** MEDICINE Red Cross **2.** MILITARY Reserve Corps **3.** CHRISTIANITY Roman Catholic

**RCA** ARTS Royal College of Art

**rcd** COMMERCE received

**RCGP** MEDICINE Royal College of General Practitioners

**RCM** MUSIC Royal College of Music

**RCMP** POLICE Royal Canadian Mounted Police

**RCN 1.** NAVY Royal Canadian Navy **2.** HEALTH SERVICES Royal College of Nursing

**RCOG** MEDICINE Royal College of Obstetricians and Gynaecologists

**RCP** MEDICINE Royal College of Physicians

**RCPC** *US* BANKING regional check processing center

**RCPsych** PSYCHIATRY Royal College of Psychiatrists

**rcpt** COMMERCE receipt

**RCS 1.** SCIENCE Royal College of Science **2.** MEDICINE Royal College of Surgeons **3.** ARMY Royal Corps of Signals

**rct** MILITARY recruit

**RCT 1.** MEDICINE randomized controlled trial **2.** MILITARY Royal Corps of Transport

**RCVS** VETERINARY MEDICINE Royal College of Veterinary Surgeons

**rd 1.** COMMERCE rendered **2.** ROADS road **3.** MEASUREMENTS rod **4.** round

**Rd** ROADS Road (NOTE: The abbreviation **Rd** is used in addresses.)

**RD 1.** BANKING refer to drawer (NOTE: The abbreviation **RD** (or R/D) is used on a bounced cheque.) **2.** MAIL Rural Delivery

**RDA 1.** HEALTH the amount of a nutrient that is needed in the diet for a person to stay healthy, as recommended by the Food and Nutrition Board. Full form **recommended daily allowance 2.** BUSINESS Regional Development Agency

**RDBMS** COMPUTING relational database management system

**RDF 1.** RADIO radio direction finder **2.** INDUST refuse-derived fuel

**RDG** BUSINESS regional development grant

**RDO** *Aus* HUMAN RESOURCES a day off given by some employers in lieu of extra hours worked, sometimes on a regular basis. Full form **rostered day off**

**RDPR** BANKING refer to drawer please represent

**RDS 1.** RADIO a system for tuning radio receivers automatically by sending digital signals with normal radio programmes. Full form **radio data system 2.** MEDICINE respiratory distress syndrome

**RDZ** ECOLOGY resource depletion zone

**re** ONLINE Réunion (NOTE: The abbreviation **re** is seen at the end of Internet addresses, preceded by a dot.)

**'re** /ər/ are

**Re 1.** PHYSICS Reynold's number **2.** CHEMICAL ELEMENTS rhenium **3.** MONEY rupee

**RE 1.** CHRISTIANITY Reformed Episcopal **2.** EDUCATION Religious Education ○ *RE teacher* (NOTE: The abbreviation **RE** is used as a noun in its own right.) **3.** Right Excellent **4.** ARMY Royal Engineers

**rec. 1.** COMMERCE receipt **2.** COMMERCE received **3.** COOKERY recipe **4.** recommended **5.** recorded **6.** recorder **7.** recording **8.** recreation

**recd** COMMERCE received

**recip. 1.** MATHEMATICS reciprocal **2.** COMMERCE reciprocity

**recit.** MUSIC recitative

**rec. sec.** recording secretary

**rect** COMMERCE receipt

**rect.** MATHEMATICS rectangle

**Rect.** CHRISTIANITY **1.** Rector **2.** Rectory

**red. 1.** FINANCE redeemable **2.** reduced **3.** reduction

**REE** CHEMISTRY rare-earth element

**ref. 1.** reference **2.** INDUSTRY refining **3.** reformed **4.** refunding

**Ref. Ch.** CHRISTIANITY Reformed Church

**refl. 1.** reflection **2.** reflective **3.** PHYSIOLOGY reflex **4.** GRAMMAR reflexive

**reg. 1.** GEOGRAPHY region **2.** registered **3.** registrar **4.** registry **5.** GRAMMAR regular **6.** regularly **7.** regulation **8.** regulator

**Reg. 1.** Regent **2.** Regina **3.** MEASUREMENTS, INDUST a trademark for a gas mark (i.e. a gradation of heat in the temperature regulation of gas ovens). Full form **Regulo**

**regd** registered

**Reg. Prof.** EDUCATION Regius Professor

**Regt 1.** Regent **2.** MILITARY Regiment

**REIT** *N Am* FINANCE real-estate investment trust

**rel. 1.** relating **2.** relative **3.** relatively **4.** released **5.** religion **6.** religious

**relig.** religion

**rem** /rem/ MEASUREMENTS, PHYSICS a unit for measuring amounts of radiation, equal to the effect that one roentgen of X-rays or gamma-rays would produce in a human being. It is used in radiation protection and monitoring. Full form **roentgen equivalent (in) man**

**REM** /rem/ **1.** PHYSIOLOGY rapid eye movement (NOTE: *REM sleep* is a stage of sleep that recurs several times during the night and is marked by dreaming, rapid eye movements under closed lids, and elevated pulse rate and brain activity.) **2.** COMPUTING a note embedded in a computer program that is purely explanatory and not interpreted as part of the programming code. Full form **remark**

**REME** /'riːmi/ MILITARY Royal Electrical and Mechanical Engineers

**rep. 1.** repair **2.** report **3.** reported **4.** reporter **5.** PUBLISHING reprint

**Rep.** POLITICS **1.** Representative **2.** Republic **3.** Republican

**repr. 1.** representative **2.** represented **3.** representing **4.** PUBLISHING reprint

**rept 1.** COMMERCE receipt **2.** report

**Repub.** POLITICS **1.** Republic **2.** Republican

**req. 1.** request **2.** require **3.** required **4.** requirement **5.** requisition

**RES 1.** INDUST renewable energy source **2.** INDUST renewable energy system **3.** MEDICINE a defence system of cells widely distributed in the body that are able to attack hostile particles such as bacteria. Full form **reticuloendothelial system 4.** INSECTS Royal Entomological Society

**res. 1.** research **2.** reservation **3.** reserved **4.** reservoir **5.** residence **6.** resident **7.** resigned **8.** resolution

**resp. 1.** respective **2.** respectively **3.** respiration **4.** LAW respondent

**ret. 1.** retain **2.** retired **3.** return **4.** COMMERCE returned

**retd 1.** retained **2.** retired **3.** COMMERCE returned

**rev. 1.** revenue **2.** reverse **3.** review **4.** PUBLISHING revised **5.** PUBLISHING revision **6.** revolution **7.** ARMS revolver **8.** revolving

> When *rev* is used informally as a noun in this sense (with reference to a single revolution of a vehicle's engine), or as a verb meaning 'to increase a vehicle's engine speed', it is written without a full stop.

**Rev.** CHRISTIANITY Reverend

**Revd** CHRISTIANITY Reverend

**Rev. Ver.** BIBLE Revised Version

**rf** GEOGRAPHY reef

**Rf 1.** MONEY rufiyaa **2.** CHEMICAL ELEMENTS rutherfordium

**RF 1.** RADIO radio frequency **2.** AIR FORCE reconnaissance fighter **3.** MILITARY regular forces **4.** BIOCHEMISTRY a hormone produced by the hypothalamus that causes the pituitary gland to secrete other hormones. Full form **releasing factor 5.** MAPS the system of relating scale to real distance on a map. Full form **representative fraction 6.** GEOGRAPHY the official name of France. Full form **République Française 7.** MILITARY Reserve Force **8.** CHEMISTRY in chromatography, a measure of how quickly a compound dissolved in a solvent travels relative to the solvent itself. Full form **retention factor 9.** BASEBALL right fielder **10.** MILITARY Royal Fusiliers **11.** MONEY Rwanda franc

**rf.** COMMERCE refund

**r.f. 1.** RADIO radio frequency **2.** ARMS rapid fire **3.** TELECOMMUNICATIONS reception fair **4.** PAPER rough finish

**RFC 1.** COMPUTING request for comment **2.** AIR FORCE Royal Flying Corps **3.** RUGBY Rugby Football Club

**RFD 1.** RADIO radio-frequency device **2.** MILITARY reporting for duty

**RFLP** BIOTECHNOLOGY a variation between individuals in the length of the DNA fragments produced by a specific restriction enzyme (an enzyme that splits DNA into segments at precise locations, used in genetic engineering). Full form **restriction fragment length polymorphism**

**Rfn** MILITARY Rifleman

**RG** AMERICAN FOOTBALL right guard

**RGB** COMPUTING the standard model for display devices in which all colours are described in terms of the quantity of red, green, and blue they contain. Printers use the CMYB (cyan, magenta, yellow, black) model. Full form **red, green, blue**

**RGN** HEALTH SERVICES Registered General Nurse

**RGS** GEOGRAPHY Royal Geographical Society

**Rgt** MILITARY regiment

**rh 1.** METEOROLOGY relative humidity **2.** right hand

**rH** CHEMISTRY a measure of the oxidising power of a solution. Full form **redox potential**

**Rh 1.** BIOCHEMISTRY rhesus (NOTE: A person who is *Rh negative* lacks the rhesus factor in the blood; a person who is *Rh positive* has blood containing the rhesus factor.) **2.** BIOCHEMISTRY rhesus factor (NOTE: The *Rh factor* is a group of antigens present in most people's red blood cells.) **3.** CHEMICAL ELEMENTS rhodium

**RH 1.** METEOROLOGY relative humidity **2.** right hand **3.** Royal Highness

**RHA 1.** HEALTH SERVICES Regional Health Authority **2.** MILITARY Royal Horse Artillery

**rhd** AUTOMOTIVE right-hand drive

**RHG** MILITARY Royal Horse Guards

**rhp** MEASUREMENTS rated horsepower

**RHS** GARDENING Royal Horticultural Society

**RI 1.** King and Emperor (NOTE: From the Latin *rex et imperator.*) **2.** Queen and Empress **3.** EDUCATION religious instruction ○ *RI teacher* (NOTE: The abbreviation **RI** is used as a noun in its own right.) **4.** MAIL Rhode Island (NOTE: The abbreviation **RI** is part of the US sorting code on the last line of a Rhode Island address.) **5.** SCIENCE Royal Institution

**RIA 1.** MEDICINE the technique of measuring the levels of antibodies in the blood by introducing into the bloodstream a substance that has a radioactive tracer attached to it. Full form **radioimmunoassay 2.** Royal Irish Academy

**RIB** BOAT rigid inflatable boat

**RIBA** /'riːbə/ ARCHITECTURE Royal Institute of British Architects

**RICS** Royal Institution of Chartered Surveyors

**RIE** FINANCE recognized investment exchange

**RIF** *US* HUMAN RESOURCES the laying off of members of a workforce. Full form **reduction in force**

**RIFF** /rɪf/ COMPUTING resource interchange file format

**RIP 1.** COMPUTING raster image processor **2.** rest in peace (NOTE: The abbreviation **RIP** is seen on gravestones.) **3.** COMPUTING routing information protocol

**RISC** /rɪsk/ COMPUTING reduced-instruction-set computer

**rit.** MUSIC **1.** ritardando **2.** ritenuto

**riv.** GEOGRAPHY river

**RJ** ROADS road junction

**RK** EDUCATION religious knowledge

**RL 1.** ONLINE real life (*used in e-mails and text messages*) **2.** RUGBY Rugby League

**RLG** ARMS rocket-launched grenade

**Rls** MONEY rials

**rly** RAIL railway

**rm 1.** MEASUREMENTS, PAPER ream **2.** room

**Rm** BIBLE Romans

**RM 1.** HEALTH SERVICES Registered Midwife **2.** MAIL Royal Mail **3.** MILITARY Royal Marines

**RMA** MILITARY **1.** Royal Marine Artillery **2.** Royal Military Academy

**RMB** *Aus* MAIL roadside mail box (NOTE: The abbreviation **RMB** is used in addresses in rural areas of Australia.)

**RMD** *Aus* MAIL roadside mail delivery (NOTE: The abbreviation **RMD** is used in addresses in rural areas of Australia.)

**RMDIR** COMPUTING a command to remove an empty subdirectory. Full form **remove directory**

**RMM** CHEMISTRY relative molecular mass

**RMN** HEALTH SERVICES Registered Mental Nurse

**rms** MATHEMATICS the square root of the mean of the squares of a set of numbers. Full form **root mean square**

**RMS 1.** MAIL Royal Mail Service **2.** SHIPPING Royal Mail Ship

**RMT** HUMAN RESOURCES National Union of Rail, Maritime, and Transport Workers

**Rn** CHEMICAL ELEMENTS radon

**RN 1.** HEALTH SERVICES Registered Nurse **2.** ONLINE right now (*used in e-mails and text messages*) **3.** NAVY Royal Navy

**RNA** GENETICS a nucleic acid containing ribose found in all living cells, essential for protein synthesis. Full form **ribonucleic acid** (NOTE: The abbreviation **RNA** is used as a noun in its own right.)

**RNAS** NAVY **1.** Royal Naval Air Service **2.** Royal Naval Air Station

**RNase** /ˌɑː en ˈeɪz/ BIOCHEMISTRY an enzyme that splits or degrades RNA. Full form **ribonuclease**

**rnd** round

**RNIB** Royal National Institute for the Blind

**RNLI** NAUTICAL Royal National Lifeboat Institution

**RNMH** HEALTH SERVICES Registered Nurse for the Mentally Handicapped

**RNP** BIOCHEMISTRY a complex of RNA and a protein formed during the synthesis of RNA. Full form **ribonucleoprotein**

**RNR** NAVY Royal Naval Reserve

**rns** CRICKET runs

**RNVR** NAVY Royal Naval Volunteer Force

**RNZAF** AIR FORCE Royal New Zealand Air Force

**RNZN** NAVY Royal New Zealand Navy

**ro 1.** PRINTING recto **2.** ONLINE Romania (NOTE: The abbreviation **ro** is seen at the end of Internet addresses, preceded by a dot.)

**ro.** MEASUREMENTS rood

**ROA** FINANCE return on assets

**ROB** BUSINESS defines an advertisement which is placed wherever space is available, at the publisher's discretion, instead in a stand-alone insert. Full form **run of book**. Same as **ROP**

**ROC** MILITARY Royal Observer Corps

**ROCE** FINANCE return on capital employed

**ROE** FINANCE return on equity

**ROI 1.** GEOGRAPHY region of interest **2.** FINANCE return on investment

**ROM** /rɒm/ COMPUTING read-only memory

**rom.** PRINTING roman (type)

**Rom. 1.** Roman **2.** LANGUAGE Romance **3.** GEOGRAPHY Romania **4.** LANGUAGE Romanian **5.** BIBLE Romans

**RON** BUSINESS defines an advertisement which is placed wherever space is available within an advertising network. Full form **run of network**

**RONA** FINANCE return on net assets

**ROP** BUSINESS defines an advertisement which is placed wherever space is available, at the publisher's discretion, instead in a stand-alone insert. Full form **run of paper / press**. Same as **ROB**

**ro-ro** /ˈrəʊ rəʊ/ TRANSPORT used to describe a ferry (or other method of transport) designed so that vehicles are driven on one end and, on arrival at their destination, off the other end. Full form **roll-on roll-off**

**ROS 1.** FINANCE return on sales **2.** BUSINESS defines an Internet advertisement which is placed wherever space is available within a specified website. Full form **run of site 3.** BUSINESS defines an advertisement which is placed whenever space is available within a given time period. Full form **run of station**

**ROSCO** /ˈrɒskəʊ/ a company that leases trains to train-operating companies under the arrangements by which the UK national railway system was privatized. Full form **rolling stock operating company**

**RoSPA** /ˈrɒspə/ DOMESTIC Royal Society for the Prevention of Accidents

**rot.** MATHEMATICS rotation

**ROTFL** ONLINE rolling on the floor laughing (*used in e-mails and Internet chat rooms*)

**ROTM** ONLINE right on the money

**ROU** GEOGRAPHY Republic of Uruguay

**ROW** BUSINESS defines an advertisement which is placed whenever space is available within a given week. Full form **run of week**

**RP 1.** PHONETICS the accent of British English that educated people from the southern part of England traditionally use, widely regarded as the least regionally modified of all British accents. Full form **Received Pronunciation 2.** EDUCATION Regius Professor **3.** GEOGRAPHY Republic of the Philippines **4.** role-play

**RPB** BUSINESS recognized professional body

**RPC 1.** COMPUTING a method of communication between two programs running on separate, but connected, computers. Full form **remote procedure call 2.** COMMERCE Restrictive Practices Court

**RPG 1.** COMPUTING a high-level computer language used primarily for business reports. Full form **report program generator 2.** MILITARY rocket-propelled grenade **3.** COMPUTER GAMES a computer or other game in which the participants assume roles, often as fantasy characters such as heroes or elves, in a scenario that develops as the game progresses. Full form **role-playing game**

**RPI** COMMERCE a measure of inflation taken from the average change in prices of a representative sample of goods and services over a period of time. Full form **retail price index**

**RPIX** FINANCE a measure of the underlying rate of inflation, that is the retail price index not taking into account mortgage payments

**RPIY** FINANCE a measure of the core rate of inflation, that is the retail price index not taking into account indirect taxes and council tax

**rpm** MEASUREMENTS revolutions per minute
> Before the advent of the compact disc for audio recordings, the abbreviation **rpm** was most frequently encountered as an indication of the speed at which the various types and sizes of gramophone record were played.

**RPM** COMMERCE the setting by the manufacturer of a minimum price at which its goods are to be sold at retail. Full form **resale (or retail) price maintenance**

**RPN** MATHEMATICS a method of expressing complex mathematical equations without the need for brackets. Full form **reverse Polish notation**

**RPO** MUSIC Royal Philharmonic Orchestra

**rps** MEASUREMENTS revolutions per second

**RPS** PHOTOGRAPHY Royal Photographic Society

**rpt 1.** repeat **2.** report

**RPV** MILITARY remotely piloted vehicle

**RQ** MEASUREMENTS, PHYSIOLOGY the ratio of the volume of carbon dioxide released to the volume of oxygen absorbed by an organism, cell, or tissue over a given time period. Full form **respiratory quotient**

**RR 1.** *US* RAIL railroad **2.** MEDICINE recovery room **3.** MEDICINE relative risk **4.** CHRISTIANITY Right Reverend

**rRNA** BIOCHEMISTRY ribosomal RNA

**RRP** COMMERCE recommended retail price

**Rs** MONEY rupees

**RS 1.** recording secretary **2.** right side **3.** SCIENCE Royal Society

**RSA 1.** BUSINESS a grant scheme operating in certain areas of the UK to encourage business to set up or expand in that area. Full form **regional selective assistance 2.** GEOGRAPHY Republic of South Africa **3.** MILITARY an organization in New Zealand to provide help for former members of the armed forces and their families. Full form **Returned Services Association 4.** ARTS Royal Scottish Academician **5.** ARTS Royal Scottish Academy **6.** ARTS Royal Society of Arts **7.** COMPUTING a public-key cryptography system used to provide high-level security

**RSC 1.** THEATRE Royal Shakespeare Company **2.** CHEMISTRY Royal Society of Chemistry

**RSCN** HEALTH SERVICES Registered Sick Children's Nurse

**RSFSR** POLITICS the former name for Russia before the collapse of the Soviet Union in 1991. Full form **Russian Soviet Federated Socialist Republic**

**RSI** MEDICINE a painful condition affecting some people who overuse muscles as a result of activities such as regularly operating a computer keyboard. Full form **repetitive strain injury** (NOTE: The abbreviation **RSI** is used as a noun in its own right.)

**RSJ** CONSTRUCTION rolled steel joist (NOTE: The abbreviation **RSJ** is used as a noun in its own right.)

**RSL 1.** MILITARY an organization established in Australia in 1916 to provide help for former members of the armed forces and their families. Full form **Returned Services League 2.** LITERATURE Royal Society of Literature

**RSM 1.** MILITARY Regimental Sergeant Major **2.** GEOGRAPHY Republic of San Marino **3.** MEDICINE Royal Society of Medicine

**RSNC** ECOLOGY Royal Society for Nature Conservation

**RSP** COMMERCE retail service provider

**RSPB** BIRDS Royal Society for the Protection of Birds

**RSPCA** VETERINARY MEDICINE Royal Society for the Prevention of Cruelty to Animals

**RSV 1.** MICROBIOLOGY a virus causing infection of the lungs and respiratory tract, most usually in young children. Full form **respiratory syncytial virus 2.** BIBLE Revised Standard Version

**RSVP** BUSINESS répondez s'il vous plaît (NOTE: The abbreviation **RSVP**, from the French, 'please reply', is used on an invitation to request a response to it.)

**rt** right

**RT 1.** TELECOMMUNICATIONS radio telegraph **2.** TELECOMMUNICATIONS radio telegraphy **3.** TELECOMMUNICATIONS radiotelephone **4.** TELECOMMUNICATIONS radiotelephony **5.** COMPUTING real time **6.** AMERICAN FOOTBALL right tackle **7.** room temperature **8.** US TRAVEL round trip

**RTDS** COMPUTING real-time data system

**Rte** ROADS route (NOTE: The abbreviation **Rte** is used in addresses.)

**RTE 1.** BROADCASTING Radio Telefis Éireann (NOTE: From the Irish, 'Irish Radio and Television'.) **2.** COMPUTING real-time execution

**RTF** COMPUTING a format for a computer file that contains text with formatting codes (e.g. for bold or italic). Full form **rich text format**

**RTFM** ONLINE a more offensive variant of RTM. Full form **read the fucking manual**

**RTGS** BUSINESS a system of settling large payments between banks by paying throughout the day rather than totting up debits against credits at the end of the day. Full form **real-time gross settlement**

**Rt Hon.** POLITICS Right Honourable

**RTM** ONLINE read the manual (*used in e-mails and text messages*)

**RTN** HEALTH SERVICES Registered Theatre Nurse

**RTP** COMPUTING real-time transport protocol

**Rt Rev.** CHRISTIANITY Right Reverend

**RTS 1.** BUSINESS the rate at which a manufacturer can reduce one input and increase another while keeping output constant. Full form **rate of technical substitution 2.**

COMPUTING a signal used to inform a sending device such as a modem that a receiving device is ready to accept more data. Full form **request to send**

**RTSC** COMPUTING read the source code

**RTW** CLOTHING ready-to-wear

**ru** ONLINE Russia (NOTE: The abbreviation **ru** is seen at the end of Internet addresses, preceded by a dot.)

**Ru** CHEMICAL ELEMENTS ruthenium

**RU** 1. GEOGRAPHY Republic of Burundi (NOTE: The abbreviation **ru** comes from the country's original name, the *R*epublic of *U*rundi.) 2. ONLINE are you (*used in e-mails and text messages*) 3. RUGBY Rugby Union

**RUC** POLICE Royal Ulster Constabulary

**rv** STATISTICS random variable

**RV** 1. AEROSPACE re-entry vehicle 2. CAMPING the US and Canadian name for a camper van. Full form **recreational vehicle** 3. BIBLE Revised Version

**rw** ONLINE Rwanda (NOTE: The abbreviation **rw** is seen at the end of Internet addresses, preceded by a dot.)

**RW** 1. Right Worshipful 2. Right Worthy

**R/W** COMPUTING read/write

**RWD** AUTOMOTIVE rear-wheel drive

**rwy** RAIL railway

**RX** COMPUTING receive(r)

**RYS** ONLINE read your screen (*used in e-mails and text messages*)

# S

**S 1.** MEASUREMENTS, TIME second **2.** semi- **3.** MONEY shilling **4.** GRAMMAR singular **5.** ZOOLOGY the male parent of an animal. Full form **sire 6.** sister **7.** MUSIC solo **8.** son **9.** MUSIC soprano **10.** MEASUREMENTS stere **11.** FINANCE stock **12.** QUANTUM PHYSICS strange quark **13.** GRAMMAR substantive

**S 1.** QUANTUM PHYSICS entropy **2.** JUDAEO-CHRISTIAN Sabbath **3.** CHRISTIANITY Saint **4.** BIBLE Samuel **5.** EDUCATION satisfactory **6.** CALENDAR Saturday **7.** HISTORY Saxon **8.** MONEY the former unit of currency in Austria, replaced by the euro in 2002. Full form **schilling 9.** GEOGRAPHY Sea **10.** CALENDAR September **11.** MEASUREMENTS, PHYSICS siemens **12.** CLOTHING small (*used in e-mails and text messages*) **13.** ONLINE smile (*used in e-mails and text messages*) **14.** ONLINE smiling (NOTE: The abbreviation **S** is used as a size of clothing.) **15.** POLITICS Socialist **16.** south **17.** southern **18.** QUANTUM PHYSICS strangeness **19.** CHEMICAL ELEMENTS sulphur **20.** CALENDAR Sunday

**sa** ONLINE Saudi Arabia (NOTE: The abbreviation **sa** is seen at the end of Internet addresses, preceded by a dot.)

**SA 1.** CHRISTIANITY Salvation Army **2.** COMMERCE a private limited company in Spain. Full form **sociedad anónima 3.** COMMERCE a private limited company in France. Full form **sociedade anónima 4.** COMMERCE a private limited company in Portugal. Full form **société anonyme 5.** GEOGRAPHY South Africa **6.** GEOGRAPHY South America **7.** GEOGRAPHY South Australia

**s.a. 1.** semiannual **2.** COMMERCE subject to approval **3.** without date

**SAA** COMPUTING systems application architecture

**Sab.** JUDAEO-CHRISTIAN Sabbath

**SABC** BROADCASTING South African Broadcasting Corporation

**SACEUR** /ˈsækɜː/ MILITARY Supreme Allied Commander, Europe

**SAD** MEDICINE depression associated with the onset of winter and thought to be caused by decreasing amounts of daylight. Full form **seasonal affective disorder**

**SADS** MEDICINE another name for SAD. Full form **seasonal affective disorder syndrome**

**s.a.e.** MAIL **1.** self-addressed envelope **2.** stamped addressed envelope

**SAEF** /seɪf/ STOCK EXCHANGE Stock Exchange Automatic Execution Facility

**S. Afr.** GEOGRAPHY South Africa

**SAIF** FINANCE savings association insurance fund

**St. Ex.** Stock Exchange

**StHA** HEALTH SERVICES Strategic Health Authority

**SALT** /sɔːlt/ MILITARY Strategic Arms Limitation Talks (or Treaty)

**SAM** /sæm/ ARMS surface-to-air missile

**Sam.** BIBLE Samuel

**S & H** COMMERCE shipping and handling

**S & L** BANKING savings and loan (association)

**S & M** sadism and masochism

**S & P** STOCK EXCHANGE Standard and Poor's

**S & P 500** STOCK EXCHANGE Standard and Poor's 500-stock index

**S-A node** ANATOMY a small mass of specialized cardiac muscle fibres in the wall of the heart. The S-A node originates the regular electrical impulses that stimulate the heartbeat. Full form **sinoatrial node**

**SAR 1.** MEDICINE the rate at which a mass, especially human tissue, absorbs radiated electrical energy (e.g. when using a mobile phone), measured in watts or milliwatts per kilogram. Full form **specific absorption rate 2.** COMPUTING store address register

**SARL** COMMERCE a small private limited company in France which may not have more than 40 shareholders. Full form **société anonyme à responsabilité limitée** (NOTE: From the French, 'limited company'.)

**SARS** /sɑːz/ MEDICINE severe acute respiratory syndrome

**SAS 1.** COMPUTING single attachment station **2.** MILITARY a British army regiment that is specially trained to undertake dangerous clandestine operations. Full form **Special Air Service**

**SASE** MAIL self-addressed stamped envelope

**Sask.** GEOGRAPHY Saskatchewan

**SAT** /sæt/ EDUCATION standard assessment task (NOTE: The acronym **SAT** is used as a noun in its own right, often in the plural.)

**Sat.** CALENDAR Saturday

**SATB** MUSIC soprano, alto, tenor, bass

**SAW** /sɔː/ ELECTRONICS surface acoustic wave

**SAYE** FINANCE a savings plan in which monthly deposits are made over a five-year period. Full form **save as you earn**

**sb** ONLINE Solomon Islands (NOTE: The abbreviation **sb** is seen at the end of Internet addresses, preceded by a dot.)

**Sb** CHEMICAL ELEMENTS antimony (NOTE: From the Latin *stibium*.)

**SB** BROADCASTING simultaneous broadcast

**SBA 1.** BUSINESS small business administration **2.** AVIAT a system of radio navigation that provides an aircraft with lateral guidance and marker beam indicators at set points during its landing approach. Full form **standard beam approach**

**SbE** south by east

**SBF** STOCK EXCHANGE Société des Bourses Françaises (NOTE: From the French, 'Association of French Stock Exchanges'.)

**SBM** COMPUTING a trademark for an acoustic technology developed by Sony. Full form **Super Bit Mapping**

**SBS 1.** HEALTH a group of symptoms typically including headaches and respiratory problems that affect workers in usually new or remodelled office buildings and are attributed to toxic building materials or poor ventilation. Full form **sick building syndrome 2.** MILITARY an elite British Royal Marines force that is used to spearhead amphibious operations and to reconnoitre beach landings. Full form **Special Boat Service 3.** *Aus* BROADCASTING Special Broadcasting Service

**SBU** BUSINESS strategic business unit

**SbW** south by west

**sc 1.** ONLINE Seychelles (NOTE: The abbreviation **sc** is seen at the end of Internet addresses, preceded by a dot.) **2.** PRINTING small capital

**Sc** CHEMICAL ELEMENTS scandium

**SC 1.** STOCK EXCHANGE Securities Commission **2.** INTERNATIONAL RELATIONS the permanent committee of the United Nations that oversees its peacekeeping operations throughout the world. Full form **Security Council 3.** MILITARY Signal Corps **4.** MAIL South Carolina (NOTE: The abbreviation **SC** is part of the US sorting code on the last line of a South Carolina address.) **5.** MEDICINE subcutaneous

**sc. 1.** THEATRE scene (NOTE: The abbreviation **sc.** (or Sc.) is used in references to a particular subdivision of a play, as in *Hamlet Act I Sc. 4*.) **2.** used to introduce a word or phrase of clarification, or a missing word or phrase. Full form **scilicet 3.** MEASUREMENTS scruple

**s/c** BUILDINGS self-contained (*used in property advertisements*)

**ScB** SCIENCE Bachelor of Science (NOTE: From the Latin *Scientiae Baccalaureus*.)

**SCC 1.** MEDICINE a common type of cancer that usually develops in the epithelial layer of the skin but sometimes in various mucous membranes of the body. Full form **squamous cell carcinoma 2.** ELECTRONICS storage connecting circuit

**ScD** SCIENCE Doctor of Science (NOTE: From the Latin *Scientiae Doctor*.)

**SCE** EDUCATION in Scotland, any of three levels of examinations in a wide range of subjects taken in the last three years of secondary school. Standard Grades are usually taken at the age of 16, Highers at 17, and Sixth Year Studies at 18. Full form **Scottish Certificate of Education**

**SCF** Save the Children Fund

**SCG** CRICKET Sydney Cricket Ground

**sch.** school

**sci** PRINTING single column inch

**sci. 1.** science **2.** scientific

**SCID** MEDICINE a rare but severe inherited disorder of the immune system. Full form **severe combined immunodeficiency**

**ScM** SCIENCE Master of Science (NOTE: From the Latin *Scientiae Magister*.)

**SCM 1.** HEALTH SERVICES State Certified Midwife **2.** CHRISTIANITY Student Christian Movement

**SCN** ANATOMY a discrete area of the brain responsible for regulating circadian rhythms (the 'biological clock') in mammals. Full form **suprachiasmatic nucleus**

**Scot. 1.** BEVERAGES Scotch **2.** GEOGRAPHY Scotland **3.** GEOGRAPHY Scottish

**SCPO** MILITARY Senior Chief Petty Officer

**SCPS** PUBLIC ADMINISTRATION Society of Civil and Public Servants

**SCR 1.** EDUCATION a common room for the use of academic staff in some colleges and universities. Full form **senior common room 2.** COMPUTING sequence control register

**Script.** RELIGION Scripture

**SCSI** /'skʌzi/ COMPUTING a specification for a high-speed computer interface used to connect peripheral devices to a computer. Full form **small computer systems interface**

**scuba** /'skuːbə/ ◊ see note at **Aids**

**sculp.** ARTS sculptor

**sd** ONLINE Sudan (NOTE: The abbreviation **sd** is seen at the end of Internet addresses, preceded by a dot.)

**SD 1.** COMPUTING secure digital **2.** COMPUTING single density (disk) **3.** MAIL South Dakota (NOTE: The abbreviation **SD** is part of the US sorting code on the last line of a South Dakota address.) **4.** STATISTICS standard deviation

**s.d.** without a day being fixed for a further meeting. Full form **sine die** (NOTE: From the Latin, 'without a day'.)

**SDA** BUSINESS Scottish Development Agency

**SDB** COMMERCE sales day book

**SDI** MILITARY Strategic Defense Initiative

**SDLC** COMPUTING synchronous data link control

**SDLP** POLITICS Social Democratic and Labour Party

**Sdn** COMMERCE Sendirian (NOTE: *Sdn berhad* is a Malay term for a private limited company.)

**SDP** POLITICS Social Democratic Party

**SDR 1.** ECONOMICS a method of settling international debts through the International Monetary Fund in order to stabilize exchange rates. Full form **special drawing right(s) 2.** COMPUTING store data register

**SDRAM** COMPUTING synchronous dynamic random-access memory

**SDRs** ECONOMICS special drawing rights

**se** ONLINE Sweden (NOTE: The abbreviation **se** is seen at the end of Internet addresses, preceded by a dot.)

**Se** CHEMICAL ELEMENTS selenium

**SE 1.** southeast **2.** southeastern **3.** STOCK EXCHANGE stock exchange

**SEAQ** /'si:æk/ STOCK EXCHANGE a computerized system for displaying prices and transactions in securities on the UK Stock Exchange. Full form **Stock Exchange Automated Quotation**

**SEATO** /'si:təʊ/ INTERNATIONAL RELATIONS Southeast Asia Treaty Organization

**SEATS** /si:ts/ STOCK EXCHANGE Stock Exchange Alternative Trading Service

**SEbE** southeast by east

**SEbS** southeast by south

**sec** MATHEMATICS secant

**SEC 1.** ONLINE (wait a) second (*used in e-mails and text messages*) **2.** STOCK EXCHANGE an agency of the US government set up to regulate transactions in securities and protect investors against malpractice. Full form **Securities and Exchange Commission**

**sec. 1.** MEASUREMENTS, TIME second **2.** secondary **3.** secretary **4.** section **5.** sector **6.** security

**SECAM** /'si:kæm/ TV a broadcasting system for colour television used in France, Russia, and a number of other countries. Full form **séquentiel couleur à mémoire**

**secy** secretary

**SED** GOVERNMENT Scottish Education Department

**SEDD** GOVERNMENT Scottish Executive Development Department

**SEED** GOVERNMENT Scottish Executive Education Department

**SEERAD** /'si:ræd/ GOVERNMENT Scottish Executive Environment and Rural Affairs Department

**SEHD** GOVERNMENT Scottish Executive Health Department

**SEM** PHYSICS scanning electron microscope

**SEN 1.** EDUCATION special educational needs **2.** HEALTH SERVICES a grade for nurses before 1988, when clinical grading came into effect. Most **SENs** converted to clinical grade C or D. Full form **State Enrolled Nurse**

**Sen. 1.** POLITICS senate **2.** POLITICS senator **3.** senior

**SEP** ONLINE someone else's problem (*used in e-mails and text messages*)

**Sep. 1.** CALENDAR September **2.** Septuagint

**sepd** separated

**SEPP** COMPUTING secure encryption payment protocol

**Sept. 1.** CALENDAR September **2.** BIBLE Septuagint

**seq.** sequel

**Sergt** MILITARY sergeant

**SERM** MEDICINE a simulated oestrogen which has some but not all of the effects of oestrogen, e.g. protecting against bone deterioration. Full form **selective oestrogen receptor modulator**

**SERPS** /sɜ:ps/ PENSIONS a pension paid by the government to people who have been employed during their lives. Full form **state earnings-related pension scheme**

**sess.** session

**SET** /set/ COMPUTING the standards created by a group of banks and Internet companies that allow users to buy goods over the Internet without risk. Full form **secure electronic transactions**

**SETI** /'setiː/ SCIENCE a scientific attempt to detect or communicate with intelligent beings from beyond Earth, especially using radio signals. Full form **search for extraterrestrial intelligence**

**SETS** STOCK EXCHANGE Stock Exchange Electronic Trading System

**sf 1.** LITERATURE science fiction **2.** MUSIC sforzando

**SF 1.** LITERATURE science fiction **2.** FINANCE a fund created by setting aside regular sums for investment, usually in bonds, in order to repay a debt that will fall due at a future date. Full form **sinking fund**

**SFA 1.** FOOTBALL Scottish Football Association **2.** STOCK EXCHANGE Securities and Futures Authority

**SFAS** FINANCE Statement of Financial Accounting Standards

**SFD** MEDICINE small for dates (NOTE: The abbreviation **SFD** is used of a baby with an abnormally low birth weight in relation to the length of the pregnancy.)

**SFE** STOCK EXCHANGE Sydney Futures Exchange

**SFO 1.** CRIME Serious Fraud Office **2.** FINANCE Superannuation Funds Office

**sfz.** MUSIC sforzando

**sg** ONLINE Singapore (NOTE: The abbreviation **sg** is seen at the end of Internet addresses, preceded by a dot.)

**Sg 1.** CHEMICAL ELEMENTS seaborgium **2.** BIBLE Song of Songs

**SG 1.** GRAMMAR singular **2.** LAW Solicitor General **3.** PHYSICS specific gravity

**sgd** signed

**SGHWR** INDUST steam-generating heavy-water reactor

**SGM** *US* MILITARY Sergeant Major

**SGML** COMPUTING an international standard for the definition of system-independent methods of representing texts in electronic form by describing the relationship between a document's form and its structure. Full form **Standard Generalized Markup Language**

**SGOT** BIOCHEMISTRY an enzyme manufactured in the liver, elevated levels of which can indicate decreased liver function. Full form **serum glutamic-oxalacetic transaminase**

**SGPT** BIOCHEMISTRY an enzyme manufactured in the liver and heart, the presence of which in the blood indicates damage to these organs. Full form **serum glutamic-pyruvic transaminase**

**Sgt** MILITARY Sergeant

**Sgt Maj.** MILITARY Sergeant Major

**SGX** STOCK EXCHANGE Singapore Exchange

**sh** ONLINE St Helena (NOTE: The abbreviation **sh** is seen at the end of Internet addresses, preceded by a dot.)

**sh. 1.** STOCK EXCHANGE share **2.** AGRICULTURE sheep **3.** PRINTING sheet

**SHA** NAVIGATION a measure of a star's position in relation to the meridian passing through Aries. Full form **sidereal hour angle**

**SHAEF** /ʃeɪf/ MILITARY Supreme Headquarters Allied Expeditionary Forces

**shan't** /ʃɑːnt/ shall not

**SHAPE** /ʃeɪp/ MILITARY Supreme Headquarters Allied Powers Europe

**she'd** /ʃiːd/ **1.** she had **2.** she would

**she'll** /ʃiːl/ **1.** she shall **2.** she will

**she's** /ʃiːz/ **1.** she has **2.** she is

**SHF** RADIO a radio frequency between 3,000 and 30,000 megahertz. Full form **superhigh frequency**

**shipt** MAIL shipment

**SHM** PHYSICS simple harmonic motion

**SHO** HEALTH SERVICES Senior House Officer

**shouldn't** /'ʃʊd(ə)nt/ should not

**should've** /'ʃʊd(ə)v/ should have

**shp** MECHANICAL ENGINEERING shaft horsepower

**shpt** shipment

**shr.** STOCK EXCHANGE share

**sht** PRINTING sheet

**shtg.** shortage

**S-HTTP** COMPUTING Secure HyperText Transfer Protocol

**si** ONLINE Slovenia (NOTE: The abbreviation **si** is seen at the end of Internet addresses, preceded by a dot.)

**Si** CHEMICAL ELEMENTS silicon

**SI 1.** MEASUREMENTS Système International (d'Unités) (NOTE: The abbreviation **SI**, from the French, 'International System (of Units)', refers to a set of units adopted for international use in science and technology. The coulomb, for example, is the *SI unit* of electric charge.) **2.** *NZ* GEOGRAPHY South Island **3.** FINANCE statutory instrument

**SIA** FINANCE Securities Institute of Australia

**SIB** FINANCE Securities and Investments Board

**SIC** COMMERCE Standard Industrial Classification

**SICAV** FINANCE a limited company in Luxembourg. Full form **société d'investissement à capital variable**

**SIDS** /sɪds/ MEDICINE the technical name for cot death. Full form **sudden infant death syndrome**

**SIG** /sɪg/ ONLINE special-interest group

**sig.** signature

**Sig. 1.** the Italian equivalent of Mr. Full form **Signor 2.** a title used before the name of a highly respected man or a man of advanced age in Italy and other Italian-speaking countries. Full form **Signore**

**sigint** /'sɪgɪnt/ intelligence data acquired electronically. Full form **signals intelligence**

**Signa** the Italian equivalent of Miss. Full form **Signorina**

**Sigra** the Italian equivalent of Mrs. Full form **Signora**

**sim.** similar

**SIM card** /'sɪm ˌkɑːd/ TELECOMMUNICATIONS a smart card inserted into a mobile phone that holds the personal information relating to the subscriber (e.g. the subscriber's PIN or stored phone numbers). Full form **Subscriber Identity Module card**

**SIMD** COMPUTING single instruction stream multiple data stream

**SIMM** /sɪm/ COMPUTING a module plugged into the motherboard of a computer to add memory. Full form **single in-line memory module**

**sin** MATHEMATICS sine

**SINBAD** /'sɪnbæd/ SOCIAL SCIENCES ◊ see note at **dinky**

**sing.** GRAMMAR singular

**Singh.** LANGUAGE Singhalese

**SINK** /sɪŋk/ SOCIAL SCIENCES ◊ see note at **dinky**

**SIO** COMPUTING serial input/output

**SIP** COMPUTING single in-line package

**SIPC** FINANCE Securities Investor Protection Corporation

**SIPO** COMPUTING serial input/parallel output

**SIPP** /sɪp/ PENSIONS self-invested personal pension

**SIR** GOVERNMENT Singapore Immigration and Registration

**SIS** INFORMATION SCIENCE strategic information systems

**SISD** COMPUTING single instruction stream single data stream

**SISO** COMPUTING serial input/serial output

**SITD** ONLINE still in the dark (*used in e-mails*)

**SIV** MICROBIOLOGY simian immunodeficiency virus

**sj** ONLINE Svalbard and Jan Mayen Islands (NOTE: The abbreviation **sj** is seen at the end of Internet addresses, preceded by a dot.)

**SJ** CHRISTIANITY Society of Jesus (NOTE: The abbreviation **SJ** is used after the name of a Jesuit.)

**SJA** MEDICINE Saint John Ambulance (Brigade or Association)

**SJD** Doctor of Juridical Science (NOTE: From the Latin *Scientiae Juridicae Doctor.*)

**sk** ONLINE Slovakia (NOTE: The abbreviation **sk** is seen at the end of Internet addresses, preceded by a dot.)

**SK** GEOGRAPHY Saskatchewan

**Skr.** LANGUAGE Sanskrit

**SKU** /,es keɪ 'juː, skjuː/ COMMERCE a unique code, consisting of numbers or letters and numbers, assigned to a product by a retailer for identification and stock control. Full form **stockkeeping unit**

**sl** ONLINE Sierra Leone (NOTE: The abbreviation **sl** is seen at the end of Internet addresses, preceded by a dot.)

**SL 1.** INSURANCE salvage loss **2.** GEOGRAPHY sea level **3.** LAW Solicitor-at-Law **4.** LINGUISTICS source language **5.** GEOGRAPHY south latitude

**SLA** COMMERCE service level agreement

**SLADE** /sleɪd/ ARTS Society of Lithographic Artists, Designers, Engravers, and Process Workers

**s.l.a.n.** PUBLISHING without place, year, or name (NOTE: From the Latin *sine loco, anno, vel nomine.*)

**SLBM** ARMS submarine-launched ballistic missile

**SLCM** ARMS sea-launched cruise missile

**SLE** MEDICINE a condition of the immune system in which it wrongly attacks the body's own tissues, most common in young women. Full form **systemic lupus erythematosus**

**SLIP** /slɪp/ ONLINE the older of two protocols for dial-up access to the Internet using a modem. It has now been largely replaced by point-to-point protocol (PPP). Full form **serial line Internet protocol**

**SLOSS** ENVIRONMENT a term in ecology relating to the debate over whether it is better to protect one large area or many smaller ones. Full form **single large or several small**

**SLP** POLITICS Scottish Labour Party

**SLR** PHOTOGRAPHY a camera in which the light passes through one lens to the film and, by means of a mirror and prism system, to the focusing screen. Full form **single-lens reflex**

**SLSI** ELECTRONICS super large scale integration

**SLV** AEROSPACE **1.** space launch vehicle **2.** standard launch vehicle

**sm** ONLINE San Marino (NOTE: The abbreviation **sm** is seen at the end of Internet addresses, preceded by a dot.)

**Sm** CHEMICAL ELEMENTS samarium

**SM** MILITARY Sergeant Major

**sm.** small

**S/M** sadomasochism

**SMA** METALLURGY shape memory alloy

**SMATV** TV satellite master antenna television

**SMB** COMPUTING server message block

**SME** BUSINESS small and medium-sized enterprises

**SMED** COMMERCE the concept of reducing the time involved in setting up a manufacturing process, ideally to under ten minutes. Full form **single minute exchange of dies**

**SMI** BUSINESS the stock market index of the Zurich stock exchange in Switzerland. Full form **Swiss Market Index**

**S/MIME** /ˌes ˈmaɪm/ COMPUTING Secure/Multipurpose Internet Mail Extensions

**SMP** HUMAN RESOURCES statutory maternity pay

**SMR** MEDICINE submucous resection

**SMS** TELECOMMUNICATIONS a service that allows short text messages to be sent to and from mobile phones. Full form **short message service**

> Text messaging has introduced a new form of shorthand that can seem daunting to the uninitiated, although it is largely based on well-established principles that date from long before the introduction of this technology. These include omitting letters from words (e.g. tlk = 'talk', wn = 'when', yr = 'your'), using letters and numbers in place of words or syllables that sound the same (e.g. C = 'see', R = 'are', U = 'you', 2 = 'to', 4 = 'for', 8 as in GR8 = 'great', L8R = 'later', and W8 = 'wait'), and reducing phrases to their initial letters (e.g. CB = 'call back', IDK = 'I don't know', MYOB = 'mind your own business', SYS = 'see you soon').

**SMT** COMPUTING surface-mount technology

**SMTP** COMPUTING the main protocol used to send electronic mail on the Internet, consisting of rules for how programs sending mail should interact with programs receiving mail. Full form **simple mail transfer protocol**

**sn** ONLINE Senegal (NOTE: The abbreviation **sn** is seen at the end of Internet addresses, preceded by a dot.)

**Sn** CHEMICAL ELEMENTS tin

**SN** *US* MILITARY seaman

**SNA** COMPUTING systems network architecture

**SNAFU** /ˈsnæfuː/ situation normal all fouled up (NOTE: The acronym **SNAFU** (or *snafu*) is used as a noun to denote any mishap or mistake generally caused by incompetence and resulting in delay or confusion.)

**SNCF** RAIL the national railway system in France. Full form **Société Nationale des Chemins de Fer** (NOTE: From the French, 'National Railway Association'.)

**SNG** INDUST substitute (or synthetic) natural gas

**SNMP** COMPUTING simple network management protocol

**SNOBOL** /ˈsnəʊbɒl/ COMPUTING a high-level computer programming language designed for dealing with strings of symbols. Full form **StriNg-Oriented symBOlic Language** (NOTE: The form of the acronym **SNOBOL** is humorously modelled on that of COBOL, an otherwise unrelated language.)

**SNP 1.** POLITICS Scottish National Party **2.** BIOTECHNOLOGY a commonly found change in a single nucleotide base in a DNA sequence, occurring about every 1,000 bases. It is of significance in biomedical research. Full form **single nucleotide polymorphism**

**Snr** Senior

**so** ONLINE Somalia (NOTE: The abbreviation **so** is seen at the end of Internet addresses, preceded by a dot.)

**SO 1.** a spouse or long-term sexual partner (*used in Internet chat rooms and text messages*) Full form **significant other 2.** BANKING standing order

**s.o.** FINANCE seller's option

**sociol.** sociology

**SOCKS** /sɒks/ COMPUTING a network protocol developed to support the transfer of TCP/IP (Internet) traffic through a proxy server. It is commonly used to enable users on a local area network to access the Internet via a single shared connection. Full form **sockets**

**S. of Sol.** BIBLE Song of Solomon

**soln** solution

**SOM** ECOLOGY soil organic matter

**Som.** GEOGRAPHY **1.** Somalia **2.** Somerset

**sonar** /ˈsəʊnɑː/ ◊ see note at **Aids**

**SOP** standard operating procedure

**sop.** MUSIC soprano

**SOR** COMMERCE sale or return

**SORN** /sɔːn/ AUTOMOTIVE a formal declaration by the owner that a vehicle does not require a road-fund licence (i.e. a current tax disc) because it is not being used on public roads. Full form **statutory off-road notification** (NOTE: The acronym **SORN** is used as a noun in its own right.)

**SOS** a call or signal requesting help (NOTE: The abbreviation **SOS**, popularly said to stand for 'save our souls', was chosen as an international distress signal because it could be easily transmitted and received in Morse code.)

**Sov.** Soviet

**SOW** ONLINE speaking of which (*used in e-mails and text messages*)

**Sow.** a title used in India before the name of a married woman whose husband is still alive. Full form **Sowbhagyawati**

**SP 1.** COMPUTING the address register containing the address of the most recently-stored piece of data or the location of the next piece of data to be retrieved. Full form **stack pointer 2.** HORSERACING starting price **3.** NAVY submarine patrol

**sp. 1.** special **2.** BIOLOGY species **3.** specific **4.** specimen **5.** spelling

**Sp. 1.** GEOGRAPHY Spain **2.** Spaniard **3.** LANGUAGE Spanish

**s.p.** LAW without children (NOTE: From the Latin *sine prole*.)

**SpA** COMMERCE società per azioni (NOTE: From the Italian, 'limited company'.)

**Span.** LANGUAGE Spanish

**SPC** COMMERCE statistical process control

**SPCK** CHRISTIANITY Society for Promoting Christian Knowledge

**spec. 1.** special **2.** specification

**specif. 1.** specific **2.** specifically

**SPECT** MEDICINE a technique used in diagnosing some diseases that generates a three-dimensional computer image of the distribution of a radioactive tracer in a particular organ. Full form **single photon emission computed tomography**

**SPF** the degree to which a sun cream, lotion, screen, or block provides protection for the skin against the sun. Full form **sun protection factor**

**Spgs** Springs (NOTE: The abbreviation **Spgs** is used in placenames.)

**sp ht** PHYSICS specific heat

**SPL** MEASUREMENTS, ACOUSTICS sound pressure level

**SPOT** ENVIRONMENT Système Probatoire d'Observation de la Terre

**spp.** BIOLOGY species (NOTE: The abbreviation **spp.** is the plural form of sp.)

**SPQR** ANCIENT HIST Senatus Populusque Romanus (NOTE: From the Latin, 'the senate and people of Rome'.)

**Spr** MILITARY Sapper

**SPS** PHYSICS standard pressure setting

**spt** GEOGRAPHY seaport

**SPUC** /spʌk/ Society for the Protection of the Unborn Child

**SPX** COMPUTING simplex

**sq. 1.** sequence **2.** sequens **3.** MILITARY squadron **4.** MEASUREMENTS square

**Sq. 1.** MILITARY Squadron **2.** ROADS Square (NOTE: The abbreviation **Sq.** is used in addresses.)

**SQA** COMPUTING software quality assurance

**SQL** /'siːkw(ə)l/ COMPUTING a standardized language that approximates the structure of natural English for obtaining information from databases. Full form **structured query language**

**Sqn** MILITARY Squadron

**sr 1.** MEASUREMENTS, MATHEMATICS steradian **2.** ONLINE Suriname (NOTE: The abbreviation **sr** is seen at the end of Internet addresses, preceded by a dot.)

**Sr 1.** CHEMICAL ELEMENTS strontium **2.** the Portuguese equivalent of Mr. Full form **Senhor 3.** senior **4.** the Spanish equivalent of Mr. Full form **Señor 5.** the Italian equivalent of Mr. Full form **Signor 6.** Sir **7.** Sister

**Sra 1.** the Portuguese equivalent of Mrs. Full form **Senhora 2.** the Spanish equivalent of Mrs. Full form **Señora**

**SRA** RAIL Strategic Rail Authority

**SRAM** /'es ræm/ COMPUTING static random-access memory

**SRB** COMMERCE sales returns book

**SRCN** HEALTH SERVICES State Registered Children's Nurse

**SRDS** BUSINESS Standard Rate and Data Service

**SRI** FINANCE socially responsible investor

**Srl** COMMERCE società a responsabilità limitata (NOTE: From the Italian, 'limited company'.)

**SRN** HEALTH SERVICES State Registered Nurse

**sRNA** BIOCHEMISTRY soluble RNA

**SRO 1.** BUSINESS self-regulatory organization **2.** TRAVEL single room occupancy **3.** standing room only **4.** Statutory Rules and Orders

**SRT** COMPUTING source transparent routing

**Srta 1.** the Portuguese equivalent of Miss. Full form **Senhorita 2.** the Spanish equivalent of Miss. Full form **Señorita**

**ss** PUBLISHING sections

**SS 1.** Saints **2.** SOCIAL WELFARE Social Security **3.** BOAT steamship **4.** CHRISTIANITY Sunday school **5.** LAW sworn statement

**SSADM** MANAGEMENT structured systems analysis and design method

**SSAP** ACCOUNTING Statement of Standard Accounting Practice

**SSB** RADIO single sideband (transmission)

**SSC 1.** *S Asia* EDUCATION a qualification given to students in India on passing out of secondary school. Full form **Secondary School Certificate 2.** LAW Solicitor to the Supreme Court

**SSD** COMPUTING single-sided disk

**SSE** south-southeast

**SSG** *US* MILITARY Staff Sergeant

**SSgt** MILITARY Staff Sergeant

**SSHA** SOCIAL WELFARE Scottish Special Housing Association

**SSI 1.** ELECTRONICS small-scale integration **2.** BUSINESS instructions from one bank to other banks as to the procedure to be followed when making payments to it. Full form **standing settlement instructions**

**SSL** COMPUTING a protocol designed by Netscape that provides secure communications over the Internet. Full form **secure sockets layer**

**SSM** ARMS surface-to-surface missile

**SSN** *US* SOCIAL WELFARE Social Security Number

**SSP** HUMAN RESOURCES statutory sick pay

**ssp.** BIOLOGY subspecies

**SSR** POLITICS Soviet Socialist Republic (NOTE: The abbreviation **SSR** was used in the names of constituent members of the Soviet Union, such as the *Latvian SSR* (now Latvia).)

**SSRI** PHARMACOLOGY an antidepressant drug that increases serotonin levels in synapses, resulting in elevation of mood. Full form **selective serotonin reuptake inhibitor**

**SSSI** /ˌtrɪp(ə)l es ˈaɪ/ ENVIRONMENT Site of Special Scientific Interest

**SST** TRANSPORT supersonic transport

**SSW** south-southwest

**st 1.** ONLINE São Tomé and Príncipe (NOTE: The abbreviation **st** is seen at the end of Internet addresses, preceded by a dot.) **2.** MEASUREMENTS short ton

**St 1.** CHRISTIANITY Saint **2.** GEOGRAPHY Strait **3.** ROADS Street (NOTE: The abbreviation **St** is used in addresses.)

**ST** TIME standard time

**st. 1.** POETRY stanza **2.** start **3.** state **4.** LAW statute **5.** PRINTING stet **6.** HANDICRAFT stitch

**Sta** Santa (NOTE: The abbreviation **Sta**, from Spanish and Italian, is used before the name of a woman who is a saint, especially in placenames.)

**stacc.** MUSIC staccato

**Staffs.** GEOGRAPHY Staffordshire

**START** /stɑːt/ MILITARY Strategic Arms Reduction Talks

**STB** BUSINESS the joining together of unions so as to enter negotiations as one entity, to ensure fairness to all members of a profession. Full form **single table bargaining**

**stbd** NAUTICAL starboard

**std** standard

**STD 1.** MEDICINE sexually transmitted disease **2.** TELECOMMUNICATIONS subscriber trunk dialling

**Ste** Sainte (NOTE: The abbreviation **Ste**, from French, is used before the name of a woman who is a saint, and is often used in the names of wines.)

**ster.** MONEY sterling

**stg** MONEY sterling

**stge** storage

**Sth** south

**STI** MEDICINE sexually transmitted infection

**stk** COMMERCE stock

**STM** RELIGION Master of Sacred Theology (NOTE: From the Latin *Sacrae Theologiae Magister.*)

**STOL** /stɒl/ AVIAT a flying system that gives an aircraft the ability to take off and land on a very short runway. Full form **short takeoff and landing**

**STP 1.** COMPUTING shielded twisted pair (cable) **2.** PHYSICS standard temperature and pressure

**s.t.p. 1.** COMPUTING shielded twisted pair (cable) **2.** PHYSICS standard temperature and pressure

**str. 1.** GEOGRAPHY strait **2.** ROWING stroke

**Str.** GEOGRAPHY Strait

**STRESS** /stres/ COMPUTING structural engineering system solver

**STS** GENETICS sequence tagged site

**STUC** POLITICS Scottish Trades Union Congress

**STV 1.** TV Scottish Television **2.** POLITICS a system of voting in a multimember constituency in which voters list the candidates in order of preference and any candidate receiving the required number of votes is elected. Full form **single transferable vote**

**STX** COMPUTING start of text

**STYS** ONLINE speak to you soon (*used in e-mails and text messages*)

**SU** MEASUREMENTS, NUCLEAR PHYSICS strontium unit

**subj. 1.** GRAMMAR subject **2.** subjective **3.** GRAMMAR subjunctive

**Suff.** GEOGRAPHY Suffolk

**Sun.** CALENDAR Sunday

**sup. 1.** superior **2.** GRAMMAR superlative **3.** GRAMMAR supine **4.** supplement **5.** supplementary **6.** supply **7.** supra (NOTE: The abbreviation **sup.** is used in formal writing to refer the reader back to something at an earlier point in the same text.)

**Supdt** Superintendent

**super. 1.** superfine **2.** superior

**Supt** Superintendent

**supvr** supervisor

**Sur.** GEOGRAPHY Suriname

**surg. 1.** surgeon **2.** surgery **3.** surgical

**SUV** *N Am* VEHICLES a tough four-wheel-drive vehicle built on a truck chassis, usually used for everyday driving. Full form **sport-utility vehicle**

**sv** ONLINE El Salvador (NOTE: The abbreviation **sv** is seen at the end of Internet addresses, preceded by a dot.)

**Sv** MEASUREMENTS, SCIENCE sievert

**SV** CHRISTIANITY **1.** Holy Virgin (NOTE: From the Latin *Sancta Virgo*.) **2.** Your Holiness

**s.v. 1.** BOAT sailing vessel **2.** ENGINEERING side valve **3.** under the word or term (NOTE: The abbreviation **s.v.** is used in textual references, e.g. to direct the reader to a particular headword in a dictionary or encyclopedia.)

**SVA** FINANCE shareholder value analysis

**SVGA** a modified specification for video display controllers used in personal computers. Full form **super video graphics array**

**SW 1.** RADIO short wave **2.** southwest **3.** southwestern

**Sw. 1.** GEOGRAPHY Sweden **2.** LANGUAGE Swedish

**SWALK** /swɔːlk/ sealed with a loving kiss

> The acronym **SWALK**, traditionally written on the back of an envelope containing a letter to a beloved person, is falling into disuse along with the practice of letter-writing itself. Nonetheless, it is probably the most enduring of a set of acronyms formerly used in the same way. Many of the others share a geographical theme; they include *BURMA* 'be undressed and ready my angel', *HOLLAND* 'hope our love lasts and never dies', *ITALY* 'I trust and love you', and *NORWICH* '(k)nickers off ready when I come home'.

**SWAT** /swɒt/ *US* POLICE a police unit that is trained in the use of military weapons and tactics. Full form **Special Weapons and Tactics**

**swbd** TELECOMMUNICATIONS switchboard

**SWbS** southwest by south

**SWbW** southwest by west

**SWELL** /swel/ SOCIAL SCIENCES ◊ see note at **dinky**

**SWG** MEASUREMENTS, MECHANICAL ENGINEERING standard wire gauge

**SWIFT** /swɪft/ BANKING Society for Worldwide Interbank Financial Telecommunications

**SWIM** /swɪm/ see what I mean? (*used in e-mails and text messages*)

**Switz.** GEOGRAPHY Switzerland

**SWP** POLITICS Socialist Workers Party

**SWPA** GEOGRAPHY Southwestern Pacific Area

**SX** COMPUTING a type of processor chip derived from the basic 80386 or 80486 processor that is slightly cheaper to manufacture and buy

**sy** ONLINE Syria (NOTE: The abbreviation **sy** is seen at the end of Internet addresses, preceded by a dot.)

**SYHA** Scottish Youth Hostels Association

**sym. 1.** symbol **2.** symmetrical **3.** MUSIC symphony **4.** MEDICINE symptom

**synd.** syndicate

**SYS** ONLINE see you soon (*used in e-mails and text messages*)

**syst.** system

**sz** ONLINE Swaziland (NOTE: The abbreviation **sz** is seen at the end of Internet addresses, preceded by a dot.)

# T

**t 1.** PHYSICS time **2.** MEASUREMENTS, FREIGHT tare **3.** MEASUREMENTS, COOKERY teaspoon(ful) **4.** MUSIC tempo **5.** MUSIC tenor **6.** GRAMMAR tense **7.** MEASUREMENTS ton **8.** GRAMMAR transitive **9.** MEASUREMENTS troy

**T 1.** PHYSICS absolute temperature **2.** PHYSICS kinetic energy **3.** PHYSICS period **4.** PHYSICS surface tension **5.** MEASUREMENTS, COOKERY tablespoon(ful) **6.** TELECOMMUNICATIONS telephone (number) (NOTE: The abbreviation **T** is used to contrast with E (e-mail address) and F (fax number).) **7.** MEASUREMENTS temperature **8.** MEASUREMENTS tera- **9.** PHYSICS tesla **10.** CALENDAR Thursday **11.** CHEMICAL ELEMENTS tritium **12.** true **13.** CALENDAR Tuesday

**Ta** CHEMICAL ELEMENTS tantalum

**TA 1.** ARMY Territorial Army **2.** ONLINE thanks again (*used in e-mails and text messages*) **3.** PSYCHOLOGY a form of psychotherapy that emphasizes the interactions within and between individuals and classifies these interactions as 'adult', 'parent', or 'child'. Full form **transactional analysis 4.** TRANSPORT Transit Authority

**TAB 1.** COMPUTING tabulate **2.** /tæb/ GAMBLING in Australia and New Zealand, the agency or company that runs legal betting on horseracing, greyhound racing, and other sporting events. Full form **Totalizator Agency Board 3.** IMMUNOLOGY typhoid-paratyphoid A-paratyphoid B (vaccine)

**tab.** table

**TAC** /tæk/ FISHERIES total allowable catch

**TAFE** /teɪf/ EDUCATION in Australia, a system of higher education providing instruction in technical subjects. Full form **Technical and Further Education**

**TAFN** ONLINE that's all for now (*used in e-mails and Internet chat rooms*)

**'tain't** /taɪnt/ it ain't

**TALISMAN** /'tælɪzmən/ STOCK EXCHANGE a computer system used for buying and selling securities on the London Stock Exchange. Full form **Transfer Accounting Lodgement for Investors and Stock Management**

**TAM** /tæm/ TV Television Audience Measurement

**tan** MATHEMATICS tangent

**T & E** an informal euphemism describing somebody who is slightly drunk. Full form **tired and emotional**

**TAO** BUSINESS an application for specific relief from taxes on the grounds that they are causing you significant hardship. Full form **taxpayer assistance order**

**TAPI** COMPUTING telephony application programming interface

**TAS** AEROSPACE true air speed

**Tas.** GEOGRAPHY Tasmania

**TAT 1.** PSYCHOLOGY thematic apperception test **2.** COMPUTING turnaround time

**TAURUS** /'tɔːrəs/ STOCK EXCHANGE a computerized system used for buying and selling securities on the International Stock Exchange. Full form **Transfer of Automated Registration of Uncertified Stock**

**Tb** CHEMICAL ELEMENTS terbium

**TB 1.** NAVY torpedo boat **2.** ACCOUNTING trial balance **3.** MEDICINE tuberculosis (NOTE: The abbreviation **TB** is used as a noun in its own right in this sense.)

**TBA 1.** to be agreed **2.** to be announced **3.** WINE the highest grade of German table wine, made from individually selected shrivelled grapes and typically very sweet. Full form **Trockenbeerenauslese**

**TBC** ONLINE to be continued (*used in e-mails and text messages*)

**TBD 1.** to be determined **2.** to be discussed

**TBI** MEDICINE total body irradiation

**T-bill** FINANCE a financial security issued by the Treasury payable to the bearer after a fixed period, usually three months. Full form **Treasury bill**

**tbs.** MEASUREMENTS, COOKERY tablespoon(ful)

**TBT** ECOLOGY a compound used in marine antifouling paints, banned in many counties because of its devastating effect on wildlife. Full form **tributyl tin**

**tc** ONLINE Turks and Caicos Islands (NOTE: The abbreviation **tc** is seen at the end of Internet addresses, preceded by a dot.)

**Tc** CHEMICAL ELEMENTS technetium

**TC 1.** BUSINESS till countermanded **2.** AUTOMOTIVE twin carburettors

**TCA** WINE a chemical that can form on wine bottle corks during the manufacturing process, causing the wine to become musty and 'corked' in storage. Full form **trichloranisole**

**TCCB** CRICKET Test and County Cricket Board

**TCDD** CHEMISTRY an extremely toxic by-product of herbicide manufacture. Full form **tetrachlorodibenzodioxin**

**TCO** BUSINESS total cost of ownership

**TCOB** ONLINE taking care of business (*used in e-mails and text messages*)

**TCP/IP** ONLINE a protocol used for transmitting data between computers and as the basis for standard protocols on the Internet. Full form **transmission control protocol/Internet protocol**

**TCS** FINANCE Tariff Concession Scheme

**TD 1.** GOVERNMENT Member of the Dáil (the lower house of the Irish parliament) (NOTE: From the Irish *Teachta Dála*.) **2.** ARMS tank destroyer **3.** TECHNOLOGY technical drawing **4.** MILITARY Territorial Decoration **5.** AMERICAN FOOTBALL touchdown

**TDB** COMMERCE Trade Development Board

**TDD** TELECOMMUNICATIONS telecommunications device for the deaf

**TDM 1.** TELECOMMUNICATIONS time-division multiplexing **2.** ONLINE too damn many (*used in e-mails and text messages*)

**TDR** COMPUTING a method of testing a conductor such as a fibre-optic cable for faults, by sending a controlled pulsed signal into it and monitoring the reflections of this. Full form **time domain reflectometry**

**TDS** COMPUTING transaction-driven system

**Te** CHEMICAL ELEMENTS tellurium

**TEC** /tek/ BUSINESS Training and Enterprise Council

**tec.** technician

**tech. 1.** technical **2.** technician **3.** technology

**technol.** technology

**TED** MEDICINE supportive elastic stockings that help to maintain circulation in the lower legs and prevent conditions such as deep-vein thrombosis. Full form **thromboembolic deterrent (stocking)**

**TEE** RAIL Trans-Europe Express (train)

**TEFL** /'tef(ə)l/ EDUCATION teaching of English as a foreign language

**TEL** CHEMISTRY an extremely poisonous oily liquid formerly used as an antiknock agent in petrol. Full form **tetraethyl lead**

**tel. 1.** telegram **2.** telegraph **3.** telegraphic **4.** telephone

**teleg. 1.** telegram **2.** telegraph **3.** telegraphic **4.** telegraphy

**temp. 1.** temperance **2.** temperate **3.** temperature **4.** template **5.** temporal **6.** temporary

**TENS** /tens/ MEDICINE a method of treating chronic pain by applying electrodes to the skin and passing small electric currents through sensory nerves and the spinal cord, thus suppressing the transmission of pain signals. Full form **transcutaneous electrical nerve stimulation**

**TEPP** /tep/ CHEMISTRY a crystalline compound used as an insecticide and in medicine as a stimulant for the nervous system. Full form **tetraethyl pyrophosphate**

**TER** EDUCATION in parts of Australia, a measure on a scale of 0 to 100 of a student's performance in the HUSK (Higher School Certificate) examinations, used to assess eligibility for tertiary courses. Full form **tertiary entrance rank**

**ter. 1.** terrace **2.** territorial **3.** territory

**Ter.** Terrace (NOTE: The abbreviation **Ter.** is used in addresses.)

**term.** terminal

**terr. 1.** territorial **2.** territory

**Terr.** Terrace (NOTE: The abbreviation **Terr.** is used in addresses.)

**TE score** EDUCATION in Australia, a score awarded on the basis of final secondary school examinations that determines whether or not a student is accepted into some tertiary education institutions. Full form **tertiary entrance score**

**TESL** /'tes(ə)l/ EDUCATION teaching of English as a second language

**TESOL** /'tiːsɒl/ EDUCATION teaching of English to speakers of other languages

**TESSA** /'tesə/ FINANCE a tax-free savings account, now superseded by the ISA (although **TESSAs** opened before the introduction of ISAs may still be held or transferred). Full form **tax-exempt special savings account**

**Test.** BIBLE Testament

**Teut.** Teutonic

**Tex.** GEOGRAPHY Texan

**TFN** FINANCE tax file number

**TFR** ECOLOGY total fertility rate

**TFTP** COMPUTING a simple form of the standard FTP (file transfer protocol) system, commonly used to load the operating system software onto a diskless workstation from a server. Full form **trivial file transfer protocol**

**tg** ONLINE Togo (NOTE: The abbreviation **tg** is seen at the end of Internet addresses, preceded by a dot.)

**TG** LINGUISTICS transformational grammar

**TGAL** ONLINE think globally, act locally

**TGAT** /'tiːgæt/ EDUCATION Task Group on Assessment and Testing

**TGI** MARKETING Target Group Index

**TGIF** thank God (or goodness) it's Friday

**TGV** RAIL in France and some other countries, a very high-speed train. Full form **train à grande vitesse** (NOTE: The abbreviation **TGV**, from French, is used as a noun in its own right.)

**TGWU** HUMAN RESOURCES Transport and General Workers' Union

**th** ONLINE Thailand (NOTE: The abbreviation **th** is seen at the end of Internet addresses, preceded by a dot.)

**Th** CHEMICAL ELEMENTS thorium

**Th. 1.** BIBLE Thessalonians **2.** CALENDAR Thursday

**ThB** RELIGION Bachelor of Theology (NOTE: From the Latin *Theologiae Baccalaureus*.)

**THC** CHEMISTRY the main active chemical in cannabis. Full form **tetrahydrocannabinol**

**ThD** RELIGION Doctor of Theology (NOTE: From the Latin *Theologiae Doctor.*)

**theat.** **1.** theatre **2.** theatrical

**theol.** RELIGION **1.** theologian **2.** theological **3.** theology

**theos.** RELIGION **1.** theosophical **2.** theosophy

**therap.** MEDICINE **1.** therapeutic **2.** therapeutics

**therm.** thermometer

**Thess.** BIBLE Thessalonians

**they'd** /θeɪd/ **1.** they had **2.** they would

**they'll** /θeɪl/ **1.** they shall **2.** they will

**they're** /θeə/ they are

**they've** /θeɪv/ they have

**THI** PHYSICS temperature-humidity index

**THNQ** ONLINE thank you (*used in e-mails and text messages*)

**thp** MEASUREMENTS, MECHANICAL ENGINEERING thrust horsepower

**3G** /θriːˈdʒiː/ TELECOMMUNICATIONS a wireless communications technology that, when fully functional, will provide high-speed mobile access to the Internet, entertainment, information, and intranets. Full form **Third Generation**

**Thur.** CALENDAR Thursday

**Thurs.** CALENDAR Thursday

**THX** ONLINE thanks (*used in e-mails and text messages*)

**THz** MEASUREMENTS, PHYSICS terahertz

**Ti** CHEMICAL ELEMENTS titanium

**TIA** **1.** ONLINE thanks in advance (*used in e-mails and text messages*) **2.** MEDICINE a temporary disruption to normal body function caused by a restriction of blood flow to the brain, commonly called a 'mini-stroke'. Full form **transient ischaemic attack**

**TIBOR** /ˈtiːbɔː/ BANKING Tokyo Interbank Offered Rate

**TIC** ONLINE tongue in cheek (*used in e-mails*)

**t.i.d.** PHARMACOLOGY three times a day (NOTE: The abbreviation **t.i.d.**, from the Latin *ter in die*, is used in prescriptions.)

**TIFF** /tɪf/ COMPUTING tagged image file format

**TIGR** /ˈtaɪɡə/ FINANCE a bond linked to US treasury bonds, profits from which are subject to UK tax when the bond is cashed or redeemed. Full form **Treasury Investment Growth Receipts**

**TILA** FINANCE Truth in Lending Act

**Tim.** BIBLE Timothy

**tinct.** PHARMACEUTICAL INDUSTRY tincture

**TIR** TRANSPORT Transports Internationaux Routiers (NOTE: The abbreviation **TIR**, from the French, 'international road transport', is seen on trucks.)

**'tis** /tɪs/ it is

**Tit.** BIBLE Titus

**tj** ONLINE Tajikistan (NOTE: The abbreviation **tj** is seen at the end of Internet addresses, preceded by a dot.)

**tk** TRANSPORT truck

**TKO** BOXING technical knockout

**tkt** ticket

**Tl** CHEMICAL ELEMENTS thallium

**t.l.** INSURANCE total loss

**TLA** three-letter acronym

**TLA** has come to be used of many terms that are not strictly acronyms (which can be pronounced as a word) but abbreviations or initialisms (which are pronounced letter by letter). **CAMRA** is a TLA, for instance, but **BBC** is an initialism.

**TLC 1.** tender loving care **2.** SCIENCE thin-layer chromatography
The abbreviation **TLC** is used as a noun in its own right in this sense. It principally denotes the care and attention required by people (as in *She just needs a bit of TLC*), but can also refer to plants, animals, and even inanimate objects.

**t.l.o.** INSURANCE total loss only

**tm** ONLINE Turkmenistan (NOTE: The abbreviation **tm** is seen at the end of Internet addresses, preceded by a dot.)

**Tm** CHEMICAL ELEMENTS thulium

**TM 1.** trademark **2.** transcendental meditation **3.** ONLINE trust me (*used in e-mails and text messages*)

**TMJ** ANATOMY either of the joints connecting the lower part of the jaw (the mandible) with the temporal bone on each side of the head. Full form **temporomandibular joint** (NOTE: *TMJ syndrome* is a painful condition involving the temporomandibular joint and the muscles used for chewing, sometimes causing clicking sounds and restricted jaw movement.)

**TMT** BUSINESS technology, media, and telecommunications ○ *companies in the TMT sector*

**tn** ONLINE Tunisia (NOTE: The abbreviation **tn** is seen at the end of Internet addresses, preceded by a dot.)

**TN** MAIL Tennessee (NOTE: The abbreviation **TN** is part of the US sorting code on the last line of a Tennessee address.)

**TNA** HUMAN RESOURCES training-needs analysis

**tng** training

**TNT** CHEMISTRY a yellow flammable crystalline compound used as an explosive. Full form **trinitrotoluene** (NOTE: The abbreviation **TNT** is used as a noun in its own right, and the full form is rarely encountered.)

**TNX** ONLINE thanks (*used in e-mails and text messages*)

**to** ONLINE Tonga (NOTE: The abbreviation **to** is seen at the end of Internet addresses, preceded by a dot.)

**Tob.** BIBLE Tobit

**TOC** /tɒk/ RAIL train operating company

**Toc H** /ˌtɒk ˈeɪtʃ/ CHRISTIANITY an interdenominational association formed in England after World War I to encourage Christian fellowship (NOTE: **Toc H** was telegraphic code for TH, the initials of Talbot House, a Belgian recreation centre on which the association was modelled.)

**TOE** MEASUREMENTS tonnes of oil equivalent

**TOIL** /tɔɪl/ HUMAN RESOURCES time off in lieu

**TOPIC** /ˈtɒpɪk/ STOCK EXCHANGE Teletext Output of Price Information by Computer

**topog.** GEOGRAPHY topography

**tox.** toxicology

**TOY** ONLINE thinking of you (*used in e-mails and text messages*)

**tp** MILITARY troop

**TP** COMPUTING **1.** teleprocessing **2.** transaction processing

**t.p.** PUBLISHING title page

**TPA** BIOCHEMISTRY an anticlotting enzyme that is produced naturally in blood vessel linings and is genetically engineered for use in treating heart attacks, to dissolve blood clots, and to prevent heart muscle damage. Full form **tissue plasminogen activator**

**TPC** *Aus* COMMERCE Trade Practices Commission

**TPI 1.** FINANCE tax and price index **2.** COMPUTING tracks per inch

**TPM** COMMERCE total productive maintenance

**TPN** BIOCHEMISTRY another name for NADP. Full form **triphosphopyridine nucleotide**

**TPO** ECOLOGY tree preservation order

**Tpr** MILITARY Trooper

**TPWS** RAIL a safety system that automatically causes the brakes of a train to be applied if it passes a signal set at danger. Full form **Train Protection and Warning System**

**TQM** MANAGEMENT total quality management

**tr** ONLINE Turkey (NOTE: The abbreviation **tr** is seen at the end of Internet addresses, preceded by a dot.)

**TR** TELECOMMUNICATIONS transmit-receive

**tr. 1.** GRAMMAR transitive **2.** PUBLISHING translator **3.** PRINTING transpose **4.** PRINTING transposition **5.** FINANCE treasurer **6.** MUSIC trill **7.** MILITARY troop **8.** FINANCE trust **9.** FINANCE trustee

**trad.** traditional (NOTE: When *trad* is used informally as an adjective or noun referring to traditional jazz, it is written without a full stop.)

**trans. 1.** COMMERCE transaction **2.** transferred **3.** GRAMMAR transitive **4.** PUBLISHING translated **5.** PUBLISHING translation **6.** transport **7.** transpose **8.** transverse

**transf.** transferred

**transl.** PUBLISHING **1.** translated **2.** translation **3.** translator

**transp. 1.** transport **2.** transportation

**treas.** FINANCE **1.** treasurer **2.** treasury

**TRH 1.** Their Royal Highnesses **2.** BIOCHEMISTRY a hormone released by the hypothalamus which stimulates the pituitary gland to produce thyroid stimulating hormone. Full form **thyroid-releasing hormone 3.** BIOCHEMISTRY a peptide hormone that is produced by the hypothalamus and controls the release of thyrotropin (TSH) by the pituitary gland. Full form **thyrotropin-releasing hormone**

**trig.** MATHEMATICS **1.** trigonometric(al) (NOTE: When *trig* is used in the phrase *trig point*, short for 'trigonometrical point', it is written without a full stop.) **2.** trigonometry (NOTE: When *trig* is used informally in this sense, especially with reference to trigonometry as a school subject, it is written without a full stop.)

**tripl.** triplicate

**tRNA** BIOCHEMISTRY transfer RNA

**trop. 1.** GEOGRAPHY tropic **2.** tropical

**trp** MILITARY troop

**trs.** PRINTING transpose (NOTE: The abbreviation **trs.** is used in proofreading to mean 'change the order of the indicated words'.)

**TS** transsexual

**TSA** STOCK EXCHANGE The Securities Association

**TSAPI** COMPUTING telephony services application programming interface

**TSE** MEDICINE a disease that affects the nervous system and can be transmitted from one species to another. Full form **transmissible spongiform encephalopathy**

**TSH** BIOCHEMISTRY a hormone that is secreted by the pituitary gland and stimulates release of hormones by the thyroid gland. TSH is also called thyrotropin. Full form **thyroid-stimulating hormone**

**tsp.** MEASUREMENTS, COOKERY teaspoon(ful)

**TSR 1.** HUMAN RESOURCES telephone sales representative **2.** COMPUTING a program which loads itself into main memory and carries out a function when activated. Full form **terminate and stay resident (program)**

**TSS** MEDICINE acute circulatory failure, commonly associated with the use of vaginal tampons, which can create conditions promoting the growth of a toxin-producing staphylococcal bacterium. Full form **toxic shock syndrome**

**TSW** COMPUTING telesoftware

**tt** ONLINE Trinidad and Tobago (NOTE: The abbreviation **tt** is seen at the end of Internet addresses, preceded by a dot.)

**TT 1.** teetotal **2.** BANKING telegraphic transfer **3.** MOTORCYCLES a series of motorcycle races held every year in the Isle of Man. Full form **Tourist Trophy 4.** AGRICULTURE tuberculin-tested

**TTFN** ta-ta for now

> The abbreviation **TTFN**, used informally in place of 'goodbye', originated in the 1940s as a catchphrase on the BBC radio programme *ITMA* (*It's That Man Again*), featuring the comedian Tommy Handley.

**TTL 1.** PHOTOGRAPHY through-the-lens ○ *TTL metering* **2.** ELECTRONICS a method of constructing electronic logic circuits. Full form **transistor-transistor logic**

**TTL4N** ONLINE that's the lot for now (*used in e-mails*)

**TTT** ONLINE **1.** that's the ticket (*used in e-mails*) **2.** to the top (NOTE: The abbreviation **TTT** is used in Internet bulletin boards to move a message to a more prominent position and stop it being overlooked.)

**TTY** COMPUTING teletype

**TU** HUMAN RESOURCES trade union

**Tu.** CALENDAR Tuesday

**TUC** POLITICS Trades Union Congress

**Tue.** CALENDAR Tuesday

**Tun.** GEOGRAPHY **1.** Tunisia **2.** Tunisian

**Tur. 1.** GEOGRAPHY Turkey **2.** LANGUAGE Turkish

**Turk. 1.** GEOGRAPHY Turkey **2.** LANGUAGE Turkish

**tv** ONLINE Tuvalu (NOTE: The abbreviation **tv** is seen at the end of Internet addresses, preceded by a dot.)

**TV 1.** television **2.** transvestite

**TVEI** EDUCATION Technical and Vocational Education Initiative

**TVP** FOOD INDUSTRY a high-protein product made from processed soya beans that are formed into chunks or minced and flavoured to taste like meat. Full form **textured vegetable protein**

**TVR** TV television rating(s)

**TVRO** TV an aerial used for receiving television signals from a broadcasting satellite. Full form **television receive only**

**tw** ONLINE Taiwan (NOTE: The abbreviation **tw** is seen at the end of Internet addresses, preceded by a dot.)

**TW** MEASUREMENTS, ELECTRICITY terawatt

**TWAIN** /tweɪn/ COMPUTING an application programming interface standard developed by Hewlett-Packard, Logitech, Eastman Kodak, Aldus, and Caere that allows software to control image hardware. Full form **Technology Without an Interesting Name**

**'twas** /twɒz/ it was

**'twere** /twɜː/ it were

**'twill** /twɪl/ it will

**'twould** /twʊd/ it would

**TX 1.** MAIL Texas (*used in e-mails and text messages*) **2.** ONLINE thanks (NOTE: The abbreviation **TX** is part of the US sorting code on the last line of a Texas address.) **3.** COMPUTING transmit(ter)

**TY** ONLINE thank you (*used in e-mails and text messages*)

**typ.** PRINTING **1.** typographer **2.** typographical **3.** typography

**typo.** PRINTING **1.** typographer **2.** typographical (NOTE: When *typo* is used informally as a noun, short for 'typographical error', it is written without a full stop.) **3.** typography

**typw.** **1.** COMMERCE typewriter **2.** typewritten

**tz** ONLINE Tanzania (NOTE: The abbreviation **tz** is seen at the end of Internet addresses, preceded by a dot.)

# U

**u 1.** uncle **2.** unit **3.** upper

**U 1.** PHYSICS internal energy **2.** JUDAISM kosher certification **3.** ELECTRICITY potential difference **4.** united **5.** CINEMA a rating indicating that a film can be seen by everybody, regardless of age. Full form **universal 6.** EDUCATION university **7.** *US* EDUCATION unsatisfactory **8.** CHEMICAL ELEMENTS uranium

The abbreviation **U** applies when a student in the US chooses to take a study course under a less strict marking scheme than is usually applied, for personal enrichment rather than for an official grade.

**ua** ONLINE Ukraine (NOTE: The abbreviation **ua** is seen at the end of Internet addresses, preceded by a dot.)

**UAE** GEOGRAPHY United Arab Emirates

**UAM** ARMS underwater-to-air missile

**UART** /'juːɑːt/ COMPUTING universal asynchronous receiver/transmitter

**UBC** COMPUTING universal block channel

**UBE** ONLINE unsolicited bulk e-mail

**UBR** BUSINESS uniform business rate

**uc** PRINTING uppercase

**UCAS** /'juːkæs/ EDUCATION Universities and Colleges Admissions Service (NOTE: The acronym **UCAS** is used as a noun in its own right.)

**UCATT** /'juːkæt/ Union of Construction, Allied Trades, and Technicians

**UCC** CHRISTIANITY United Church of Christ

**UCCA** /'ʌkə/ EDUCATION the former name of UCAS. Full form **Universities Central Council on Admissions**

**UCE** ONLINE unsolicited commercial e-mail

**UCL** EDUCATION University College London

**UCLA** EDUCATION University of California at Los Angeles

**UDA** POLITICS Ulster Defence Association

**UDI** POLITICS unilateral declaration of independence (NOTE: Probably the most famous **UDI** was that made in 1965 by Ian Smith, prime minister of Rhodesia (now Zimbabwe), which led to thirteen years of UN sanctions against the country.)

**UDM** HUMAN RESOURCES Union of Democratic Mineworkers

**UDR** POLITICS Ulster Defence Regiment

**UEFA** /juˈeɪfə/ FOOTBALL Union of European Football Associations (NOTE: The acronym **UEFA** is used as a noun in its own right.)

**UFO** /ˌjuː ef 'əʊ, 'juːfəʊ/ AEROSPACE a flying object that cannot be identified and is thought by some to be an alien spacecraft. Full form **unidentified flying object**

The abbreviation **UFO** has entered the language as a noun in its own right and has spawned the derivative *ufology*, denoting the study of UFOs and the investigation of recorded sightings of them.

**ug** ONLINE Uganda (NOTE: The abbreviation **ug** is seen at the end of Internet addresses, preceded by a dot.)

**UGC** EDUCATION University Grants Committee

**UHF** RADIO any or all radio frequencies between 300 and 3,000 megahertz, typically used for television transmission. Full form **ultrahigh frequency**

**UI** /'juːiː/ COMPUTING user interface

**uk** ONLINE United Kingdom (NOTE: The abbreviation **uk** is seen at the end of Internet addresses, preceded by a dot.)

**UK** GEOGRAPHY United Kingdom

**UKAEA** INDUST United Kingdom Atomic Energy Authority

**UKCC** HEALTH SERVICES United Kingdom Central Council for Nursing, Midwifery and Health Visiting

**ULA** COMPUTING a chip containing a number of unconnected logic circuits and gates which can then be connected by a customer to provide a required function. Full form **uncommitted logic array**

**ult. 1.** ultimate **2.** of the previous month. Full form **ultimo** (NOTE: The abbreviation **ult.** was formerly used in business correspondence, as in *your letter of the 13th ult.*)

**UMIST** /ˈjuːmɪst/ EDUCATION University of Manchester Institute of Science and Technology

**UN** INTERNATIONAL RELATIONS United Nations

**unb.** PUBLISHING unbound

**unbd** PUBLISHING unbound

**UNCED** ENVIRONMENT United Nations Conference on Environment and Development

**UNCTAD** /ˈʌnktæd/ BUSINESS United Nations Conference on Trade and Development

**UNDP** BUSINESS United Nations Development Programme

**UN/EDIFACT** E-COMMERCE United Nations electronic data interchange for administration, commerce, and transport (or trade)

**UNEP** ENVIRONMENT United Nations Environment Programme

**UNESCO** /juːˈneskəʊ/ INTERNATIONAL RELATIONS a United Nations agency that promotes international collaboration on culture, education, and science. Full form **United Nations Educational, Scientific, and Cultural Organization**

**UNHCR** LAW United Nations High Commission for Refugees

**UNICEF** /ˈjuːnɪsef/ INTERNATIONAL RELATIONS a United Nations agency that works for the protection and survival of children around the world. Full form **United Nations Children's Fund** (NOTE: The agency was formerly called the United Nations International Children's Emergency Fund, hence the abbreviation.)

**UNIDO** /juːˈniːdəʊ/ INDUSTRY United Nations Industrial Development Organization

**UNISON** /ˈjuːnɪs(ə)n/ HUMAN RESOURCES a trade union for public service employees, the largest trade union in the United Kingdom (NOTE: **UNISON** is not an abbreviation. The name reflects the fact that the union was formed by the merger of three unions, COHSE, NALGO, and NUPE, in July 1993.)

**univ.** EDUCATION university

**UNO** INTERNATIONAL RELATIONS United Nations Organization

**unp.** PUBLISHING unpaged

**UNPROFOR** /ʊnˈprəʊˌfɔː(r)/ MILITARY United Nations Protection Force

**UNRRA** /ˈʌnrə/ INTERNATIONAL RELATIONS United Nations Relief and Rehabilitation Administration

**UNRWA** INTERNATIONAL RELATIONS United Nations Relief and Works Agency

**UNSF** ECONOMICS United Nations Special Fund for Economic Development

**UP** GEOGRAPHY Uttar Pradesh

**up.** upper

**UPC** *US* COMMERCE an early form of bar code containing 12 digits, used in the US before the advent of the EAN-UCC system in 1977. Full form **Universal Product Code**

**UPI** PRESS United Press International

**UPPP** uvulopalatopharyngoplasty

**UPS** COMPUTING uninterruptable power supply

**uPVC** INDUSTRY a rigid form of PVC. Full form **unplasticized polyvinyl chloride**

**URC** CHRISTIANITY United Reformed Church

**URL** ONLINE an address identifying the location of a webpage on the Internet, consisting of the protocol, the domain name of the service, and the directory or file name. Full form **Uniform (formerly Universal) Resource Locator**

**urol.** MEDICINE **1.** urological **2.** urology

**Uru.** Uruguay

**us** ONLINE United States (NOTE: The abbreviation **us** is seen at the end of Internet addresses, preceded by a dot.)

**US** GEOGRAPHY United States (of America) (NOTE: The abbreviation **US** can be used as a noun or adjective. The nickname *Uncle Sam*, a personification of the US government, is a jocular expansion of these initials.)

**u.s. 1.** ubi supra (NOTE: From the Latin, 'where (mentioned) above'.) **2.** ut supra (NOTE: From the Latin, 'as (mentioned) above'.)

**U/S** unserviceable

**USA** GEOGRAPHY United States of America

**USAF** AIR FORCE United States Air Force

**USAID** /ˌjuː es ˈeɪd/ INTERNATIONAL RELATIONS a trademark for a US government agency that provides humanitarian aid and assistance for development to other countries

**USART** /ˈjuːzɑːt/ COMPUTING universal synchronous asynchronous receiver/transmitter

**USASCII** /ˌjuː es ˈæskiː/ COMPUTING USA Standard Code for Information Interchange

**USB** COMPUTING an external interface standard designed for communication between a computer and attached peripheral devices such as printers, scanners, and keyboards ○ *USB port* Full form **universal serial bus**

**USDAW** /ˈʌzdɔː/ HUMAN RESOURCES Union of Shop, Distributive, and Allied Workers

**USGS** GEOLOGY United States Geological Survey

**USM 1.** ARMS underwater-to-surface missile **2.** STOCK EXCHANGE unlisted securities market

**USN** NAVY United States Navy

**USO** MILITARY United Service Organizations

**USP 1.** MARKETING a characteristic of a product that makes it different from all similar products. Full form **unique selling proposition (or point)** (NOTE: The abbreviation **USP** is used in advertisements and marketing: *What is this product's USP?*) **2.** PHARMACOLOGY United States Pharmacopeia

**USRT** COMPUTING universal synchronous receiver/transmitter

**USS 1.** GOVERNMENT United States Senate **2.** NAVY United States Ship

**USSR** GEOGRAPHY Union of Soviet Socialist Republics

**usu.** usually

**USW** RADIO ultrashort wave

**UT 1.** TIME another name for Greenwich Mean Time (GMT). Full form **Universal Time 2.** MAIL Utah (NOTE: The abbreviation **UT** is part of the US sorting code on the last line of a Utah address.)

**UTC** TIME an internationally accepted standard for calculating time based on International Atomic Time. Full form **Universal Time Coordinated**

**ut dict.** PHARMACOLOGY as directed (NOTE: The abbreviation **ut dict.**, from the Latin *ut dictum*, is used in prescriptions.)

**UTI** MEDICINE urinary tract infection

**util.** utility

**UTP** COMPUTING unshielded twisted pair (cable)

**UU 1.** POLITICS Ulster Unionist **2.** RELIGION Unitarian Universalist

**Uub** CHEMICAL ELEMENTS ununbium

**UUCP** COMPUTING UNIX-to-UNIX copy

**Uuq** CHEMICAL ELEMENTS ununquadium

**Uuu** CHEMICAL ELEMENTS unununium

**UV** PHYSICS ultraviolet (radiation)

**UVA** PHYSICS ultraviolet radiation, especially from the sun, with a relatively long wavelength. Full form **ultraviolet A**

**UVB** PHYSICS ultraviolet radiation, especially from the sun, with a relatively short wavelength. Full form **ultraviolet B**

**UVF** POLITICS Ulster Volunteer Force

**UVR** PHYSICS ultraviolet radiation

**UW** INSURANCE **1.** underwriter **2.** underwritten

**UWIST** /'juːwɪst/ EDUCATION University of Wales Institute of Science and Technology

**ux.** wife (NOTE: From the Latin *uxor.*)

**UXB** ARMS unexploded bomb

**uy** ONLINE Uruguay (NOTE: The abbreviation **uy** is seen at the end of Internet addresses, preceded by a dot.)

**uz** ONLINE Uzbekistan (NOTE: The abbreviation **uz** is seen at the end of Internet addresses, preceded by a dot.)

# V

**v 1.** PHYSICS instantaneous potential difference **2.** PHYSICS instantaneous voltage **3.** PHYSICS specific volume **4.** PHYSICS vacuum **5.** MATHEMATICS vector **6.** ANATOMY vein **7.** PHYSICS velocity **8.** MEDICINE ventilator **9.** ANATOMY ventral **10.** GRAMMAR verb **11.** GRAMMAR verbal **12.** verse **13.** PRINTING verso **14.** versus **15.** vertical **16.** very **17.** via **18.** QUANTUM PHYSICS vibrational quantum number **19.** CHRISTIANITY vicarage **20.** victory **21.** vide (NOTE: The abbreviation **v** is used in textual references.) **22.** MUSIC violin **23.** MICROBIOLOGY virus **24.** METEOROLOGY (abnormally good) visibility **25.** OPHTHALMOLOGY vision **26.** GRAMMAR vocative **27.** MUSIC voice **28.** GEOGRAPHY volcano **29.** MEASUREMENTS, ELECTRICITY voltage **30.** volume **31.** PHONETICS vowel

**V 1.** PHYSICS electric potential **2.** PHYSICS electromotive force **3.** PHYSICS potential **4.** PHYSICS potential efficiency **5.** PHYSICS potential energy **6.** PHYSICS vacuum **7.** BIOCHEMISTRY valine **8.** CHEMICAL ELEMENTS vanadium **9.** MEDICINE a region in an antibody that has many varying patterns of amino acids. Full form **variable region 10.** MONEY vatu **11.** MATHEMATICS vector **12.** ANATOMY vein **13.** PHYSICS velocity **14.** CHRISTIANITY Venerable **15.** MEDICINE ventilator **16.** ANATOMY ventral **17.** GRAMMAR verb **18.** GRAMMAR verbal **19.** verse **20.** version **21.** versus **22.** vertical **23.** very **24.** CHRISTIANITY vespers **25.** via **26.** QUANTUM PHYSICS vibrational quantum number **27.** CHRISTIANITY vicar **28.** CHRISTIANITY vicarage **29.** vice **30.** victory **31.** vide (NOTE: The abbreviation **V** is used in textual references.) **32.** village **33.** MUSIC violin **34.** MICROBIOLOGY virus **35.** Viscount **36.** Viscountess **37.** METEOROLOGY (abnormally good) visibility **38.** OPHTHALMOLOGY vision **39.** GRAMMAR vocative **40.** MUSIC voice **41.** GEOGRAPHY volcano **42.** MEASUREMENTS, ELECTRICITY volt **43.** MEASUREMENTS, ELECTRICITY voltage **44.** PHYSICS voltmeter **45.** volume **46.** Volunteer(s) **47.** PHONETICS vowel

**va 1.** ONLINE Vatican City (NOTE: The abbreviation **va** is seen at the end of Internet addresses, preceded by a dot.) **2.** GRAMMAR verb active **3.** GRAMMAR verbal adjective **4.** MUSIC viola

**VA 1.** COMMERCE value analysis **2.** COMMERCE value-added **3.** MEDICINE ventricular arrhythmia **4.** CHRISTIANITY vicar apostolic **5.** MILITARY Vice Admiral **6.** MILITARY (Royal Order of) Victoria and Albert **7.** MAIL Virginia (NOTE: The abbreviation **VA** is part of the US sorting code on the last line of a Virginia address.) **8.** OPHTHALMOLOGY visual acuity **9.** visual aid **10.** WINE volatile acidity **11.** MEASUREMENTS, ELECTRICITY volt-ampere **12.** MILITARY Volunteer Artillery

**V/A** COMMERCE voucher attached

**vac. 1.** vacancy **2.** vacant **3.** PHYSICS vacuum

**val. 1.** GEOLOGY valley **2.** FINANCE valuation **3.** COMMERCE value

**VAN** /væn/ COMPUTING a computer network that enables private companies to exchange information with other registered subscribers. Full form **value-added network**

**van.** vanilla

**V & A** ARTS Victoria and Albert Museum

**var** MEASUREMENTS, ELECTRICITY volt-ampere reactive

**VAR 1.** /vɑː/ COMPUTING a retail seller of computers who adds products to computers produced by manufacturers or performs services such as product integration or customization before selling the computers to customers. Full form **value-added reseller 2.** visual aural range **3.** ELECTRICITY volt-ampere reactive

**var. 1.** variable **2.** variant **3.** variation

**VAT** /væt/ FINANCE a tax added to the estimated value of a product or material at each stage of its manufacture or distribution, ultimately paid by the consumer. Full form **value-added tax** (NOTE: The abbreviation **VAT** is used as a noun in its own right.)

**Vat.** Vatican

**vb** GRAMMAR **1.** verb **2.** verbal

**VBAC** /'viːbæk/ MEDICINE a vaginal delivery of a baby by a woman whose first baby was delivered by Caesarean section. Full form **vaginal birth after Caesarean**

**vc** ONLINE St Vincent and the Grenadines (NOTE: The abbreviation **vc** is seen at the end of Internet addresses, preceded by a dot.)

**VC 1.** FINANCE venture capital **2.** FINANCE venture capitalist **3.** vice chairman **4.** vice chancellor **5.** POLITICS vice consul **6.** MILITARY Victoria Cross **7.** POLITICS Vietcong **8.** WINE a category for Spanish wines falling just below the standards set out by the DO appellation. Full form **Vino Comarcal**

**vCJD** MEDICINE a form of Creutzfeldt-Jakob disease (CJD) that has a much shorter incubation period than previously recognized types but is clinically identical. Full form **variant CJD**

**VCM** FINANCE venture capital market

**VCR 1.** HOUSEHOLD video cassette recorder **2.** AVIAT visual control room (on an airfield)

**VCT** FINANCE venture capital trust

**vd 1.** PHYSICS vapour density **2.** various dates **3.** void

**VD 1.** MEDICINE venereal disease (NOTE: The abbreviation **VD** is used as a noun in its own right. Both the abbreviation and the full form are somewhat dated, *sexually transmitted disease (STD)* being the current term.) **2.** MILITARY Volunteer Decoration

**VDC** *Aus* MILITARY Volunteer Defence Corps

**VDH** MEDICINE valvular disease of the heart

**VdlT** WINE a category for Spanish wines equivalent to the French 'vin de pays'. Full form **Vino de la Tierra**

**VdM** WINE Vino de Mesa (NOTE: From the Spanish, 'table wine'.)

**VDN** WINE a French fortified wine made from naturally sweet grapes such as Muscat. Full form **vin doux naturel**

**VDQS** WINE the second-highest quality of French wine after AOC. Full form **Vin Délimité de Qualité Supérieure**

**VDR** VIDEO **1.** videodisk recorder **2.** videodisk recording

**VDRL** MEDICINE venereal disease research laboratory

**VDSL** TELECOMMUNICATIONS very-high-data-rate (or very-high-bit-rate) digital subscriber line

**VDT 1.** COMPUTING video / visual display terminal **2.** WINE Vino da Tavola

**VDU** COMPUTING visual display unit (NOTE: The abbreviation **VDU** is used as a noun in its own right.)

**ve** ONLINE Venezuela (NOTE: The abbreviation **ve** is seen at the end of Internet addresses, preceded by a dot.)

**'ve** /əv/ have

**vel. 1.** PAPER vellum **2.** PHYSICS velocity

**Ven. 1.** CHRISTIANITY Venerable **2.** GEOGRAPHY Venezuela

**Venez.** GEOGRAPHY Venezuela

**VER** COMMERCE voluntary export restraint

**ver. 1.** verse **2.** version

**vers** MATHEMATICS versed sine

**vert.** vertical

**VESA** COMPUTING Video Electronics Standards Association

**vet. 1.** MILITARY veteran **2.** veterinarian **3.** veterinary

**VF 1.** MEDICINE ventricular fibrillation **2.** TV video frequency **3.** TELECOMMUNICATIONS voice frequency

**VFR** AEROSPACE visual flight rules

**VFT** RAIL very fast train

**VFU** COMPUTING part of the control system of a printer that controls the vertical format of the page to be printed, e.g. the line spacing. Full form **vertical format unit**

**vg 1.** very good **2.** ONLINE (British) Virgin Islands (NOTE: The abbreviation **vg** is seen at the end of Internet addresses, preceded by a dot.)

**VG** CHRISTIANITY Vicar General

**VGA** COMPUTING a specification for video display controllers used in personal computers. Full form **video graphics array**

**vgc** very good condition (NOTE: The abbreviation **vgc** is used in classified advertisements of items for sale, for example cars.)

**VHF** RADIO very high frequency

**vi 1.** GRAMMAR verb intransitive **2.** ONLINE (US) Virgin Islands (NOTE: The abbreviation **vi** is seen at the end of Internet addresses, preceded by a dot.)

**VI** GEOGRAPHY Vancouver Island

**v.i.** vide infra (NOTE: From the Latin, 'see below'.)

**vic.** RELIGION vicar

**Vic.** Victoria

**Viet. 1.** GEOGRAPHY Vietnam **2.** LANGUAGE Vietnamese

**VIF** COMMERCE variable import fee

**vign.** vignette

**vil.** village

**vill.** village

**vin.** FOOD vinegar

**VIP 1.** MEDICINE a peptide secreted by the intestines that has been shown to have beneficial effects for arthritis sufferers. Full form **vasoactive intestinal peptide 2.** very important person (NOTE: The abbreviation **VIP** is used as a noun in its own right.)

**VIR** Victoria Empress and Queen (NOTE: From the Latin *Victoria Imperatrix Regina*.)

**Vir. 1.** LITERATURE Virgil **2.** ASTRONOMY Virgo

**Vis. 1.** Viscount **2.** Viscountess

**visc.** PHYSICS viscosity

**Visc. 1.** Viscount **2.** Viscountess

**ViSCA** /ˈvɪskə/ COMPUTING a trademark for a protocol used to synchronize multiple video devices, developed by Sony. Full form **video system control architecture**

**Visct. 1.** Viscount **2.** Viscountess

**VJ** VIDEO somebody who plays videos, especially music videos, on television. Full form **video jockey**

**vl** LITERATURE an alternative translation for a piece of literature. Full form **variant reading** (NOTE: From the Latin *varia lectio*.)

**VL** LANGUAGE Vulgar Latin

**VLCC** INDUSTRY very large crude carrier

**VLDL** BIOCHEMISTRY a lipoprotein that is associated with coronary and heart diseases as it deposits cholesterol on the walls of arteries. Full form **very low density lipoprotein**

**VLF** RADIO very low frequency

**VLSI** ELECTRONICS very large scale integration

**VM** COMPUTING virtual machine

**VMD** EDUCATION Doctor of Veterinary Medicine

**vn** ONLINE Vietnam (NOTE: The abbreviation **vn** is seen at the end of Internet addresses, preceded by a dot.)

**vo** PRINTING verso

**VO 1.** MILITARY Royal Victorian Order **2.** an spoken order, sometimes delivered by telephone, by a physician to administer treatment to a patient. Full form **verbal order 3.** BEVERAGES very old (NOTE: The abbreviation **VO** is used on brandy, whisky, or port labels.) **4.** TV, CINEMA voiceover

**VOC** CHEMISTRY an organic compound such as ethylene, propylene, benzene, or styrene that evaporates at a relatively low temperature and contributes to air pollution. Full form **volatile organic compound**

**voc.** GRAMMAR vocative

**vocat.** GRAMMAR vocative

**VoIP** /vɔɪp/ ONLINE a technology that enables voice messages to be sent via the Internet, often simultaneously with data in text or other forms. Full form **voice over Internet protocol**

**vol. 1.** GEOGRAPHY volcano **2.** volume **3.** volunteer

**vols.** volumes

**VOR** AEROSPACE very-high-frequency omnidirectional radio range

**vou.** voucher

**VP 1.** GRAMMAR verb phrase **2.** vice president

**VPL** CLOTHING visible panty line

**VQPRD** WINE **1.** a European classification for French wines of high quality produced under strict controls, such as AOC wines. Full form **Vins de Qualité Produits dans des Régions Déterminées 2.** a European classification for Portuguese wines of high quality produced under strict controls. Full form **Vinho de Qualidade Produzido em Região Determinada**

**vr** GRAMMAR verb reflexive

**VR 1.** Victoria Regina **2.** COMPUTING virtual reality **3.** MILITARY Volunteer Reserve

**VRC** COMPUTING an odd parity check on each character of a block received, to detect any errors. Full form **vertical redundancy check**

**VRI** Victoria Queen and Empress (NOTE: From the Latin *Victoria Regina Imperatrix*.)

**VRML** a computer-graphics programming language used to create images of three-dimensional scenes. Full form **Virtual Reality Modelling Language**

**vs** versus

**VS** COMPUTING virtual storage

**v.s.** vide supra (NOTE: From the Latin, 'see above'.)

**VSD** MEDICINE ventricular septal defect

**VSO** an organization that sends volunteers to work and teach in developing countries. Full form **Voluntary Service Overseas**

**vss. 1.** verses **2.** versions

**V/STOL** /ˈviː stɒl/ AVIAT a system used by some aircraft that enables them to take off and land vertically or using a short runway. Full form **vertical/short takeoff and landing**

**vt** GRAMMAR verb transitive

**VT 1.** PHYSICS vacuum tube **2.** a type of fuse more commonly known as a proximity fuse. Full form **variable time 3.** MAIL Vermont (NOTE: The abbreviation **VT** is part of the US sorting code on the last line of a Vermont address.)

**VTOL** /ˈviːtɒl/ AVIAT a system used by some aircraft that enables them to take off and land vertically. Full form **vertical takeoff and landing**

**VTR** HOUSEHOLD video tape recorder

**vu** ONLINE Vanuatu (NOTE: The abbreviation **vu** is seen at the end of Internet addresses, preceded by a dot.)

**VU** ECOLOGY vulnerable (species)

**Vul.** BIBLE Vulgate

**vulg. 1.** vulgar **2.** vulgarly

**Vulg.** BIBLE Vulgate

**vv** vice versa

**vv. 1.** MUSIC (first and second) violins **2.** verses **3.** volumes

**VW** Very Worshipful

**VxD** COMPUTING a device driver used to control one part of the Windows operating system or to link a peripheral device to the Windows operating system. Full form **virtual device driver**

**w 1.** TIME week **2.** CRICKET wicket(s) **3.** CRICKET a ball bowled beyond the reach of the batsman or batswoman, for which one run is awarded to the batting side. Full form **wide(s) 4.** MEASUREMENTS width **5.** wife **6.** with

**W 1.** CHEMICAL ELEMENTS tungsten **2.** GEOGRAPHY Wales **3.** Warden **4.** MEASUREMENTS, ELECTRICITY watt **5.** ONLINE web (address) **6.** Wednesday **7.** PHYSICS weight **8.** LANGUAGE Welsh **9.** west **10.** western **11.** CLOTHING women's (NOTE: The abbreviation **W** is used of clothing sizes.) **12.** PHYSICS work

**W3** ONLINE World Wide Web

**W3C** ONLINE a consortium of organizations, programmers, developers, industry executives, and users that seeks to guide the evolution of the World Wide Web and ensure that all its technologies are compatible with one another

**W8** ONLINE wait (*used in e-mails and text messages*)

**W8ING** ONLINE waiting (*used in e-mails and text messages*)

**WA 1.** MAIL Washington (State) (NOTE: The abbreviation **WA** is part of the US sorting code on the last line of an address in the state of Washington.) **2.** GEOGRAPHY Western Australia **3.** INSURANCE with average

**WAAAF** /wæf/ AIR FORCE Women's Auxiliary Australian Air Force

**WAAC** /wæk/ ARMY an voluntary association of women working with the British Army in World War 2, though with fewer rights and privileges and a lower status than men. Full form **Women's Army Auxiliary Corps**

**WAAF** /wæf/ AIR FORCE a branch of the Royal Air Force for women, established in 1939 to release men for active service in World War II. In 1949 it was renamed the Women's Royal Air Force. Full form **Women's Auxiliary Air Force**. Former name for **Women's Royal Air Force** (NOTE: The acronym **WAAF** was used as a noun to denote a member of the Women's Auxiliary Air Force.)

**WACA** /ˈwækə/ CRICKET a cricket club and ground in Perth, Western Australia. Full form **West Australian Cricket Association**

**WAEF** ONLINE when all else fails (*used in e-mails and text messages*)

**Wal.** LANGUAGE Walloon

**WAN** /wæn/ COMPUTING a network of computers and peripheral devices linked by cable and satellite over a broad geographic area. Full form **wide area network**

**wanna** /ˈwɒnə/ want to

**WAP** /wæp/ **1.** COMPUTING wireless access point **2.** ONLINE a standard protocol for the transmission of electronic data between devices such as mobile phones and pagers and other sources of digital information such as the Internet. Full form **wireless application protocol**

**war.** warrant

**War.** GEOGRAPHY Warwickshire

**Warks.** GEOGRAPHY Warwickshire

**wasn't** /ˈwɒz(ə)nt/ was not

**WAVES** /weɪvs/ NAVY the women's branch of the US Naval Reserve that was organized in World War II. It no longer exists as a separate entity. Full form **Women Accepted for Volunteer Emergency Service** (NOTE: A member of the **WAVES** was known as a *Wave*.)

**wb 1.** FREIGHT waybill **2.** westbound

**Wb** MEASUREMENTS, PHYSICS weber

**WB 1.** describes a boat that has specially designed compartments to hold water to act as ballast. Full form **water ballast 2.** FREIGHT waybill **3.** ONLINE welcome back (*used in Internet chat rooms*) **4.** westbound

**WBA** BOXING World Boxing Association

**WBC 1.** MEDICINE white blood cell **2.** BOXING World Boxing Council

**WbN** west by north

**WbS** west by south

**WC 1.** water closet (NOTE: Although 'water closet' is a rather old-fashioned name for a toilet, the abbreviation **WC** is still in use on signs, in lists of facilities, and as a noun in its own right.) **2.** ONLINE who cares (*used in e-mails and text messages*)

**w.c.** COMMERCE without charge

**WCC** CHRISTIANITY World Council of Churches

**WCED** ENVIRONMENT World Commission on Environment and Development

**WCMC** ECOLOGY World Conservation Monitoring Centre

**wd 1.** HEALTH SERVICES ward **2.** COMMERCE warranted **3.** wood **4.** word

**WD** MILITARY War Department

**w/d** COMMERCE warranted

**WDA 1.** BUSINESS Welsh Development Agency **2.** ACCOUNTING writing-down allowance

**WDM** COMPUTING a method of increasing the data capacity of an optic fibre by transmitting several light signals at different wavelengths along the same fibre. Full form **wavelength division multiplex(ing)**

**wdth** MEASUREMENTS width

**WDV** ACCOUNTING written-down value

**WDYT** ONLINE what do you think (*used in e-mails and text messages*)

**WEA** EDUCATION Workers' Educational Association

**we'd** /wiːd/ **1.** we had **2.** we would

**Wed.** CALENDAR Wednesday

**WEF** ECONOMICS World Economic Forum

**we'll** /wiːl/ **1.** we shall **2.** we will

**we're** /wɪə/ we are

**weren't** /wɜːnt/ were not

**Westm.** Westminster

**WET** TIME Western European Time

**WEU** INTERNATIONAL RELATIONS Western European Union

**we've** /wiːv/ we have

**wf 1.** ONLINE Wallis and Futuna Islands (NOTE: The abbreviation **wf** is seen at the end of Internet addresses, preceded by a dot.) **2.** PRINTING wrong font

**wff** LOGIC well-formed formula

**WFTC** FINANCE Working Families' Tax Credit

**WFTU** HUMAN RESOURCES World Federation of Trade Unions

**wg 1.** water gauge **2.** wire gauge

**Wg Cdr** MILITARY Wing Commander

**W Glam.** GEOGRAPHY West Glamorgan

**Wh** MEASUREMENTS, ELECTRICITY watt-hour

**wh.** white

**WHA** ENVIRONMENT World Heritage Area

**what's** /wɒts/ **1.** what does **2.** what has **3.** what is

**whf** wharf

**WHO** /ˌdʌbəljuːeɪtʃ ˈəʊ/ MEDICINE World Health Organization

**who'd** /huːd/ **1.** who had **2.** who would

**who'll** /huːl/ **1.** who shall **2.** who will

**who's** /huːz/ **1.** who has **2.** who is

**whs.** COMMERCE warehouse

**whsle** COMMERCE wholesale

**WI 1.** SOCIAL SCIENCES West Indian **2.** GEOGRAPHY West Indies **3.** MAIL Wisconsin (NOTE: The abbreviation **WI** is part of the US sorting code on the last line of a Wisconsin address.) **4.** Women's Institute

**Wilts.** GEOGRAPHY Wiltshire

**WIMP** /wɪmp/ **1.** PHYSICS a hypothetical subatomic particle that has been proposed as a possible form of dark matter. Full form **weakly interacting massive particle 2.** COMPUTING a graphical user interface for computers that includes windows, icons, and other features designed to make them more user-friendly. Full form **windows, icons, mouse, pull-down menu / windows, icons, menus, pointers**

**WIP** BUSINESS work in progress

**WIPO** /ˈwaɪpəʊ/ World Intellectual Property Organization

**WISC** /wɪsk/ COMPUTING writable instruction set computer

**Wisd.** BIBLE Wisdom of Solomon

**wk 1.** weak **2.** week **3.** work

**wkly** weekly

**wkt** CRICKET wicket

**WL 1.** NAUTICAL water line **2.** PHYSICS wavelength

**WLTM** would like to meet

The abbreviation **WLTM** is one of several that are routinely used in personal ads and online dating. Because of the original cost of newspaper advertising a shorthand has evolved which includes terms such as *ALA* ('all letters answered'), *GSOH* ('good sense of humour'), *LTR* ('long-term relationship'), *n/s* ('non-smoker'), and the somewhat terse *NTW* ('no time-wasters').

**Wm.** William

**WMD** ARMS weapons of mass destruction

**wmk.** watermark

**WML** COMPUTING **1.** WAP markup language **2.** wireless markup language

**WMO** METEOROLOGY World Meteorological Organization

**WNF** MEDICINE West Nile fever

**WNV** MICROBIOLOGY West Nile virus

**WNW** west-northwest

**WO 1.** GOVERNMENT War Office **2.** MILITARY warrant officer **3.** *S Africa* WINE a guarantee of the place of origin for South African wines. Full form **Wine of Origin 4.** MILITARY wireless operator

**w/o** without

**WOB** ONLINE without a boyfriend (*used in Internet chat rooms*)

**w.o.b.** INSURANCE washed overboard

**WOG** ONLINE without a girlfriend (*used in Internet chat rooms*)

**WOM** ONLINE word of mouth (*used in e-mails and text messages*)

**WOMBAT** /ˈwɒmbæt/ ONLINE waste of money, brains, and time (*used in e-mails and text messages*)

**won't** /wəʊnt/ will not

**WOOF** MARKETING older people in or past middle age with a comfortable lifestyle and significant disposable income (*humorous*) Full form **well-off older folks**

**woopy** SOCIAL SCIENCES ◊ see note at **dinky**

**Worcs.** GEOGRAPHY Worcestershire

**WORM** /wɜːm/ COMPUTING a computer storage medium, usually optical, in which data cannot be changed after it is stored but can be read. Full form **write once read many (times)**

**wouldn't** /'wʊd(ə)nt/ would not

**would've** /'wʊd(ə)v/ would have

**WOW** INDUST waiting on weather (NOTE: The abbreviation **WOW** is used in relation to outdoor construction activities that rely on favourable weather conditions.)

**WP 1.** METEOROLOGY weather permitting **2.** LAW without harming somebody's legal rights. Full form **without prejudice 3.** COMPUTING word processing **4.** COMPUTING word processor

**WPA** Work Projects Administration

**WPB** wastepaper basket

**WPC** POLICE Woman Police Constable

**WPGA** GOLF Women's Professional Golfers' Association

**WPI** COMMERCE wholesale price index

**wpm** MEASUREMENTS words per minute (NOTE: The abbreviation **wpm** is most frequently used with reference to typing speed.)

**wpn** ARMS weapon

**WR** MEDICINE a blood test for syphilis. Full form **Wassermann reaction**

**WRAAC** /ræk/ ARMY Women's Royal Australian Army Corps

**WRAAF** /ræf/ AIR FORCE Women's Royal Australian Air Force

**WRAC** ARMY an association of women formed in 1949 to undertake non-combat roles in the army, disbanded in 1992. Full form **Women's Royal Army Corps**

**WRAF** AIR FORCE a branch of the Royal Air Force for women, established in 1939 to release men for active service in World War II. Before 1949 it was called the Women's Auxiliary Air Force (WAAF). Full form **Women's Royal Air Force**

**WRANS** /rænz/ NAVY Women's Royal Australian Naval Service

**WRNS** NAVY Women's Royal Naval Service (NOTE: The **WRNS** no longer exists as a separate entity. Its members were called 'Wrens', from the informal pronunciation of the abbreviation.)

**wrnt** LAW warrant

**WRP** POLITICS Worker's Revolutionary Party

**WRT** ONLINE, POLITICS (*used in e-mails and text messages*) **1.** with regard to **2.** with respect to

**WRULD** MEDICINE work-related upper limb disorder

**WRVS** SOCIAL WELFARE Women's Royal Voluntary Service

**ws** ONLINE Samoa (NOTE: The abbreviation **ws** comes from the country's original name, Western Samoa. It is seen at the end of Internet addresses, preceded by a dot.)

**WSW** west-southwest

**wt** MEASUREMENTS weight

**WTA** TENNIS **1.** Women's Tennis Association **2.** World Tennis Association

**WTC** COMMERCE World Trade Center

**WTG** ONLINE an informal expression of congratulations (*used in e-mails and text messages*) Full form **way to go**

**WTH** ONLINE what the heck (*used in e-mails and text messages*)

**WTO** COMMERCE World Trade Organization

**WV** MAIL West Virginia (NOTE: The abbreviation **WV** is part of the US sorting code on the last line of a West Virginia address.)

**WWF 1.** ECOLOGY World Wildlife Fund **2.** WRESTLING World Wrestling Federation
The World Wildlife Fund changed its name to the World Wide Fund for Nature in 1986; however, the abbreviation **WWF** was so well-known that it did not fall out of use. In 2000 it became the official name for the organization.

**WWI** HISTORY World War One

**WWII** HISTORY World War Two

**WWW** ONLINE World Wide Web

**WWW** ONLINE World Wide Web

**WY** MAIL Wyoming (NOTE: The abbreviation **WY** is part of the US sorting code on the last line of a Wyoming address.)

**WYSIAYG** /ˈwɪziːeɪg/ COMPUTING what you see is all you get (NOTE: The abbreviation **WYSIAYG** is used to describe a *WYSIWIG* word processing program that is not complex enough for an advanced user's needs.)

**WYSIWYG** /ˈwɪziːwɪg/ COMPUTING what you see is what you get (NOTE: The abbreviation **WYSIWYG** is used to indicate that what appears on the screen (especially in word processing) will appear in the same form on the printout.)

# X

**x 1.** MATHEMATICS an algebraic variable **2.** MEASUREMENTS by (NOTE: The symbol **x** is used in giving two or more dimensions.) **3.** BRIDGE a card that is not an honour, i.e. a picture card or a ten **4.** MATHEMATICS a coordinate along the x-axis (conventionally the horizontal one) **5.** COMMERCE ex **6.** extension **7.** MATHEMATICS multiplied by

**X 1.** exchange **2.** extension **3.** PHYSICS, ELECTRONICS reactance

**xa** BUSINESS describes shares in a company that are sold without any of the accompanying rights, e.g. current dividends. Full form **ex-all**

**XA** COMPUTING Extended Architecture

**xc** BUSINESS ex-capitalization

**XD** STOCK EXCHANGE without the right to the current dividend on purchase. Full form **ex dividend**

**xdiv** STOCK EXCHANGE without the right to the current dividend on purchase. Full form **ex dividend**

**Xe** CHEMICAL ELEMENTS xenon

**XGA** COMPUTING extended graphics array

**XL** CLOTHING extra large (NOTE: The abbreviation **XL** is used as a size of clothing.)

**XML** ONLINE a programming language designed for web documents that allows for the creation of customized tags for individual information fields. Full form **Extensible Markup Language**

**XMODEM** /ˈeks ˌməʊdem/ COMPUTING a file transfer protocol for asynchronous communications in which data is sent in 128-byte blocks

**Xn** CHRISTIANITY Christian

> The letter 'X' is used in place of 'Christ' in various other contexts, notably the word *Xmas*. It is a transliteration of the Greek letter 'chi', the first letter of the Greek name for Christ.

**Xnty** CHRISTIANITY Christianity

**XP** COMPUTING **1.** Athlon XP **2.** Windows XP

**xr** BUSINESS ex-rights

**XS** CLOTHING extra small (NOTE: The abbreviation **XS** is used as a size of clothing.)

**Xt** Christ

**XT** COMPUTING a version of the original IBM PC, developed by IBM, that used an 8088 processor and included a hard disk

**Xtian** Christian

**xtn** extension

**Xty** Christianity

**y 1.** MATHEMATICS an algebraic variable **2.** MATHEMATICS a coordinate along the y-axis (conventionally the vertical one) **3.** TIME year **4.** MEASUREMENTS yocto-

**Y 1.** ELECTRICITY admittance **2.** MATHEMATICS an unknown factor **3.** MONEY yen **4.** MEASUREMENTS yotta- **5.** CHEMICAL ELEMENTS yttrium **6.** MONEY yuan

**Y2K** TIME year 2000

> The abbreviation **Y2K** was used in the closing years of the 20th century, especially with reference to the millennium bug, an anticipated problem for computer software that coded dates using only the last two digits of the year.

**YA** ONLINE yet another (*used in e-mails and text messages*)

**YAC** /jæk/ BIOTECHNOLOGY a sequence of DNA taken from another organism and inserted in a yeast to reveal its function. Full form **yeast artificial chromosome**

**YAG** /jæg/ a synthetic mineral used in infrared lasers and as a gemstone. Full form **yttrium, aluminium, garnet**

**yappy** /ˈjæpi/ SOCIAL SCIENCES ▷ see note at **dinky**

**Yb** CHEMICAL ELEMENTS ytterbium

**YBS** ONLINE you'll be sorry (*used in e-mails and text messages*)

**YC** POLITICS Young Conservative

**Y/C** COMPUTING two parts of a video signal representing the luminance (Y) and the chrominance (C) of the image

**yd** MEASUREMENTS yard

**YDT** TIME Yukon Daylight Time

**ye** ONLINE Yemen (NOTE: The abbreviation **ye** is seen at the end of Internet addresses, preceded by a dot.)

**YER** BANKING yearly effective rate

**YHA** Youth Hostels Association

**YHWH** /ˈjɑːweɪ/ JUDAISM the usual transliteration of the Tetragrammaton, the four letters representing the Hebrew name of God in the Bible, sometimes expanded to Yahweh

**YIU** ONLINE yes, I understand (*used in e-mails and text messages*)

**YK** FINANCE yugen kaisha

**YM** ONLINE you mean (*used in e-mails and text messages*)

**YMCA** CHRISTIANITY Young Men's Christian Association

> The abbreviation **YMCA** is used as a noun, especially denoting a centre where social, sports, or educational facilities (and sometimes accommodation) are provided for members of the association and others.

**YMHA** JUDAISM Young Men's Hebrew Association

**YMODEM** /ˈwaɪ ˌməʊdem/ COMPUTING a variation of the XMODEM file transfer protocol that uses 1024-byte blocks and can send multiple files

**YNK** ONLINE you never know (*used in e-mails and text messages*)

**YOB** year of birth

**Yorks.** GEOGRAPHY Yorkshire

**you'd** /juːd/ **1.** you had **2.** you would

**you'll** /juːl/ **1.** you shall **2.** you will

**you're** /jɔː/ you are

**you've** /jɔː/ you have

**YOYO** ONLINE you're on your own (*used in e-mails and text messages*)

**yr 1.** year **2.** younger **3.** your

**Yrs** Yours (NOTE: The abbreviation **Yrs** is used at the end of a letter.)

**YST** TIME Yukon Standard Time

**yt** ONLINE Mayotte (NOTE: The abbreviation **yt** is seen at the end of Internet addresses, preceded by a dot.)

**YT 1.** ONLINE yours truly (*used in e-mails and text messages*) **2.** GEOGRAPHY Yukon Territory

**YTD** ACCOUNTING year to date

**YTS** HUMAN RESOURCES Youth Training Scheme

**yu** ONLINE Yugoslavia (NOTE: The abbreviation **yu** is seen at the end of Internet addresses, preceded by a dot.)

**Yug.** GEOGRAPHY Yugoslavia

**Yugo.** GEOGRAPHY Yugoslavia

**yuppie** /'jʌpi/ SOCIAL SCIENCES a young educated city-dwelling professional, especially when regarded as materialistic. Full form **young urban (or upwardly mobile) professional**

> **Yuppie** is the most enduring of a number of acronyms coined in the late 20th century to denote various socioeconomic groups. It has given rise to various derivatives, notably the verb *yuppify* and the noun *yuppification*, referring to an influx of such people into an area or to modifications made in accordance with their tastes, needs, and values.

**YWCA** CHRISTIANITY Young Women's Christian Association

> The abbreviation **YWCA** is used as a noun, especially denoting a centre where social, sports, or educational facilities (and sometimes accommodation) are provided for members of the association and others.

**YWHA** Young Women's Hebrew Association

# Z

**z 1.** MATHEMATICS a Cartesian coordinate along the z-axis **2.** MATHEMATICS an algebraic variable **3.** CHEMISTRY atomic number **4.** MONEY zaïre **5.** MEASUREMENTS zepto- **6.** MEASUREMENTS zetta- **7.** GEOGRAPHY zone

**Z 1.** CHEMISTRY atomic number **2.** PHYSICS impedance **3.** MEASUREMENTS zetta- **4.** GEOGRAPHY zone

**za** ONLINE South Africa (NOTE: The abbreviation **za** is seen at the end of Internet addresses, preceded by a dot.)

**ZANU** /'zɑːnuː/ POLITICS a nationalist political party that helped bring about majority rule in Zimbabwe. It merged with the opposition party ZAPU in 1988 to form ZANU-PF. Full form **Zimbabwe African National Union**

**ZAPU** /'zæpuː/ POLITICS a nationalist political party that helped bring about majority rule in Zimbabwe. It merged with ZANU in 1988 to form ZANU-PF. Full form **Zimbabwe African People's Union**

**ZBB** FINANCE zero-based budgeting

**ZDPS** BUSINESS zero dividend preference shares

**ZEV** ECOLOGY zero emission vehicle

**ZIF** COMPUTING zero insertion force (socket)

**Zin** WINE Zinfandel

**Zl** MONEY zloty

**zm** ONLINE Zambia (NOTE: The abbreviation **zm** is seen at the end of Internet addresses, preceded by a dot.)

**ZMODEM** /'zed ˌməʊdem/ COMPUTING an enhanced version of the XMODEM file transfer protocol that includes error detection and the ability to restart a transfer where it left off if the connection is cut

**Zn** CHEMICAL ELEMENTS zinc

**zod.** ASTROLOGY zodiac

**zool. 1.** zoological **2.** zoology

**ZPG** SOCIAL SCIENCES zero population growth

**zr** ONLINE Zaire (NOTE: The abbreviation **zr** is seen at the end of Internet addresses, preceded by a dot.)

**Zr** CHEMICAL ELEMENTS zirconium

**zw** ONLINE Zimbabwe (NOTE: The abbreviation **zw** is seen at the end of Internet addresses, preceded by a dot.)